Multicultural education

Towards good practice

Edited by

R.K. Arora

and

C.G. Duncan

Routledge & Kegan Paul

London, Boston and Henley

First published in 1986
by Routledge & Kegan Paul plc

14 Leicester Square, London WC2H 7PH, England

9 Park Street, Boston, Mass. 02108, USA and

Broadway House, Newtown Road,
Henley on Thames, Oxon RG9 1EN, England

Set in Times, 10 on 11pt
by Columns of Reading
and printed in Great Britain
by St Edmundsbury Press, Bury St Edmunds, Suffolk

Library of Congress Cataloging in Publication Data

Main entry under title:
Multicultural education.

(Routledge education books)
1. Children of minorities – Education – Great Britain – Addresses, essays, lectures. 2. Intercultural education – Great Britain – Addresses, essays, lectures.
I. Arora, R. K. (Ranjit K.) II. Duncan, C. G. (Carlton G.), 1941- . III. Series.
LC3736.G6M84 1986 371.97 85-10796

ISBN 0-7102-0229-6

British Library CIP Data also available

Contents

Contributors vii
Acknowledgments xi

1 Editorial
Ranjit Arora and Carlton Duncan 1
2 Strategies for change
Gerry Davis 9
3 Black response to white definitions
Tuku Mukherjee 25
4 Developing a multicultural approach to the curriculum: The role of the headteacher (A case study at Wyke Manor)
Carlton Duncan 36
5 Towards a multicultural curriculum – primary
Ranjit Arora 47
6 Towards a multicultural curriculum – secondary
Carlton Duncan 62
7 Approaches to multicultural curriculum – humanities
Sylvia Collicott 74
8 Arts education as an element of multicultural education
Horace Lashley 84
9 A second language or language for learning
Ranjit Arora 101
10 Multicultural approach to mathematics
Derek Dyson 117
11 Science education for a multicultural society
Sue Watts 135
12 Resources for multicultural education (Where to find them and how to choose them)
Gillian Klein 147

13 Initial teacher training (A case study of a decade of change in Bradford)
Ranjit Arora 161
14 In-service mis-education
Dave Dunn 182
15 The multicultural community and the school
Carlton Duncan 200
16 Pastoral care and guidance in the multicultural school
Carlton Duncan 213

Contributors

Ranjit Arora is at present Head of Department at Bradford and Ilkley Community College, where she is in charge of multicultural education throughout the institution. She is chairperson of the Asian Women's Centre and of the Community Relations Council Education Panel in Bradford and an active member of several national organisations. She is also on the editorial committees of *Multiracial Education* (NAME journal) and *Multicultural Teaching*. Her previous publications include: 'Supply and Training of Teachers of Community Languages' (1983), NCMTT Discussion paper; *English as a Second Language for Adults* (1982), national study for ACACE; *'Parosi' Tutors' Handbook* (1977) with S. Nicholls, BBC.

Ms Arora took her first degree at the University of Punjab in Chandigarh and received higher degrees there and at the University of London. She lectured in English at various degree colleges in the Punjab and at Delhi University before coming to England in 1968. Since then she has taught in primary and secondary schools in a number of local authorities in the Greater London area, been an Education Officer with the BBC and co-ordinated English language teaching provision for Asian adults in a London borough. Before taking up her present job, Ms Arora lectured in Education at Roehampton Institute of Higher Education and at Bradford College where she was engaged in initial and in-service training of teachers.

Carlton Duncan was born in Jamaica, West Indies, in 1941 where he was educated up to the General Level of Education standard. On arrival in the UK in January 1961 he discovered that it was necessary to repeat his general education, which he did between the years 1961 and 1965 at Kilburn Polytechnic in north west

London. In 1965 he entered the University of Wales (Swansea), where he read for and obtained a joint honours BSc (Econ) in Economics and Sociology by 1968. He spent a further year at Swansea obtaining his Postgraduate Certificate in Education and began his first teaching post for the Inner London Education Authority in 1969. By 1971 he moved to the Brent (London) Authority on his first promotion to a Departmental Headship. By 1975 he was again promoted to a faculty headship with the same authority.

In 1976 he took up the Deputy Headship of Sidney Stringer School and Community College in Coventry, where he was to spend the next five years, during which time he privately prepared for and obtained an External London Law degree – LLB(Hons) 1979.

Whilst in Coventry, he was invited to serve on the Rampton (later Swann) Department of Education and Science National Inquiry into the education of ethnic minorities. His service extended to the level of sub-committee chairmanship. During 1980 he was appointed one of Her Majesty's Justices of the Peace, West Midlands Commission, Coventry Bench.

In April 1982 he took up the headship of a large comprehensive school (Wyke Manor Upper) in Bradford where he is still. He has also served on the Home Office Working Party on the Recruitment of Ethnic Minorities to the Police Forces; is currently serving on the DES Statistic (Ethnic) Working Party: Regional Sub-group and on the National Union of Teachers' Working Party for Multi-Ethnic Education, and is a consultant for Anti-Racist Teaching at Sunderland Polytechnic Education Department. Finally, Duncan is now an assessor in County Court cases involving Race Relations under the 1976 Race Relations Act.

Sylvia Collicott gained both her History Honours degree and the Postgraduate Certificate of Education at Leeds University. She worked for four years at Kenyatta College, Nairobi, as a history teacher. On her return to England, she went into infant teaching. She completed a part-time MPhil in December 1981 and has written a number of articles for *Child Education*. Now seconded to the Multicultural Curriculum Support Group, Haringey, she is at present writing a book tracing Haringey's local–world links over the past four hundred years.

Gerry Davis (BEd, MA), was born in St Vincent, West Indies, in 1948. He came with his parents to England in 1959 and attended primary and secondary school in the London area. Before studying mathematics and physical education at a college of education, he worked as a chemist at the Atomic Energy Authority, Harwell and studied part-time day release for the ONC in sciences. Having taught in three London comprehensive schools, he was seconded to the Multicultural Curriculum Support Group in Haringey, where he began the development of a strategy for change to a multicultural curriculum, particularly in primary schools. He is currently Adviser for Multicultural Education in Brent and is married with two children attending a Brent infants school.

Dave Dunn started teaching in Sussex, in what used to be the largest comprehensive school in Europe. He then moved to Yorkshire to work on education for international understanding. Since 1978 he has been a research fellow at the University of Keele in Staffordshire, at first studying in-service teacher education. At present he is working on 'The Educational and Vocational Experiences of Young People of Minority Ethnic Groups'.

Derek J. Dyson is a mathematics teacher at Wyke Manor Upper School, Bradford, West Yorkshire. He is chairman of a working party on multicultural education in the Faculty of Mathematics and Commerce.

Gillian Klein joined ILEA as a school librarian in 1967. As librarian for ILEA's Centre for Urban Education Studies, she set up the first consultative collection of books for teachers and students in a multicultural society. She left in 1981 to prepare a list for the Schools Council: *Resources for Multicultural Education: An introduction*, which she has just extensively revised for its second edition. Then followed a year as teacher fellow at the London Institute of Education, one outcome of which was a report on the role of the school librarian as a changed agent towards multicultural education.

She has written widely for the *Times Educational Supplement* and other journals, contributed chapters to several books and is the author of a book published by Routledge & Kegan Paul: *Reading into Racism: Bias in children's literature and learning materials*. With artists Simon Willey and Bridgett Hill, she has produced two series of infant books, *The Fancy Dress Party* and *Scrapbooks* (Methuen) and she edits the termly journal *Multicultural Teaching*.

Horace Lashley was born in Trinidad and came to Britain in 1961. He joined the RAF on arrival in the UK. On leaving the RAF in 1967 he went to Trent Park College of Education. He has subsequently done postgraduate work at Manchester University and Brunel University. He has taught in a number of schools and has had considerable experience in youth work. He has also been a visiting lecturer to a variety of higher educational institutions on the subject of multicultural education. At present he works as the Senior Education Officer at the Commission for Racial Equality.

Tuku Mukherjee is a senior lecturer in Multicultural Studies at Southlands College (constituent college of the Roehampton Institute, London). He is a member of the Racism Awareness Training Programme and secretary of Sri Guru Singh Sabha Education Committee, Southall. He is also a consultant to Berkshire LEA's Education for Equality Service.

Sue Watts has taught science in London schools and is currently an advisory teacher in the Secondary Curriculum Development Unit which works for the ILEA Multi-Ethnic Inspectorate. She has worked with a number of science teachers in the ILEA and elsewhere looking at science education in a multicultural society. She was formerly head of science at Central Foundation Girls' School in Bow, east London.

Note: Biographical data for editors and all contributors were correct at the time the manuscript was completed.

Acknowledgments

The editors wish to express their thanks to all contributors. They are also grateful for the support they have received from their families and friends during the preparation of this volume. They are particularly indebted to Janice Sugden for her invaluable secretarial assistance.

Ranjit Arora would also like to acknowledge the generous help received from Arthur Arnold, Peter Chambers and Dave Dunn in the preparation of her contributions.

Abbreviations

ACER	Afro-Caribbean Educational Research Project
CILT	Centre for Information on Language Teaching and Research
IMTEC	International Movements Towards Educational Change
IRR	Institute of Race Relations
NAAY	National Association for Asian Youth
NAME	National Association for Multiracial Education
NARTAR	National Association for Race Relations Teaching and Action Research
NATE	National Association for Teachers of English
SLIPP	Second Language Learning in the Primary Classroom Project

Chapter 1

Editorial

Ranjit Arora and Carlton Duncan

It is not always easy to recognize when one is caught up in a revolution. Yet only the most careless and reluctant of educationists will not have observed the revolutionary thrust of educational thought and practice both nationally and internationally in recognizing the true nature of the composition of the world's population.

Of course, it is still possible, though not strictly accurate, to speak of pockets, either locally, nationally or internationally, of monocultural/racial groupings of people, but such a picture would represent the exception to the greater reality. For this reason, plus the rapidly shrinking size of our world in relation to travel, communication and business, together with the important virtues of truth, justice and equality, the demand for education to reflect positively all races of people and to make a concerted attack against stereotypes, negative and racist attitudes to some races is at last becoming commonplace.

Some of these views have found expression in one way or the other in no fewer than four government publications all in the early 1980s.[1] All these reports recognize the experience of racial discrimination and prejudice as the one special factor shared by all minority groups in this country. At the time of writing an increasing number of local authorities are also issuing statements of policies which strongly indicate their commitment to multicultural education coupled with their anti-racism policies.

At the same time, not only are new authors and publishers emerging in these fields, but even more familiar authors and established publishers are now coming to terms with this new dawn on the education frontiers.

Many publications, especially in the early 1980s, have appeared under titles similar to this one. Their aim, like ours, is to stimulate worth-while changes and a rejection of the old Eurocentric approaches to the curriculum. We, as the title suggests, intend further to emphasize models of good practice across the country: models which have been tested and found to be effective in meeting the aims and purposes which we intend. The book is in the main written for student teachers, practising teachers (probationers and experienced) and teacher trainers who we hope will find this volume of immense use from a practical point of view. But we also hope that all others with an interest in education will also find it interesting and informative.

It will be observed, throughout, that for us multicultural education is not an additional competing subject in schools. We dissociate ourselves most strongly from the view that multicultural education is about teaching black studies as per the Tulse Hill model of the 1970s or only about Asian studies or Caribbean studies. Similarly and very much in Maureen Stone's mould, we do not lend much support to 'one off' cultural evenings or the pretence of celebrating festivals outside the Christian tradition as multicultural education.

Again, we have endeavoured to get as far away as possible from the idea that multicultural education is something for ethnic minorities – rather at the expense of white children. The views which we advocate, it will be observed, are measures to benefit all children alike. Because, as the Fifth Report from the Home Affairs Committee suggests, 'School is the one shared experience of all Britons. We have no alternative but to seek there a solution to the problems which may arise elsewhere but which are at their most visible in the educational arena.'

In other words, we take the view that multicultural education in schools is about what happens via the curriculum whether planned or hidden. And if the curriculum – whether planned or hidden – is to be multicultural in approach, then it should be appropriate to the education of all pupils, whatever their background by reference to a diversity of cultures. Hence, a variety of cultural and social groups must be evident in the visual images, stories and historical, geographical or whatever type of information disseminated within the school. The selections should not be made in such a way as to reinforce stereotyping of life-styles, occupations, status, human characteristics or one particular culture. Teachers should take the responsibility of selecting not merely from preselected collections but also from a rich and wide variety of resources available in the classroom and in the community. A 'good' education cannot be based on one culture only and should therefore be multicultural by definition.

It should enable a child to understand his/her own society and to know enough about other societies to enhance that understanding.

This book is an attempt to illustrate some of the ways in which practitioners are responding positively to the changing educational needs of our multicultural, multiracial and multilingual schools. We recognize that 'the world of people's feelings and ideas, of what is happening to them in real life moves much more quickly than the long, slow development lead time in schools'. This is why changes in school curriculum and in policies are frequently met with a characteristic response of 'too little and too late' slogan.

The development lead time in schools may appear to be too slow but it certainly requires a well-thought-out overall strategy. It is to these strategies for change that the first section of our book is devoted. Gerry Davis begins this by addressing himself to individual class teachers. He offers an analysis of the factors which are in the control of individual class teachers. He also suggests strategies for effecting change within these factors which are directly associated with developing education for a multicultural democracy.

He believes, and we share this belief, that the individual teacher has a responsibility both inside and outside the classroom to eliminate the ideology of racism from the structures and procedures of education itself.

These teacher-controlled factors such as the curriculum (both stated and hidden), content and selection procedure, selection and use of material, links with home and community, communication, in-service training are later dealt with in individual chapters.

In 'Black Response to White Definitions', Tuku Mukherjee describes how black children are imprisoned by white definitions as the 'cause and victim' of the failure of the English educational system. He explains how multicultural education offers a 'liberal racist' version of reality by concentrating on interpersonal relationships and the provision of information on 'backgrounds'. He illustrates his argument by discussing courses for teachers and the police, stressing that pleas for harmony and understanding do not face up to the ideology of white racism. Even personal awareness of racism is totally inadequate unless that awareness is incorporated into one's institutional role and used to change the structures of black oppression.

It is in this context of the institutional role of the headteacher that Carlton Duncan points us towards a way forward in situations and circumstances as encountered by him at Wyke Manor School in Bradford. He suggests that strategies for overcoming difficulties and obstacles are as important as the listing of achievements. This case study will no doubt offer the readers some interesting parallels with their own situations. The message from Duncan is that challenge must be accepted with commitment and a desire to learn.

This message of accepting a challenge is further conveyed by Ranjit Arora in her focus on multicultural curriculum at a primary level. She argues that for a change within the school curriculum to be effective and even possible, it is vital that changes are initiated within the staff themselves. Since the key agents of change are classroom teachers, it is important for them to be aware of their personal position in race and culture and to question their assumptions, attitudes and expectations. They also need to step down from the role of the authority in a classroom to share experiences with children and to allow them to create their own learning experiences and to evaluate these by sharing with others.

Whilst recognizing the need for a whole school policy to ensure a non-racist selection of content and organisation of the curriculum and resources, Ms Arora emphasizes that an examination of processes used to teach skills and transmit knowledge and values is equally important to ensure a just balance in the curriculum, because it is only through analysing these processes that we can hope to address the important question: How does a school educate children against prejudice, racism and discrimination? It is suggested that employment of more ethnic minority teachers and more frequent and active contact with parents may be helpful, but most importantly schools need to create a climate where it is easier to discuss emotive issues such as race, prejudice and stereotyping in a constructive and educational way.

The view taken throughout this book is that such uninternational racist attitudes as may become evident by analysis of the process, together with a Eurocentric approach to the curriculum in the British schools, is largely responsible for the now well established social facts of underachievement amongst ethnic minority children and of misinformed indigenous white people.

Duncan's chapter on multicultural curriculum at a secondary level includes subject-by-subject pointers to avoid the consequences of the well-meant but misguided adoption of the 'equal treatment for all' principle.

The second section of our book is devoted to multicultural approaches as illustrated by practitioners in their specific curriculum areas. Sylvia Collicott believes that history has an important part to play in developing personal, local, cultural, religious and national identities. She argues that since each country's history is one of constant contact with other parts of the world, it is necessary to trace the links between England and other countries. She also suggests that history should be taught through a whole curriculum approach and that each child's family history can be a starting-point for a spiral curriculum in history followed closely by themes in the local community. We find that Collicott's chapter represents a rather refreshing style, which illustrates most effectively the technique for 'starting where the pupils are'. This technique also lends itself very readily to a multicultural approach to the history curriculum.

Horace Lashley not only sees art education as a jumping-off point for multicultural education but focuses on wider issues of arts education in a multicultural society. He argues that the omission from the curriculum of rich oral tradition and written literature of ethnic minorities has contributed to the feelings of alienation.

This chapter includes some excellent examples of good practice – not only of models such as West Indian music in Birmingham and Asian music in Harrow – but also of the introduction of non-European musical forms in all-white schools. The importance of drama as a way to improve confidence in social relations as well as in using language is highlighted. Examples of the visual arts and performing arts in schools in Manchester and Leicester lead him to conclude that it is important to see the arts as emerging from children's experiences inside and outside schools and as a means of enriching and making sense of themselves.

Ranjit Arora confirms the view that separation of ESL learners from the mainstream classroom cannot be justified on educational grounds and calls for a model of language teaching that is flexible and more sensitive to the learners' needs. She also includes examples of some of the ways in which language support across the curriculum can be provided for through integrated project work in primary schools and through collaborative efforts between subject teachers and ESL teachers in secondary schools.

Derek Dyson begins by looking at various approaches to teaching mathematics in a multicultural classroom. These range from those which merely acknowledge the presence of different cultures in the classroom to those which directly recognize the contribution of other cultures to mathematics, whether they are represented in the classroom or not. He also explores the mathematical potential of subjects such as geography and art and takes us through the history of mathematics to demonstrate specific contributions of various cultures to its development.

Sue Watts has attempted to develop some of the issues which science teachers need to consider and suggests some of the ways in which they need to rethink science education with a multicultural perspective. She begins by examining the nature of science and the way it is taught in our schools and moves on to issues of language in science education and points towards ways of locating racist bias in biology textbooks and developing anti-racist approaches to science teaching. Whilst the main thrust of this chapter is towards consideration of science as a process, it does include a brief explanation of some of the content issues such as conflicts with religious beliefs and questions of health education, genetics and evolution.

The third section of the book includes chapters on initial and in-service teacher training, the role of the community, pastoral care and resources.

Gillian Klein, in 'Resources of Multicultural Education', urges teachers to examine their aims and objectives for proposed new initiatives in the school's curriculum because resources cannot in themselves teach the students. She distinguishes resources used in the classroom from those available for teachers' use. She believes it is important for teachers to handle and evaluate materials before purchasing them and draws out attention to criteria for selection of resources. She reminds teachers of their responsibility to ensure that books offer accurate information and a multicultural perspective on the world and the people in it. As for their use, teachers would do well to remember that resources are only as good as the way in which they are used.

In 'Initial Teacher Training', Ranjit Arora describes an institutional response to the community's social, cultural, environmental, educational and industrial needs. She traces the development of a college policy for teacher education for a multicultural society and discusses key aspects of its implementation as evident in some of the current teacher training programmes. Throughout the chapter reference is made to the guiding assumptions for multicultural processes in teacher education and to the specific examples of good practice found within the institution which particularly relate to teacher training programmes. Ms Arora is aware of the dangerously false impression of coherence and integration inherent in the case study format. However, her first-hand experience of the conflict resulting from the effects of endless series of mergers has given her an insight which lends credibility to this description and her pertinent observations. She calls for a comprehensive programme of multicultural education which includes coherent approaches that span units and individuals, a policy of staff support and staff development, participation of staff from minority groups as consultants, advisers and governors and, above all, she calls for successful experience of teaching in the multicultural classrooms.

Dave Dunn examines some of the difficulties faced by providers of in-service courses in multicultural education and provides a critique of the course structures that are generally adopted. The analysis and the diversity of course participants is illustrated by frequent quotations from teachers attending courses.

He claims that these courses overemphasize issues of language and culture to the detriment of considering the importance of race and class in affecting the attainment of pupils. It is maintained, and demonstrated by examples, that knowledge of racism and structural inequality are vital for any adequate comprehension of multicultural education. A critical examination of processes of schooling considered in courses suggests that in-service provision gives undue prominence to curriculum development but fails to accord adequate attention to allocation procedures and classroom interaction.

In 'The Multicultural Community and the School', Carlton Duncan illustrates how careful thought about issues sometimes taken for granted can bring about desirable results. Many would agree with his basic philosophy that education is more meaningful when it is seen as a total community affair. But it is the translation of this philosophy into action which has not always been effectively met. It is in this respect that this chapter is most interesting, particularly in the recognition that communities are not always homogeneous. Sidney Stringer School is a living example of such recognition and this lends credibility to Duncan's ideas.

Finally, pastoral care is given a comprehensive definition in that no aspect of a child's development can be considered in isolation. The conclusion one inevitably arrives at is that, for example, where the school with a multiracial population does not adopt a multicultural approach to the curriculum, it is necessarily, albeit unconsciously, doing injustice to its ethnic minority pupils in terms of pastoral care as Duncan defines it. It is hard not to accept such an analysis, particularly since it is based on tried and tested practice in different schools.

Note

1 These include *West Indian Children in Our Schools*, the interim report of the Committee of Inquiry into the education of children from ethnic minority groups; *Fifth Report from the Home Affairs Committee, Racial Disadvantage; The Brixton Disorders*, report of an inquiry by the Rt Hon Lord Scarman, OBE, and *Experience and Participation*, report of the Review Group on the Youth Service in England.

Chapter 2

Strategies for change

Gerry Davis

An important feature of the British education system is its decentralised nature, with decisions being made at different levels in the system.[1] Multicultural education is concerned with changing the nature of teaching and learning across the board. Proponents argue that the present system is based on representing the knowledge, values, beliefs, ways of life, i.e. culture,[2] of white people on the apparent premise that they are of supreme importance. Many advocates of the status quo would argue that since Britain is a predominantly white country the current perspective may be justified. However, I have not read any serious work which attempts to justify this white ethnocentric perspective on educational grounds. I doubt that it could ever be justified on such grounds – yet it persists.

Multicultural education initiatives at school level should be concerned with changing the white ethnocentric perspective within education. This perspective serves to perpetuate the notion of racial superiority and supports racism in society. In order to change, it would be necessary to challenge the established norms, values and attitudes which have developed in custom and practice, and which perpetuate racial prejudice and racism primarily *within the education service*.

In our decentralised system this kind of broad-based change in the system is hard to achieve quickly. However, the very nature of the system does allow a degree of autonomy to individuals at each level of the service. It is therefore possible for individual classroom teachers to exercise their degree of autonomy within their realm and level of decision-making and thereby effect certain changes.

In this chapter an analysis of the factors which are in the control of individual classroom teachers is offered. Strategies are suggested for effecting change within those factors which are directly associated with developing education for a multicultural democracy.

The desire to change is really a matter of the professional integrity of the teacher. If the principles of equality, fairness and justice are really important, the buck cannot be passed to higher authorities. A teacher does not need to seek permission to do what is educationally, professionally and ethnically right. It is, however, recognised that advice is needed to enable the teacher to develop a strategy for doing what is right and just.

A realistic goal

The individual classroom teachers wishing to change the white ethnocentric perspective should not presume that their work in the classroom will directly eliminate racism and racial inequality from society at large. That would be an unrealistic goal which ignores the influence of other institutions, and if adopted would only serve to create a feeling of powerlessness and hopelessness in the committed teacher. Education cannot, indeed, compensate for society.[3]

The goal for the teacher committed to change is to teach from a perspective which is not based on an ideology of cultural (or any other) superiority. A learning environment may thus be created in which pupils would be motivated towards successful learning of skills, information, values, attitudes and beliefs which will enable them to participate effectively within a multicultural democracy. They would be motivated to question the inequalities in society and strive for structural changes to promote a fair, just and equal society.

The immediate concern of the teacher committed to the development of education for a multicultural democracy should be the elimination of the ideology of racism from the structures and procedures of education itself. In this regard the individual teacher has a responsibility both inside and outside the classroom. The goal is not only achievable; it suggests the only educationally justifiable approach to schooling within a society created out of a history of colonialism and imperialism. This approach has been referred to as 'an anti-racist approach to multicultural education'.[4]

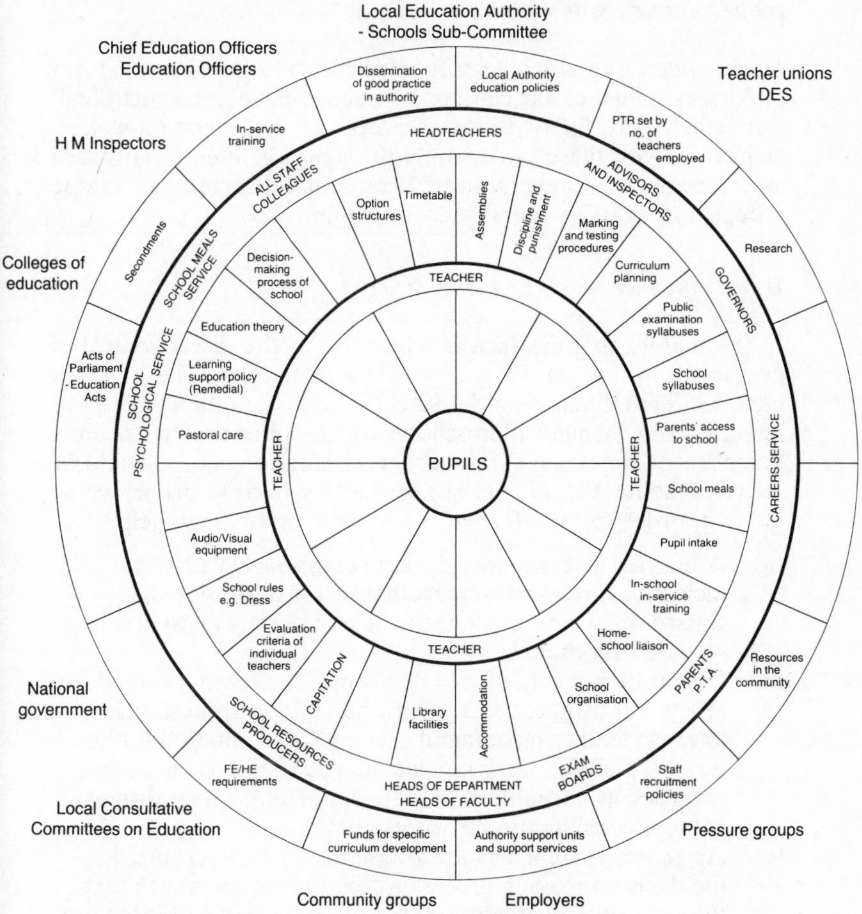

Figure 2.1 Representation of some of the factors which are central to or impinge on the work of the classroom teacher

Factors relevant to the change process

Figure 2.1 represents some of the factors which committed classroom teachers have identified to me as being important in their quest to develop an anti-racist approach to multicultural education in the classroom.

Indirect influence on classroom practice

In the outer ring some factors which have an indirect but yet important influence on classroom practice have been identified. The teacher is likely to have access to the decision-makers concerned with these factors only through organised groups such as unions or community groups. They could, therefore, join these groups and exercise pressure from within.

Direct influence on classroom practice

In the middle ring are factors which are in the direct control of people within the school and governors/managers. These factors have a direct influence on the teachers and could therefore act as limitations to change within schools which prefer to retain a white ethnocentric approach. The teacher wishing to change should be selective about the factors she/he tackles outside his/her classroom in order to be effective. Four basic points may help:

(a) A teacher with integrity cannot compromise with any incident of overt racism whether inside or outside the classroom. To be silent in the face of overtly racist acts is to collude with that racism.

(b) Covert racism is harder to deal with. The teacher should aim to confront covert racism when the confrontation is likely to lead to meaningful change. Confrontation for its own sake about everything could lead to the teacher being regarded as a troublesome staffroom crank who is dismissed without consideration by colleagues.

(c) As a priority, teachers are advised to strive to ensure that the decision-making process within the school is such that the view of individuals are allowed to be expressed (but not necessarily accepted and acted upon at all times). If as a profession we are to educate children to participate in decision-making processes implicit in democratic living, it is vital that democratic decision-making is practised by the staff.

(d) The teachers engaged in change within their classroom will soon find that certain school factors will be acting as limitations to those changes. It is on these factors that the teacher should concentrate as they arise.
Write (keeping a copy) to the appropriate person responsible for the factor (e.g. school meals, to the school meals supervisor) outlining:

1 The nature of the limitation;
2 The effect of the limitation on the children's education inside and outside the classroom;
3 Suggestions of ways in which the limiting factor could be reduced or removed;
4 The time-scale in which you hope the change to occur;
5 Request for a reply in writing and a chance to discuss the matter.

Also, raise the issue at meetings.

Strategy for influencing the whole staff

I have found that individual teachers who wish to develop certain changes find it difficult to discuss the relevant issues with colleagues. As a strategy, some of these teachers have been able to encourage their headteachers to invite a speaker to outline the issues. As a result of many such requests from primary teachers, I have developed a model for debating the issue of racism in what is selected to be taught. The model was based on an attempt to create a supportive, trusting framework in which individuals could deal constructively with racism when revealed.

A brainstorming technique was developed, based on certain principles described by Carl Rogers[5] to create a supportive atmosphere in which each person felt valued. This was vital, since the projected debate was about the need to value people. The teachers were asked to brainstorm (call out at random) the themes or topics they already taught in their curriculum. This was a necessary starting-point as it focused on what teachers perceived as their *normal* curriculum. If they could see that many of the areas they taught were inherently multicultural, they could be made to examine their own reasons (and ideology) for having taught with an ethnocentric and, in its effect, racist perspective.

The teachers were asked to call out any topics which they had taught, would be teaching or would like to teach. These were written down exactly as they were named by the teacher. One major aspect of the exercise was that every contribution had to be written down. It was very important that every member of staff present should feel that he/she has invested in the collection being amassed in front of him/her. Thus, if a stated topic was considered by others to be included in one previously stated, both topics were written down. It was more important to retain the involvement of every staff member than to worry about the number of topics written down.

Before the start of the actual brainstorm, a short introduction about the concept of multicultural education was given. The brainstorm technique was also explained. In particular the necessity for a non-censorial method was stressed. Teachers were asked not to veto any topic or give overt value-judgments on any topic either verbally or non-verbally; for example, by laughing. This was vitally important because curriculum is a personal matter with many primary teachers. To a great extent the topics they taught reflect their own interests, knowledge and skills. Any overt comment on a topic could have been seen by the contributor of that topic as a comment on him/her, reducing that teacher's inclination to be fully involved. If this did occur, the non-censorial atmosphere needed to be re-established and the 'abused' teacher encouraged to commit him/herself once more.

Using the technique, it was possible within fifteen to thirty minutes to get a whole staff to make public their 'head-held' topic curriculum. It was not necessary to divide the topic into subject areas, although this could have been done if the school worked within a definite subject framework. Also, many of the topics seemed to be distinctly multidisciplinary in nature.

The purpose of the exercise of topic collection was to separate the topics from the people. Given the large number of topics which was amassed, it was rarely possible to match a particular topic to the contributing teacher. It was thus possible to discuss the topic itself without becoming enmeshed in the person and thus personal defensiveness – itself a barrier to change.

The exercise was relatively quick, and if conducted properly was free of stress and anxiety. It could be conducted by a headteacher or other delegated member of staff and would be a useful starting-point for a school wishing to evaluate its programme. Throughout the schools visited, this sort of evaluation had not been done. While the exercise was in progress, it became obvious that many of the topics mentioned by individuals were being taught by other teachers – but in ignorance of each other's work.

It was possible to discuss this crucial point with teachers. There was a feeling that curriculum planning was about people from 'outside' telling the school what to teach. By discussing the repetition of topics in the school it was possible to show teachers that curriculum planning needed to be done by them in order to maximise the use of resources and time and to structure the child's learning as he/she progressed through the school. The isolated way in which teachers worked was criticised by Her Majesty's Inspectors in their report on Primary Schools in

England.[6] Teachers who encountered the fact that the same topics were being taught to the same children in successive years soon realised the necessity for structuring that work. This encounter was made possible by the public brainstorm technique.

This was a very important matter. Racism affects teachers' expectations of certain pupils. If they feel that black pupils are innately intellectually inferior, they are unlikely to plan and structure their work with sufficient care. The effects of racial disadvantage are compounded when work is not carefully planned and structured, and underachievement can result. Social class and sexist ideologies have similar effects by providing lazy and professionally incompetent teachers with excuses for their failure to educate all children.

It is unlikely that this strategy for starting a debate in school could be done by the individual teacher but anyone, even a newly qualified teacher, could and should suggest issues and speakers for school-based in-service training.

There are many factors which are in the direct control of the individual teacher, and which are therefore in the individual's power to change.

In the inner ring in which pupils form the central focus, some of the many factors over which the individual teacher has major control have been identified. Changes in these factors would be required to achieve the immediate goal outlined earlier in this chapter.

The curriculum

This is a strong indicator of the school's and teacher's value system. The main part of the teacher's day is taken up with the curriculum. It is important, therefore, that the teacher be held accountable for the way in which the philosophy of white ethnic superiority is perpetuated within it. There are many other things for which critics of some bad practice, which masquerades under the name of multicultural education, would like teachers to be accountable.[7] But the curriculum is the focus around which the teacher's work revolves and should therefore be the priority in terms of teachers' accountability.

The curriculum is much more than the list of subjects, faculties, topics/themes to be taught. It can be defined as the information, skills, techniques, values, beliefs and attitudes which are learned within a school. The information or knowledge may be listed as facts, rules, concepts, generalisations, principles and theories, and is usually contained in the teacher's syllabus or scheme of work.

The 'unadmitted' curriculum

The values, attitudes and beliefs implicit in the syllabus and in the school are rarely listed or stated explicitly. They are usually conveniently dismissed as being part of the 'hidden curriculum'. In my experience, this tends to be hidden from the teacher and not from the pupils. The black child (Asian/African or Caribbean) who is constantly subjected to a white ethnocentric curriculum is all too aware of the potency of that hidden (though I prefer 'unadmitted') curriculum. The hidden curriculum can be sensed within the ethos of the classroom. In a supportive learning environment in which diversity is taken as normal, the children represent a useful resource in themselves, and pupils from the various cultural backgrounds would intuitively feel that their commonsense knowledge[8] is valued and respected.

As teachers, we are daily and continuously defining what is to count as valuable knowledge to be included in the curriculum. Our selections also reveal our perception of who are to count as valuable people.

In this pluralist diverse society, the white ethnocentric perspective and its resultant curriculum suggests that white British people and their culture are superior to at least those British people who are not white. The fact that black people have been British subjects for over 150 years appears to be lost as part of the historical amnesia[9] suffered by people educated into the white ethnocentric perspective. Through a white ethnocentric curriculum, teachers are actively teaching racial superiority and racial prejudice to their white pupils. This is mainly done through a process of omitting any significant knowledge about black people (African, Asian, Caribbean) from the normal curriculum. It is through this omission that the historical racial myths, prejudices, half-truths and disadvantages are sustained and the hypocritical form of British racism perpetuated. That it is unintentional[10] is a claim which needs to be seriously questioned. It is an insult to teachers who are the guardians of the intellectual development of the nation's children to suggest that they are doing part of their work unconsciously. The vehemence with which the teaching profession on the whole (but with notable exceptions) has resisted the debate on multicultural education suggests a very conscious approach.

It is my experience that many teachers wrongly believe that multicultural education is about teaching black children their culture. That is a misguided and presumptuous view of the situation. The multicultural curriculum is concerned with the teaching of essential skills, concepts/ideas, organised in various subject disciplines, through examples appropriately selected from various cultural/ethnic groups, but with a recognition that those groups are not equally valued in the society or even in the school. It is a new perspective and content which is required, and not necessarily new subjects.

I once saw a multicultural class of pupils working on the follow-up materials of the television programme 'How We Used to Live – The Victorians'. The programme and materials depicted a white upper-middle-class family in London and their below-stairs staff. The teacher was asked about the development she had planned. None had been planned. To any onlooker it would have seemed necessary to deal with the mismatch between the 'we' present in the diversity of the class and the 'we' depicted by the materials. Those children would leave school, as did generations before them, believing that they have encountered the Victorians. However, teachers would agree that the Victorians were, at least, all those British subjects who lived under the rule of Queen Victoria. This would mean that in truth the Victorians were a multiracial and multicultural society, a group of people living in many lands. The teacher was not cognisant of that fact because she had been 'educated' with a monocultural curriculum where only the white British experience was given value. If the evidence about the Victorians had been looked at with educational rather than ideological eyes, the topic could never have been taught as it has been. Selections would have been made to depict the lives of African, Asian and West Indian Victorians so that children would come to see that they too were living and were contributing to the wealth and life of the British nation, as well as to their own countries. But the learnings from this approach would also be vital to white pupils who need to realise that 'their people' are not the centre of everything. However, the ideology on which the monocultural curriculum is based may not wish those truths to be known.

Curriculum content

In order to advise on strategies for changing the content of the 'normal curriculum', it is necessary to analyse the process teachers use to determine what is to be taught.

Selection procedure

Teachers tend to select what they teach according to the resources which are available. Even in primary schools which boast a child-centred approach the curriculum tends to be 'controlled' by the producers of school resources.[11]

In secondary schools, teachers claim that their perspective for years 1 to 3 is governed by what is embodied in the public examination syllabuses. They apparently construct the lower school curriculum content by selecting materials which reflect the values, attitudes, beliefs and concept of valuable knowledge and people, as dictated by the public examiners. Through this process of selecting curriculum content from available materials, teachers are allowing the *resources tail to wag the curriculum dog*.

While working with colleagues in Haringey, we recognised that if serious change was to be encouraged, it was necessary to develop a means of helping teachers to change their selection procedure. Colleagues in the Multicultural Curriculum Support Group in Haringey recognised that the teacher wishing to change the white ethnocentric perspective in the classroom must regain control of what is to count as valuable curriculum content. Thus, teachers were helped to decide what was worth teaching before looking at the available materials.

Changing the selection procedure

All teachers in primary and secondary schools necessarily teach in topics (within a subject discipline) or in themes (interdisciplinary).

1 The teacher must be able to justify educationally why a particular topic or theme is included in the curriculum.
2 The teacher must detail the information, skills, attitudes, values or beliefs which are inherent to the chosen topic or theme. This would also involve a description of the methods to be used to teach that topic.

This plan or scheme can be drawn up with guidance from appropriate advisers/inspectors, headteachers, post-holders, or heads of department. It is knowledge about the conceptual structure of the subject disciplines which is required to do this and not knowledge of multicultural (in its true meaning) examples. This planning should be done well in advance of teaching the topic to allow the teacher to acquire the knowledge and resources required to teach from an anti-racist/multicultural perspective.

As a general guide, the basic essential concepts of the subject disciplines could form the basis of this conceptual curriculum.[12] J.A. Banks[13] suggests some key concepts for study in a multicultural curriculum and gives a good analysis of how they could be taught from several subject-discipline perspectives. He writes in an American context, but is concerned with the development of education for genuine democratic living, which is also the goal of this chapter.

Having decided what ideas or concepts need to be taught, the teacher should, where appropriate, select examples from various ethnic/cultural groups' perspectives, through which the concept may be grasped and critically analysed. The teacher should not seek to select an example from every culture for every concept. It is sufficient to select two or three examples for each concept. However, over a term or year, examples from a wide variety of cultural/ethnic groups would be utilised. Choices should not be restricted to the groups represented in the school. This short-sighted outlook has probably resulted in the widespread view that a multicultural curriculum is valid only in multicultural schools. This is totally fallacious and misses the major educational justifications for a multicultural curriculum.

Curriculum materials

There seems to be a tacit agreement that school resources depicting the lives, achievements and contributions of Asian, African and Caribbean people are valid only for black pupils. School resources producers appear to be suggesting that there is no market for such materials because teachers in all-white schools/areas would not buy them. The producers are probably right, although paradoxically it is the pupils in those schools/areas who may be in greatest need of such resources if they are not to develop the attitude of racial superiority engendered by a white ethnocentric curriculum.

It is unlikely that teachers' demands would increase fast enough for resource producers to recognise the commercial viability. Thus the teachers themselves need to develop their own classroom materials – as many do already. In order to change, they need to expand their sources from which the information for their materials are to be gained. There are now black bookshops and specialist multicultural curriculum development centres (e.g.

Bedford, Coventry, Birmingham) that produce materials. The Commonwealth Institute has some useful materials, and the Institute of Race Relations very good materials. Ultimately, teachers engaged in change of this nature would find that curriculum materials may become a limitation. It is true that the teacher's attitude and expectation are more important, but materials are an expression of those and not a substitute for them.

In some Local Authorities, support units and centres have been established to help teachers to extend their knowledge and produce appropriate materials (e.g. Brent, Birmingham, Bristol, Coventry, Bedford, ILEA). In areas where these units/centres do not exist, the teacher should campaign through his/her head-teacher, adviser/inspector, union, for specialist resourcing, perhaps through the Teachers' Centre. In a society in which it is obvious that change is a permanent feature, it is vital that every Authority develop the means whereby teachers could engage in change as a normal process. This is relevant to all areas of schooling. In multiethnic areas, Section 11 funding may be attracted for the staffing of units designed to help schools to meet the needs of what the section of the 1966 Local Government Act calls 'New Commonwealth Immigrants'.

Display of visual materials

The images in the classroom (and around the school) convey the striking message of whom the school/teachers value as people. The teacher who is keen to display images of black people as well as those of white must ensure that they do not perpetuate occupation and status stereotypes.

The availability of capitation may be a limitation to the individual teacher. If this is the case, this is a factor about which he/she should campaign. However, there are useful arrays of images in magazines, colour supplements and posters from embassies and travel agents (though care must be taken with these). Posters and photoprints may also be available cheaply from specialised multicultural units around the country. Community and religious groups are usually happy to help with resources of this kind if approached in a sensible manner. Teachers could also utilise the talents of their design and arts colleagues to produce illustrations of people who are not white.

Finally, but most importantly, a well-thought-out and honestly taught curriculum will undoubtedly produce images of a multiracial nature by the pupils, whatever their own group. Indeed, this could be a criterion for evaluating the effectiveness of a multicultural approach.

Links with home and community

In multicultural areas, teachers may have certain fears about visiting groups which are ethnically different from their own. Parents and others in the community also appear to find schools rather forbidding places. As a teacher involved in change, I could not tolerate this gulf. Too often parent/school liaison tends to be discussed in relation to disciplinary problems and not in relation to the curriculum. The teacher with a clear conceptual curriculum, described earlier, planned well in advance, is in a good position to seek the knowledge and resources from parents and others in the community. Black parents are very interested in their children's education. They would value the chance to contribute to the most meaningful part of school life to them, i.e., the curriculum, rather than to the more peripheral, but none the less enjoyable, social functions.

Teachers in all-white areas are somewhat deprived of the rich human resources in multiethnic areas. A useful strategy for these teachers is to attend national and regional DES courses so that they may form useful links with colleagues in multiethnic areas. Visits to specialist multicultural units is also a useful strategy for the formation of contacts. Perhaps, in the future, teacher exchanges between multicultural and all-white areas could be arranged.

Verbal and non-verbal communication

Although these are important factors in all classes, they are crucial in ethnically and linguistically mixed classes.

Verbal

In classes where pupils do not come from a standard English home background, the teacher needs to develop a genuine regard and acceptance of the children's language repertoire. The good teacher will wish to value the children's language(s) while at the same time helping them to acquire standard English, especially the written form, which is the language of access in education. This would require significant but necessary self-in-service training and attendance at organised courses.

Non-verbal

The teachers' real attitudes to pupils are expressed in non-verbal (and sometimes verbal) communication. A teacher who does not have a genuine feeling of equality for certain groups of pupils is unlikely to hide it from the pupils. Some people have invented the convenient 'chip on the shoulder' excuse to explain what I regard as pupils' reaction to racist non-verbal communication.

Discipline

In my experience, the teacher who is not sure about his/her attitudes to black groups tends to have difficulty when it comes to disciplining black pupils. They tend to be reluctant to demand the highest standards of discipline from black pupils. If pupils are denied firm discipline (as distinct from punishment) by insecure teachers, they eventually reach a stage where they become incapable of exercising self-discipline. Our children need confident and secure teachers. They will, on the whole, accept the discipline of teachers whom they have assessed as being fair and just – but if the teacher is not sure about his/her attitudes, this is likely to be communicated to the pupils with disastrous results for them.

In-service training

Self-education

Teachers need to accept the responsibility for acquiring knowledge for themselves in addition to attending courses. The teacher committed to change should try to gain an insight into the various communities. This can be done by reading community newspapers, reading the black ethnic press (produced in English), listening to the radio and watching television programmes prepared from the perspective of the black community. Whenever possible the teacher should seek invitations to attend community group meetings.

Organised courses

The teacher engaged in change should attempt to keep up to date with current developments in their subject areas and in education theory. In the evaluation of any course, the teacher should remark on the appropriateness of the course in relation to education for a multicultural democracy.

Grouping in the class

Although school policy may dictate which group of children is allocated to each class, it is important that the teacher exercises control over groupings within the class. The creation of permanent groups within the class is not good educational practice. The teacher should attempt to develop different groupings according to the current task. In a class where the teacher is trying to develop an ethos of diversity, it would be unfortunate if the physical groupings revealed cultural or colour apartheid.

Conclusion

The critics are right to demand that the education service accounts for the many trivial and tokenist practices developed as multicultural education in the name of black people. However, their blanket condemnation of multicultural education as a concept reveals a naïve misunderstanding of the decentralised system and frustrates those teachers in multicultural classrooms who are seriously attempting to improve the life chances of black pupils, and to prevent white pupils from becoming racially prejudiced.

It is true that teachers (including headteachers) can do much more collectively through their Unions to address the issue of racial disadvantage in education and in society. However, this chapter has attempted to suggest some priorities and strategies for change within the realm of the individual teacher's power.

References

1 D. Lawton, *The Politics of the School Curriculum*, Routledge & Kegan Paul, 1980, p. 135.

2 D. Lawton, *Class, Culture and Curriculum*, Routledge & Kegan Paul, 1975.
3 B. Bernstein, 'Education Cannot Compensate for Society', *New Society*, 26 February 1970.
4 Brent LEA, *Education for a Multicultural Democracy*, Book 1, London Borough of Brent Education Committee, 1983.
5 C. Rogers and B. Stevens, *Person to Person: The Problems of Being Human*, Real People Press, 1967.
6 DES, *Primary Education in England: A Survey by HM Inspectors of Schools*, HMSO, 1979.
7 J. Tierney (ed.), *Race, Immigration and Schooling*, Holt, Reinhart & Winston, 1982, ch. 6.
8 R. Pring, *Knowledge and Schooling*, Open Books, 1976, ch. 5.
9 S. Hall, 'Racism and Reaction', Transcript of Lecture, BBC2 Television, 1979.
10 A. Rampton (chairman), *West Indian Children in our Schools: Interim Report of the Committee of Inquiry into the Education of Children from Ethnic Minority Groups*, Cmnd 8273, HMSO, June 1981.
11 G.V.I. Davis, 'Supporting Change to a Multicultural Curriculum', unpublished MA dissertation, University of London Institute of Education, 1981.
12 DES, *Ideas in Geography*, HMI Series, 'Matters for Discussion', no. 5, HMSO, 1978.
13 J.A. Banks, *Teaching Strategies for Ethnic Studies*, Allyn & Bacon – 2nd ed., 1979, Part 1, chs. 1–4.

Chapter 3

Black response to white definitions

Tuku Mukherjee

Over the last six years I have been involved in in-service courses directed generally at the 'caring professions', but more specifically at teachers, socially mixed all-white groups and black groups. The experience has been enriching, and the feedback rewarding. The ongoing process of involvement leaves me totally convinced of the imperative that black educationists have a decisive role to play in the crisis we face in education.

We need to reflect on our own passage through racist Britain to arrive at a precise, incisive and critical analysis, not so much to become conscious of multicultural Britain, but the more agonising reality of 'multiracist' Britain, as central to our initiative. We need to wrench ourselves free from the 'golliwoggish' definition of multicultural education dominated by white orthodox view of education, teaching and schooling, and enter the arena of discourse with a black perspective to formulate a 'revolutionary definition', not just as a theory, but as an active approach rooted in our experience of oppression, to challenge every fact of white society, 'White speech, White schooling, White law',[1] and above all the white teaching profession.

If we fail to initiate a distinct 'anti-racist' approach to a multiracist Britain, we shall be abdicating our responsibility to all those we teach. Our position then becomes untenable. Those who have 'made it' provide an acceptable 'black face' colluding and legitimating the black problematic and alien image, participating in the process of deracination, so that eventually our children would 'fit in' and be 'absorbed' within the class analysis, as an object, an underclass, sub-proletariat, structurally domesticated in British society, with ESL/and 'black underachievement' as the only enabling skills available to function. They would be imprisoned and segregated by white definition as being the 'cause and the victim' of the failure of the English educational system.

I am aware that for us to aspire to status, access to power and critically question or to challenge the layers of racist attitudes encased within a 'fair and just' liberal teacher, leads to being stereotyped as people with 'chips on our shoulders', 'polemical' in academic circles, or being racists in reverse. As black educationists we have taken on board all the risks, and the only power we have is the force of our experiential evidence to expose the authentic enemy – white racism, both institutional and general, caught within a vicious and 'hardened' bureaucracy, 'living with an unresolved, and possibly unresolvable, conflict between egalitarianism and elitism',[2] with the blacks as a dye and a mass phenomenon. Almost invisible, omitted from the mosaic of education, except contained, to be controlled by the distorted concept of multicultural education; an appendage with an organic connection between our colour and the concept; an abnormality within education, a black educational forum, separate and distinct from the norm. 'I realise more so now than before that challenging assumptions, definitions and practices is as important as challenging attitudes'; 'I also now realise why multicultural education meant so little to me. It's the black connection' (comments of white teachers in a mixed group from the 'Caring Profession', on a summer course).

The white debate on multicultural/multiracial education has gone on continuously and unremittingly, based on the concept of good and harmonious race relations. With interpersonal relationships and patronised recognition of 'ethnic cultures' as the central grid, orientated for a safe non-conflictual passage to a better 'understanding' to be achieved by providing hard information on black 'life-style'.

A recent, classic example is the response of the Metropolitan Police Planning Unit following the catalystic release of *Racist Essays* by John Fernandez. 'I was shocked . . . it was so unexpected! The attitudes were so deplorable and out of character! But one of the fine sides of this miserable affair is that it has helped us to focus on the problem and tackle it' (Commander Richard Wells, as reported in the *Guardian*, following the Panorama programme, 19 July 1983). The white thrusts to 'tackle' the racism of white cadets is the 'Black Multicultural Model' in a new guise – called 'Human Awareness Training'. Back again to the 'diversity' model with the following main components: 'Community Relations, self-awareness and interpersonal skills . . . Community Relations Training can be viewed as having two dimensions. First cultural awareness, and second race awareness, development of personal knowledge and identification of prejudice. The development of awareness of cultural/historical backgrounds to ethnic groups in G.B., and the provision of information regarding those cultures' (Human Awareness Training for the recruits' initial course – April 1982). An outdated, and yet very acceptable and predictable liberal racist response to a highly volatile and yet a static situation of 'stop, search and research' (*Guardian*, 19 April 1983). In a social and political context, a position of conflict. 'Race awareness' is reduced to 'prejudice', to be dealt with and presumably eliminated by providing 'backgrounds' and 'information'. However, every research categorically informs us that the input of hard information of a 'stereotyped' out-group can have very little impact on attitudes; quite on the contrary, it can go a long way to reinforce 'prejudiced' attitudes.

The essays hit the headlines, as though the manifestation of crude racism is unusual. In my judgment they were microcosmic views reflecting the pervasive nature of British racism. The unions' response was just as predictable – collusion with institutional racism, exposing its own hypocrisy on the issue of race, and abdicating responsibility to its rank-and-file membership across the colour line. It seems to be beyond the comprehension of most white people that 'Getting rid of the attitude behind those graffiti involves not so much sandpapering as wholesale reconstruction, a task which cries out for the skills of people like John Fernandez rather than his removal from the job' (Leader, *Guardian*, 28 March 1983).

The cataclysmic turn of events affected me personally, for I was the first person to run an in-service course for the academic staff and officers at Hendon in 1981–2. I negotiated the course with the academic staff, with racism very high on the agenda. It was entitled 'Multicultural Approaches to Police and Community Relations' and had the following aims:

1 To examine a range of issues related to policing in a multicultural/multiracial society.
2 To set them in a historical context, and examine contemporary approaches to the problem.

I found it unbelievable that this was the first time that the academic staff and officers of the Metropolitan Police, both responsible for turning out cadets as agents of law and order, had ever discussed imperative issues affecting the lives of the community.

The course was evaluated by Faith Shaw of the Roehampton

Institute of Higher Education, based on an open-ended questionnaire. The returns made it abundantly clear that 'very few respondents even mentioned in passing that they were doing the course jointly with Police Officers . . . one return only commented that a question raised was "How to establish a better partnership between Police staff and academic staff in the Cadet school?" ' Then further comments upon the 'great divide and enough understanding upon both sides'. Evaluation: 'It seems to me, as I will indicate by other quotes from the returns, that the lack of comments about the shared experience, and about two groups of staff taking part, is significant and probably indicates an absence of a sense of sharing and a considerable lack of communication. This could be summed up by the words of one return: "I feel that we perhaps were not completely open." '

The guarded qualification of this phrase was supported in other ways by comments such as: '. . . There were others who, I felt, might have benefited more.' '. . . How to convince our students, some of our colleagues . . .' '. . . Pleasantly surprised to find so many Police Officers attending . . .'

These comments in their respective contexts, and others, indicate some degree of tension and/or hostility and lack of open discussion of differing stances. Further to the above, one return quotes a Police Officer's view: 'You can't really do much in a classroom, it's only when they get out there on the job that the real lesson begins.' He then asks whether those most needing the course are the experienced officers on the beat. This particular participant was the most openly articulate about the 'great divide' and said that 'our worlds hardly meet.' Faith Shaw summed up her evaluation: 'The teachers indicated the value of grappling with abstract and ideological theories (race and class) and relating this study to themselves as individuals, to them as a group of teachers, to the Cadet School. Several commented upon the way the discussion and lectures had raised ideas and issues in a more explicit way than they had previously encountered (25 May 1982). It seemed inevitable that the Metropolitan College was preparing cadets for policing a highly diverse community without any framework of co-ordination between the academic staff and Police Officers responsible for teaching the rudiments of laws. Yet academic studies and social studies – in fact anything to do with fundamental social and political issues – have the lowest priority, and the academic staff the lowest status. The emphasis is to produce a 'breed' of 'fighting fit' men, and very few women, who are put through a process and inevitably emerge as anti-blacks and anti-working class. The course was a catalyst to throw into sharp focus not only the 'great divide' and tension between the academic staff and Police Officers, but more fundamentally the division between 'black and white' staff. The 'blacks' wanted the tutors to take up the issue of racism head on, whereas the liberal non-conflictual view suggested: 'To what extent there is now a Race Relations industry in this country with a vested interest in keeping race relations as a contentious issue' (Faith Shaw, Evaluation). Only one officer, out of eight, owned, 'My own contribution to "racism" and "liberal standpoint" and the desire to develop the "ability to critically self-examine". He also wished for more structured discussion and deeper examination of many issues, especially all aspects of racism' (Faith Shaw, Evaluation).

The 'great divide', the 'tension' and the 'hostility' that I, as a course tutor, experienced is not an exception but a rule, when we consider and examine 'black' and 'white' approaches to educational issues affecting the lives of children, both black and white, growing up in a multicultural/multiracial Britain.

'Whiteness' has its own limitations. It lacks the imagination, sensitivity, realism and a sense of identity to be able to lift itself from a state of anomie, to be able to examine critically the ideological forces of race, class and sex around which institutions are built as weapons to deal with conflict and shape an unquestioning, uncritical and non-conflictual view of life. Institutions specific to class have developed sophisticated mechanics to neutralise class conflict, especially the working-class threat. They also emanate a spurious culture of domination and destruction of 'white' identity: 'the teachers – in common with other adults – retained from their own adolescence uncertainty about identity and an unresolved ambivalence about their own worth as individuals.'[3]

In my judgment, the damage is far more pathological. Institutions have created a 'halo' around 'white professionalism' and 'individualism' which in reality does not exist. What does exist is a segmented personality: teachers teaching in a vacuum, content to transmit 'white traditional middle-class' values in a society which has undergone dramatic ethnographic changes since the post-war immigration of blacks.

In spite of our high visibility, in a sense we remain almost invisible. Recently, at the beginning of a course for an all-white group of youth workers, I asked every one to say something positive about multicultural/multiracial Britain. There was a great pause, and not a single positive response. When probed, it emerged that they were aware of the terminology, but hadn't given it much thought. The life-style of those I have met in the 'caring professions', or their work, have very little to do with each other; and the 'black presence', to them, remains a meaningless terminology and a 'mass phenomenon' even though most are professionally involved with black people. The questioning spirit, which is so often highlighted in education, is almost non-existent. 'I have never questioned the procedures and practices of my institutions', was the response of every white teacher on a day devoted to 'Institutional Racism'.

The accelerated pull towards the 'nation' state, and the oppression and domination of institutional racism to crush critical and creative thinking has left the 'semi-professional' in teaching 'divided and alienated in his/her work: he/she is alienated in his/her thinking about his/her work.'[4] A consequence of this is the almost total inability of 'white teachers' to face up to the imperative issues of race, class and sex.

High on the agenda of expectation, in nearly every course, is: Give us a 'multicultural package' of cultural differences to take back for our 'ethnic minority' children. They expose their total failure to cope with a crisis of racist attacks by the white middle-class agencies operating at the heart of a 'black community'. The following extract from an evaluation report after an intensive course on 'Racism and Dysfunctionalism' refers to the New Cross massacre and openly admits:

> It is probably true to say that many lefty alternative do-gooding agencies periodically talk about racism. Resolutions to 'be less racist' are made, as well as, for example, 'let's employ more black staff', but nothing really changes. Many such agencies were given a jolt in 1981. The Centre wanted to reform. Basically we did not know what to do. We talked and agonised about it. We put our hands in our purses and pockets, and put a '*collection jar*' [my italics] on the reception desk . . . We found it impossible to know what to do when we found that all black people did not welcome us white people to their campaign meetings.

The rejection by the black community led them to 'think and feel that we should be looking at our own house'.

The 'collection box' response is the legacy of a historical past internalised by a 'caring institution'. In the context of education, the white definitionists of multicultural education aren't far off. They still want to 'pioneer' on our backs with compassion and a helping hand for 'harmony, understanding and good practices' without even facing the ideology of white racism. They demean themselves and their readers with a 'white lie', totally removed from the reality of conflict that we know exists. They lack academic rigour, and the integrity to analyse the consequences of the Third World within the First. They are responsible for projecting and perpetuating 'black people' as an 'alien' abnormality, to be studied, controlled, contained, managed and helped within a segregated assimilationist or a cultural diversity model. They fail to realise that the model they project is racist, and implicit within it are conflict, alienation and black revolt.

I would maintain that the 'harmonious and understanding' analysis:

1 '. . . acts as a tranquilliser and dampens their critical awareness of the crisis in education, that your moral, physical and educational world is in order as long as your interpersonal relationship with pupils – especially black pupils – is full of empathy and understanding. They fail to realise that integral to the model is political, economic, cultural and religious oppression: not just of the individual, but also collective oppression of black people' (Om Dogra, Southall, September 1983).

2 At the same time, it offers a lifeline to rootless, benevolent white teachers with a distorted purpose to 'uplift' the 'abnormal' black pupils to normality, particularly since the working class have more or less bowed out of education. ESL and white teachers find the perverted view of 'multiethnic' education a field of safe operation. I'm fairly certain that if black pupils are removed, or remove themselves, from the locale of ESL and multiethnic educational initiatives, the entire edifice of white professional identity and purpose will collapse like a house of cards.

As 'black educationists', we must distance ourselves and challenge the mythical world of 'harmony, good race relations and good practices', by articulating the 'black experience' in a 'multiracist' white world, where racism is an organic facet of white culture, white society, white politics, white language and white institutions. Furthermore, it is racism which 'divides' us structurally across the colour line. Whichever institution we focus on – education, transport, media communication, law and order, etc. – we address ourselves to the dynamics of unbalanced power relationships, question the collusion of the so-called 'converted' multiculturalists, and operate from a position of strength based on our collective experiences. We are aware that racism 'attacks in a fundamental way, the concept the individual has of himself, his body, and his being, and the concept he has of the identity, the culture and the quality of his racial group.'[5]

The process has a variety of implications for black people: I would just like to take up a few. It gives us an incisive insight into the dynamics of racism. Long before anyone else had even thought of structural and state racism, it was Sivaji (A. Sivanandan, of the IRR) who first homed in to analyse the concept. Implicit to the experience is the process of politicisation, and the political skill to develop a 'revolutionary culture' to challenge racism at all levels. The commonality of racist oppression, in the context of Britain, provides a 'basis for solidarity' for all black people, since as Leo Kaper writes, it is 'experienced as a totality, and stimulates a racial . . . response, transcending class divisions'.[6]

To test out Kuper's analysis, I recently posed the question: 'What is your class position?' to an all-black group of social and community workers participating in a course on 'Black Consciousness'. The unanimous response was: 'We are black – and our class location is purely transitory. We slip into class as we enter our institutions. We fade out to our racial location as we leave.'

The argument has often been presented by white teachers that class inequality and oppression is the same as racial oppression, that it is only a question of degree. They forget that class has emerged out of economic order, and within the order each class had an economic function, location, position and relationship. Race, on the other hand, has emerged out of exploitation of 'black' people and their resources both in the national and global context. Furthermore, black people have been incorporated into class as a distinct social category to perform the lowest economic functions, but social, political and power relationships remain firmly based on the ideology of race. The 'visibility' factor makes it impossible to 'pass', as the Jewish and the Irish have managed to do. Our racialisation based on 'colour', in a sense, transcends class analysis. We carry our 'Star of David' wherever we go, and whatever we do. An attempt has also been made to neutralise the commonality of our experience of racial oppression by imposing our ethnic differences to create inter-ethnic tensions related to scarce resources, so that institutions can stay above the battle, deflect the issue and prevent us from locating the real enemy – white racism. It also serves another important political function. It neutralises inter-class conflict by scapegoating us, the cause of all the ills, in a class-ridden society based on inequality. I would maintain that white analysts act as deflectors to control the debate on race relations, and to prevent black organisations from emerging as community-based political forces, in a position to challenge the inability of schools to educate our children. My own survey, research and involvement with schools in London suggests that the romantic notion of multicultural education as the solution to the 'black presence' has wreaked havoc both on children and teachers.

Very recently I tested out my findings on a group of teachers, who were honest enough to admit to the following:

1 Acute tension and suspicion within the hierarchical power structure.
2 Pastoral care means control and an obsession with discipline.
3 Little or no inter-action between Departments.
4 There doesn't seem to be any coherence of purpose, codes or practices.
5 Hostile pupils – demoralised teachers – inconsistent and *ad hoc* controls and sanctions – leading to suspension.
6 Overt and covert racist attitudes without any policy to deal with them.
7 Enormous infrastructure – without any well-defined lines of communication – and lack of capacity to make decisions.

Given the above existing conditions in our schools, it isn't surprising that schooling is going through a crisis of confidence and near dysfunction. It is the same in other 'caring professions': for example, a Social Services Department in one outer borough has been unable to spend £700,000 because it doesn't know how, and is still 'colour blind' to the changing composition of its clientèle and their differing needs. To confuse the issue even more, there has emerged the new 'Ebony' of training – Racism Awareness courses – another euphemism either for a 'diversity model' or for a 'self-awareness' model, as if to be self-aware is sufficient to make any difference to the structural inequality, division and tension. I have personally been involved with Racism Awareness Training since 1979, and maintain that personal awareness is totally inadequate unless it is incorporated in one's institutional role and fed into the structure to expose the political dimension and consequences of dysfunctionalism.

In my view and experience, most of the courses lack any political analysis and fail to answer the key question: Why should white teachers, white social workers, white community workers, white institutions etc., be 'anti-racist'? They admit to 'racism' as a white phenomenon, arising out of ideology of race, but still come up with multiculturalism as the answer. We need to point out quite clearly, locally and nationally, that the imperative issue of race has to be faced head on, failing which we must come to terms with the fact that, 'In an ironic sense, Britain is maintaining the leadership. As it once showed the way towards democratic success, today it blazes the trail towards democratic failure' (Samuel Beer, as quoted by Peter Jenkins, *Guardian* 20 October 1982) and walking the thin red line between a police state and policing the state. We as blacks see the consequences far more clearly and sharply. Our power is our political insight and incisiveness, and we must clearly point out to the institutions, as the following 'black' members did after going through a course on 'racism awareness':

Antiracist Education Committee,
c/o Southlands College

> We the undersigned, as a result of attending the Racism Awareness Course on 20th, 22nd, 23rd September 1983, would like to make the following comments:
>
> Amongst those of us who attended the course, some people experienced opposition from their seniors. We feel that this opposition had a racist element and could account for the fact that the course was so poorly attended.
>
> The lack of publicity also contributed to the poor attendance.
>
> However, despite the low numbers, we felt that the course was a tremendous success and we feel it deplorable that others were deprived of the opportunity to get together and participate in a course that addresses itself to the issue of racism in our Borough.
>
> We observed that those who attended the course were of officer level only, and would like the course to be opened up to include ALL EMPLOYEES of the Council at ALL LEVELS, AND GRADES, from directors to manual workers.
>
> As a result of attending this course it has become very clear that the Council is structurally racist. We feel that the Council's Equal Opportunities Policy is in total contradiction to its practices. For the policy to be meaningful and effective it is imperative that the Council faces the issues of racism head on.
>
> The participants undergoing the Racism Awareness course should be given formal back-up facilities to meet in work time, at least three monthly, to monitor both the progress and constraints.

It is, I believe, our function to hold the state to the Lusaka Declaration on Racism and Racial Prejudice, August 1979:

> Inspired by the principles of freedom and equality which characterize our association, we accept the solemn duty of working together to eliminate racism and racial prejudice.

Changes are essential to Britain, not because of the black presence, but because racism, in covert and overt forms, is dragging the state, and education as an antenna of the state, to disintegration.

> We went through Racism Awareness Training during the last academic year, and have come to realize the dynamics of racism, and how liberal racism operates both at an individual and structural level. We believe that procedures, practices, contents implicit in assimilationist and integrative models have a definite racist orientation, both covert and overt – which in fact has brought education and schooling to a point of crisis – following the trail of massive alienation not only of black pupils but of white pupils, and our own alienation, operating as we do within the construct of institutional racism.
>
> We are convinced that RAT is essential for teachers in our Borough, to enable us to break from the legacy of racism and initiate changes, both at structural level, and individual racist assumptions we bring to our teaching.

This is being presented to the Chief Education Officer of the borough by an all-white group of teachers.

References

1 A. Sivanandan, *Liberation of Black Interests: A different hunger*, Pluto Press, 1982, p. 95.
2 A. Sampson, *Anatomy of Britain*, Hodder & Stoughton, 1982.
3 John Rae, quoted in Sampson, op. cit., p. 121.
4 *British Journal of Sociology*, vol. 15, 1964, p. 284.
5 Leo Kuper, *Race, Class and Power*, Duckworth, 1974, p. 224.
6 Ibid., p. 225.

Chapter 4

Developing a multicultural approach to the curriculum:

The role of the headteacher (A case study at Wyke Manor)[1]

Carlton Duncan

Let Maggie Williamson[2] introduce this chapter:

Background

'The concept of education for a multicultural society was introduced to Wyke Manor by Carlton Duncan on his appointment to the school as Headmaster in April 1982.

Prior to this the school had for many years numbered among its population children from several ethnic minority groups, the largest of these being the children of Asian origin emanating from India and Pakistan, a few of them via Uganda and Kenya. The second main group consisted of the children of Afro/Caribbean origin; in addition there have, over the years, been the occasional one or two of other ethnical origin such as Chinese, Polish, South American, etc. The breakdown of the school population for 1982–3 is 84% white, 13% Asian – mainly Muslims – 2% West Indian and 1% others. The attitude of the school towards these children from ethnic minorities during those years was to emphasise their social integration into a mainly indigenous white community, and the way to do this was seen to be by consciously treating all the children alike, regardless of their background. Special provision was of course made for those children with particular language difficulties, but in the main, and with the best of intentions, everything possible was done to make sure that no child from an ethnic minority was made to feel in any way 'different' from his peers.

In practice what this meant was that the provision in the school, and in most other schools at the time, in terms of curriculum, cultural and social development, was exactly the same for everyone and the children of different ethnic backgrounds had no alternative but to fit in with it. This is in no way intended to imply criticism of the school; there would have been quite genuine horror and indignation among the staff had it been suggested that racial discrimination was taking place. The fact is that, as with most other schools, Wyke Manor had not yet become aware of the issues involved in that children from ethnic minorities do have special needs other than language, that they are not the same as the native English children, that the latter also need educating to live in a multicultural society and that discrimination by omission can be just as harmful as active discrimination.

Conception

With the advent of the 1980s the racial tensions which for years had lain dormant in Britain began to erupt, aggravated by huge unemployment, poverty, the National Front Movement and many other social and economic factors which came to a head at that time. The eruption took the form of massive street violence in areas like Lewisham, Toxteth and Brixton, and suddenly the issues involved could no longer be ignored. As the media reported the events and in the wake of Lord Scarman's findings,[3] it quickly became evident that the problems of the ethnic minorities had been sadly neglected, and that urgent action from government and other bodies was now necessary.

Thus began a national movement whose aim was to look into and try to make provision for the needs of the ethnic minorities in all areas of society, education being one of the major fields of activity. The Rampton Committee[4] and subsequently the Swann Committee[5] of Inquiry became part of this movement, though they preceded the riots in their beginnings in response to the all-party Select Committee of the House of Commons Report[6] in the 1970s which was itself triggered into action by Bernard Coard's publication, *How the West Indian Child is Made Educationally Sub-normal in the British School System*, 1971.

It was against this background of growing awareness that there was a need to be met, a need which had also by this time been fully recognised by Bradford Council, that Duncan began his headship at Wyke Manor. He is himself a serving member of the

Swann Committee of Inquiry and even before officially taking up his position at Wyke he addressed a meeting of the staff at which he emphasised his own personal involvement in and commitment to the concept of multicultural education.

Duncan came to Wyke from the Sidney Stringer School and Community College in Coventry where his responsibilities had led him to develop a deep interest in both multicultural and community education. That position, together with his work with the Swann Committee and being a member of an ethnic-minority group himself, made him very experienced and knowledgeable in a field which is very dear to his heart.

In subsequent addresses to the staff Duncan made it clear that his aim for Wyke Manor was that it should adopt a policy of multicultural approach to the curriculum which would benefit not only the ethnic minority groups but all pupils in the school community.

Development

From the outset it was recognised that none of us at Wyke Manor is an expert in the field of multicultural education and that the introduction of such a policy must entail a process of investigation, learning, experimentation and adaptation from stage to stage. In order to facilitate the process two major but overlapping strategies were adopted initially:

(a) The appointment of a Committee for Multicultural Education within the school.
(b) A programme of visiting specialist speakers.'[7]

Maggie Williamson's introduction tells us something about the nature of Wyke Manor Upper School. I shall add a little.

The school serves a largely white working-class neighbourhood and is itself surrounded by a complex of council houses and a number of terrace houses. Well into the background, but on the school's borders, stands a large chemical factory which employs up to 600 people.

The ethnic minority contingent of the school travel to school either by private transport or buses mainly from the town centre. This is believed to be a relic of the old Bradford busing policy which had ceased to operate before my arrival at the school in April 1982.

A small contingent of middle-class children also attend the school which draws its intake from about ten to fifteen different middle schools, but from three or four in particular. Pupils first arrive at the school at age 13 and are of mixed sexes numbering approximately 1,200. Until September 1982, the school was a straightforward comprehensive occupying buildings dated 1959 and 1975. In September 1982 the school took its first step towards becoming a community school, admitting adults of all ages to its various classes with pupils – a development which has made rapid advance since.

There are some seventy members of the teaching staff, three of whom are of an ethnic minority background; an Asian, a Greek and the Headmaster who is from the West Indies (Jamaica). Most of the staff are either Yorkshire men and women or have strong Yorkshire connections. It is a truism to say that Yorkshire teachers do not change school readily, and consequently many of the staff at the school have been here for many years.

Wyke itself, as a village community, is situated on the edge of Bradford and it would be true to say it has a strong community spirit, though sadly lacking in community facilities. This part of Bradford (South) has been somewhat neglected in terms of social capital. Halifax, Huddersfield, Kirklees and Leeds are near-by towns which are of as much interest (if not more) to the people of Wyke as is Bradford. One sometimes gets the impression that no special affinity is felt for Bradford . . . but this is subjective.

Finally, the school has some eight ancillary staff and about nine community staff who are financed by the MSC. One of these is also of ethnic minority origin – an Asian young man. It is in this climate that I sought to introduce the idea of a multicultural curriculum for *all*.

The first task was to get across my educational philosophy to my colleagues, and as Maggie Williamson has already indicated, I used my first two meetings with the full staff (one before I took up my appointment and the other on the first day) to do just that. A point of particular emphasis was that multicultural education is synonymous with good practices in education. It is a different approach to all subject areas of the curriculum rather than some additional subject. It is meant to benefit *all* pupils equally, thus ensuring equality of opportunities in education. It was not a thing which had particular relevance to ethnic minorities, hence the all-white or near-all-white school was as suitable a candidate as any other. Perhaps the most essential point one had to get across was the need to admit that in these early days there were no experts and so we could all set off on a learning trek together.

The appointment of a committee for multicultural education

It became necessary to establish a team of colleagues who would set the ball rolling. But by its very nature, multicultural education could not be seen as something specially assigned to a few members of the school. This would have been a sure way of encouraging other staff to opt out on the pretext of leaving it to the specialist. For this reason alone, any appointments made with a multicultural brief had to be seen as only temporary with the function of starting things, giving it sufficient fuel, and then leaving it to gain rapidity under its own momentum. Hence, three members[8] of the existing staff (there was no room on the staff to bring in outsiders) were promoted temporarily for one year to this end.[9] A fourth, but more senior person (Maggie Williamson) was promoted permanently, not to lead initiatives – but to co-ordinate initiatives and to ensure that the whole school always knows what is happening in this field in all corners of the school. These four appointments, together with my curriculum deputy,[10] were charged with making things happen.

The next step

The staff, having acknowledged that we did not know how, but that we needed to do so, felt it would be best if we heard from those who knew.

Eric Bolton,[11] Her Majesty's Senior Inspector of Schools as he then was, willingly travelled to Bradford to address the entire staff on the subject of multicultural education. This macro address was opened to the whole Authority. The assembly hall was full with my own staff, staff from other schools, members of my governing body, advisers and other officials from the Authority and a few visitors from outside the Authority. Eric had, in fact, done this very task for me once before when I was Deputy Head and Director of Personal Development and with a curriculum brief to develop multicultural education at Sidney Stringer School and Community College in Coventry. As it was then, his lecture was well received. But, as happened then, now staff were saying 'Fine' from a general point of view, but how does it apply to . . . maths, science, etc.?

A series of micro or specialist lectures was thus indicated. There seems to be a general feeling that a multicultural approach to history, geography and the Humanities generally is possible, if not easy. But this feeling seems to disappear in relation to the other subject areas of the curriculum. That is why it was important that our micro lectures did not begin with the Humanities.

Sue Watts, whom I had heard giving evidence to the Rampton/Swann Inquiry on multicultural science and who has contributed chapter 11 to this book, had promised me a long time before that she would come to Coventry to address the staff at Sidney Stringer. She fulfilled that promise late in 1982 but at Wyke Manor, where again her lecture was not open only to Wyke Manor Science staff but also those of other schools in the Authority (some came from elsewhere too) as well as to any of my own staff whose specialisation was not science.

The chairmanship of these sessions was important. For the Eric Bolton lecture, I had invited the Authority's main secondary adviser for multicultural education (Mr Akram Khan-Cheema) to chair the session. But for the micro sessions it was vital that the Head of the relevant faculty areas would chair the session, organise the arrangements and invite the relevant advisers.

Early in January 1983, after much persuasion, we were lucky enough to have Ray Hemmings, author of 'Multiethnic mathematics'[12] to address our mathemeticians. Before the end of the second term 1982–3, three other similar lectures were given to Wyke Manor staff – Chris Power, the multicultural adviser for the London Borough of Haringey, addressed the Humanities staff; Yvonne Collymore, member of the Rampton/Swann Committee, addressed the home economists, and Joycelyn Barrow, OBE, came to address the staff of both the Communications Faculty and the Modern Languages Faculty.

It will be observed that I have omitted physical education, music and drama. This is deliberate. These are the areas where stereotypes and preconceptions about ethnic minorities are rife. It is my judgment that we need to come back to these areas, but when progress is well established in other areas. Similarly, little attention is paid to festivals, cultural evenings and shows, since all too often these kinds of efforts become synonymous with multicultural education. Of course, I recognise some worth – but I believe in an established order of priorities and a definite direction of development.

It is, however, highly important that as curriculum development takes place, the pictorial atmosphere of the school begins to come alive in its cross-cultural reflections in the same way as the textbooks, other materials and the library stocks do.

It was therefore my task to obtain visuals, to encourage their acquisition for display in key areas of the school. It was my task to ensure that the library held the most recent documentation in this field.

At this point it became clear that the school should devise its policy, allocate responsibilities, create the avenues for consultation and discussions and, above all, establish a monitoring system.

Thus the seven faculties were encouraged to set up their own working parties under the chairmanship of the faculty head to consider and research how best to adopt a multicultural approach to the curriculum covered by their faculty. From time to time I will see each working party to monitor progress and similarly, Mrs Williamson will co-ordinate developments among them.

Following various discussions, the following was unanimously adopted as the school's policy at its main decision-making body.

The Multicultural Curriculum (policy)

Rationale

1 Our present British society is composed of a variety of social and ethnic groups, and this variety should be made evident to our pupils in every way possible.
2 The content of courses offered within the curriculum of the school which are totally dominated by Britain and British values cannot be justified in the 1980s and they should be international in their content and universal in their perspective.
3 Our pupils should have access to accurate information about racial and cultural differences and similarities.
4 People from British minority groups and from other cultures should be presented as individuals with every variety of human quality and attribute. Stereotyping, whether expressed in terms of human characteristics, life-styles, social roles or occupational status, is unacceptable and likely to be damaging.
5 Other cultures and countries have their own validity and should be described in their own terms and not judged exclusively against British or European values.

Aims

1 To ensure that all our pupils have respect and tolerance for others.

2 To ensure all our pupils have dignity and self-esteem.

Objectives

1 (A) All our pupils should be aware of:
(a) the basic facts of race and racial difference;
(b) the beliefs, customs and values of the major cultures represented in Britain, and especially those of Bradford;
(c) why different ethnic groups migrated into Britain in the past, and especially how Bradford has come to acquire its present ethnic composition.
(B) All our pupils should be able to:
(a) recognise stereotyping and scapegoating in what they read, hear and see;
(b) evaluate their own cultures objectively.
(C) All our pupils should accept:
(a) the uniqueness of each individual human being;
(b) our common humanity;
(c) the concepts of justice and equal rights;
(d) the achievements of other cultures and countries;
(e) that Britain historically and currently is a multiethnic society;
(f) that cultures are dynamic and involve mutual assimilation and acceptance;
(g) that discrimination and prejudice widely exist in Britain and the factors which have fostered them;
(h) that discrimination and prejudice is destructive and humiliating to rejected groups;
(i) that we can have loyalty to more than one group;
(j) differences without feelings of insecurity.

2 (A) All our pupils should be aware of:
(a) the history, achievements and uniqueness of their own culture.
(B) All our pupils should be able to:
(a) communicate efficiently in English and their own mother tongue;
(b) master the other basic skills necessary for educational achievement.
(C) All our pupils should develop:
(a) a positive self-image;
(b) confidence in their own identity.

It is now the task of each faculty to ensure that this policy is adopted and applied throughout its area.

To monitor its effects, there are four systems, viz.:

1 The Director of Administration[13] charts the school in statistics reflecting the different ethnic groups within the school. One can readily see how the different groups perform in terms of examinations, etc., how they are placed in the different academic bands, and so forth.
2 My own need to feed information, documentary or otherwise, to the working parties directly or via the co-ordinator and to require feedback from resulting discussions.
3 The co-ordinator's role is dependent on things happening in the working parties and faculties.
4 The Deputy in Charge of the Curriculum has responsibility, after all, for all that happens or should happen curriculum-wise.

Some difficulties

(a) *Shortage of funds* This is always going to be a difficulty. Directions need to be given regarding the use of annual capitation. Its expenditure should reflect institution of the school's policy.

(b) *Conservatism* Change creates suspicions. These have to be worn down. The best technique is to surround such reluctance with effective actions and willing enthusiasm. On every staff, there is some of each. This technique will not always work, and eventually one might have to crack an egg if one is to suck it.

(c) *Attitudes do not change overnight* Quoting from Mr Sherry's contribution to the interim report on developments at Wyke, his observation is:

> After almost a year of having multicultural education on the agenda, I think everyone has a much clearer idea of what multicultural education is. However, this is not to say that we have achieved our aims. Far from it . . . keeping my ears and eyes open it has not been difficult to see that whilst the document to create a multicultural ethos at Wyke has been accepted there are many who think it is a waste of time and effort . . . statements such as 'the ethnic minority tail is wagging the indigenous dog' crudely exemplifies the problem.

Mr Sherry is right where he states: 'the nub of the problem is that changes of any kind which are foisted on a group and do not evolve from experiences always leave an inertia and opposition which takes time to eradicate.' Thus time, in-service courses, at school and abroad, discussions, constant chipping away of the block, lasting patience and even authoritative actions might all need to be employed. But remember two things: you don't win them all, and the leader should never give up.

(d) *Parents* A number of parents will come forward to ask difficult questions – many of these will be founded upon lies, rumours and fabrications – but they have to be answered nevertheless and convincing explanations must be given.

Some of my parents wanted to know 'why I had removed a picture of the Queen from the school?' No one in the school ever remembers having seen a picture of the Queen hanging in the school in all their years there. I certainly did not see one in my 1½ years. What I did was to get one for the school. It now hangs proudly in the hall. Other questions concerned the introduction of Urdu at the school and what is meant by multicultural education. These are parents' legitimate concerns. All deserve convincing replies.

(e) *Lack of knowledge and know-how* It is the Head's role to know . . . or to find out. Additionally, he should enable his staff/team to know and to find out, too. Immediate staffing sacrifices have to be made for long-run gain. Speakers, visits to other places and schools, etc. – the Head should always be willing to facilitate these.

Some major help to our efforts

1 My involvement in multi-cultural education had begun in the early 1970s as a departmental head (later faculty head) in Brent,[14] and later at Coventry.
2 My service as sub-committee chairman for the Rampton Interim Report and my continued membership on the Swann Committee meant I had access to a vast reservoir of information, people and places relevant to the field.
3 Both nationally and locally the move towards a multicultural curriculum is evident via major reports, government and otherwise. Each week the *Times Educational Supplement* carries articles, and the job columns were full of relevant posts. Only a foolish teacher would not recognise the direction of things. Consider the several Authorities that now have policy statemnts on these matters. Bradford has issued directives to

the schools on adapting for ethnic minorities and it has very recently issued all schools with its anti-racist policy and at the same time indicate its intention to issue a directive to adopt a multicultural curriculum. Wyke Manor will be in the forefront by at least some two years.

4 Within the school there are some keen, able enthusiasts who are getting on with the job and are making significant progress.
5 Bradford LEA has strengthened its multicultural advisory team.
6 It was fortunate that when I took over the headship of the school a number of points became available to assist my appointments.
7 The LEA made a sum of money available to assist my speakers' programme, and many thanks should go to Tony Rampton (chairman of the Interim Report) who helped us to get a £500 grant from the Hilden Charitable Fund to assist our programme of development.

The story, of course, continues.

Notes and references

1 Bradford Metropolitan Council (LEA).
2 Maggie Williamson is the Co-ordinator of Multicultural education initiatives at Wyke Manor School. She is also Head of Year and Head of Religious Education within the Humanities Faculty.
3 *The Brixton Disorders: 10–12 April*, Cmnd 8427, HMSO, April 1981.
4 *West Indian Children in our Schools*, Cmnd 8273, HMSO, June 1981.
5 The remainder of the Rampton Inquiry, currently sitting (November 1983), finally published March 1985.
6 House of Commons, HC 180- I-III, February 1977.
7 Extract from 'Multi-cultural Education' (A report on its conception, development and progress): An interim report, Margaret Williamson, Wyke Manor Upper School.
8 Mrs Susan Clark, Domestic Science Teacher; Miss Deborah Farrington, in charge of Drama; Mr Patrick Sherry, Head of General Studies.
9 The academic year 1982–3.
10 Mr Geoffrey Antcliffe.
11 Now the Chief HMI.
12 *NAME Journal*, vol. 8, no. 3, summer 1980, vol. 9, no. 1, autumn 1980.
13 Mr Robert Griffiths.
14 London Borough of Brent, Aylestone High School 1971–6.

Chapter 5

Towards a multicultural curriculum – primary

Ranjit Arora

The 1980 HMI discussion document, *A View of the Curriculum*,[1] stated:

> All primary schools should help their pupils to appreciate that today's world grew out of yesterday's. But today's world cannot be understood without some knowledge of Britain's role overseas today and in former years and reference to this should certainly be included in the *later* primary school curriculum in a balanced and sensitive way as a means of helping young children to understand our multicultural society.

The DES further emphasised this in the *School Curriculum*[2] document in 1981:

> What is taught in schools, and the way it is taught, must appropriately reflect fundamental values in our society. The schools have long recognised this as one of their important tasks which calls for perceptive and sensitive treatment both within the classroom and outside it . . . first our society has become multicultural; and there is now among pupils and parents a greater diversity of personal values. Second, the effect of technology on employment patterns sets a new premium on adaptability, self reliance and other personal qualities. Third, the equal treatment of men and women embodied in our law needs to be supported in the curriculum. It is essential to ensure that equal opportunity is genuinely available to both boys and girls.

Such laudable statements from the DES encourage one to hope that teachers throughout the country would be constantly engaged in reviewing their approaches to teaching, rethinking, reshaping the curriculum content to keep up with the demographic and ideological changes in our society. But such hopes as we can see from chapter 14 on 'In-service mis-education' are far from being realised.

Maureen Stone's[3] suggestion that 'Multiracial education' represents a developing feature of urban education aimed at 'watering down' the curriculum and 'cooling out' black city children while at the same time creating for teachers, both radical and liberal, the illusion that they are doing something for a particularly disadvantaged group may be seen by some as unhelpful because it focuses only on those aspects of the curriculum such as Asian studies or black studies which are specially created for certain racial groups. One also needs to remember that such an approach is a direct consequence of concentration on meeting 'special' needs. Another consequence is evident in a tendency in many multiracial authorities and schools to regard multicultural issues as matters for the specialist adviser or 'expert' teacher rather than as having implications for the staff and school as a whole. This was also confirmed by Richard Willey[4] in his review of the curriculum. He also noted that since 1979 emphasis has shifted from an 'adding on' approach to the notion of 'permeation' of the whole curriculum. It is this notion of 'permeation' and the 'whole curriculum' that I wish to focus on in this chapter.

But before that, it is important to clarify what our major educational objectives are. As explained in the introduction to this book, when we refer to multicultural education we are in fact talking about 'good education'. We know that good teachers have been and are interested in good education. But the question is: What is 'good education' for teachers who are mainly from the white middle classes and have been educated and trained in a Eurocentric, colonialist system where curriculum, staffing and materials have been overwhelmingly monocultural?

Some teachers dismiss the notion of multicultural education as a marginal matter compared with other forms of disadvantage in our school system. It may be worth mentioning that if schools adequately responded to the needs of all its children and ensured that their abilities are fully developed and that they are all equally equipped to compete for jobs in a highly competitive industrial and technological world, then other forms of disadvantage would also eventually cease to exist or at least their effects would be less accumulative.

One needs therefore to look at the content and process of schooling with the needs of all children in mind. Furthermore, such needs have to be identified in terms of present and future political, historical as well as economic context of the world we live in. I agree with Gail Meyers Sharman, when she says: 'All this will demand enormous individual tact, sensitivity and old-fashioned "guts" in order to deal with the facts, prejudice, ignorance and hostility that make up the racism that we have failed for too long to confront.'[5] The Association of Brent Teachers also feel this is to ask a great deal of teachers.[6]

> It is to expect that they will in some ways be ahead of our society in general. It is to ask teachers to beware of, analyse and discard prejudices which are deep rooted in our society and others. It is to ask teachers to achieve an understanding of cultures of which they will have had no direct experience in their own lives.

But is this really too much to ask of teachers? Teachers who believe in encouraging children to articulate their own ideas, to question, to listen to each other and who seek to broaden their approach to teaching and recognise their responsibility to enable all their pupils to benefit from good education surely don't think so. This naturally raises questions about what is regarded as good education. I am afraid any one looking for a blueprint or a finite set of practices in curriculum is likely to be disappointed because none exist. However, there is a set of principles, directions, signposts and methods for development. It is these that need to be addressed to all our actions, procedures and structures we work within.

The Multicultural Working Party at Birley High School, Manchester,[7] has perhaps come closest to looking at multicultural education as 'good education'. For them,

> Multicultural education is as much an attitude and a relationship as it is a pack of materials or a set of ideas. It is a whole curriculum which involves an attitude to life. It aims to promote positive self image and respect for the attitudes and values of others. Such an education will improve academic attainment.

Whether they achieve these aims in their everyday practice is open to debate.

Even the most conservative of educationists would not wish to dissociate themselves from the underlying assumptions of such a definition. These are:

1 Multicultural education is not for 'them', but is for the good of all children.
2 Contemporary Britain is part of the global village and

contains a wide variety of social and ethnic groups.
3 The whole curriculum should reflect these two facts.
4 The atmosphere and ethos of a school is crucial in determining equality of relationships.
5 Finally, high morale is created by expectation of high standards of attendance, work and behaviour.

One of the advantages of our decentralised system is the power and autonomy it gives individual schools. In the absence of any directives from the DES, it is the individual schools that shape the curriculum for individual pupils. The dedication and competence of the headteacher is essential as a starting-point, but the interest and involvement of the whole staff is absolutely crucial in implementing innovatory changes in the content and procedures of a school curriculum. Indeed among the factors found to be significant in initiating positive multicultural changes in first schools in Bradford,[8] the appointment of a new headteacher was found to be most significant followed closely by inservice courses for teachers.

What is curriculum?

In the words of Eric Bolton, Senior Chief HMI,[9] ' "The curriculum" is about the most difficult thing to explain to anybody who is not familiar with British schools.' It is even more difficult to explain to teachers in some British schools that 'the curriculum' is not only about examinable subjects but that, as a source of knowledge attitudes and values, it necessarily means all the educational experience that learners and teachers have under the guidance of our educational institutions. The realities of contemporary cultural diversity, and social political and economic conditions surrounding all learners, their families and communities must be reflected in all the learning arrangements that a school makes. No doubt a great deal of work has been going on in schools to develop awareness of cultural, social and linguistic diversity, not just as a description of the school population but as a positive resource for learning and teaching.

Dennis Lawton's definition of curriculum[10] focuses on central issues of selection and culture:

> the school curriculum (in the wider sense) is essentially a selection from the culture of a society. Certain aspects of our way of life, certain kinds of knowledge, certain attitudes and values are regarded as so important that their transmission to

> the next generation is *not* left to chance in our society but is entrusted to specially trained professionals (teachers) in elaborate and expensive institutions (schools). Not everything in a culture is regarded as of such importance, and in any case time is limited, so selection has to be made. Different teachers may make different kinds of selection from the culture, teachers may have different lists of priorities, *but all teachers and all schools make selections of some kind from the culture.*

Even if this were true, the selection procedure used by teachers is more than likely to be affected by the values, attitudes, personality, prejudices and knowledge of the individuals themselves. Such values and attitudes are also influenced by the adverse perception in teachers' minds against knowledge other than their own as well as such ignorance of other cultures.[11]

> But teachers are in fact merely selecting from a selection from the culture which was preselected for them by authors and publishers of books and materials; and these publishers appears to be making this selections with white people in mind . . . Thus in the very procedure they used to select knowledge, teachers were [are] abrogating the major part of their selecting role on the controllers of the media used in schools (including television) . . . By selecting their knowledge from selections already made by the powerful group of media producers, teachers are consciously or unwittingly accepting the ideology inherent in the books, television and other media.

This raises two important questions: (1) How does a school deal with books and materials which present a stereotyped or biased view of cultural or racial groups? (2) How does a school educate children against prejudice, racism and discrimination, because these are harmful and perpetuate divisive social phenomena which undermine justice and relations in school and society?

The first question will be more adequately dealt with in chapter 12 in this book. However, if good education is concerned with the preparation of all children to understand and appreciate life in a multicultural society, any school's overall collection of resources must reflect the fact that pupils are learning in a multicultural, multilingual and multiracial society. This can be done by assuring a positive place for all ethnic, cultural, linguistic and social groups in the information, literature communication and visual images of the school and its staffing.

The second question is based on an assumption that there is, among teachers, an agreement and a common concern to counter racism and racist attitudes, and the inequalities and discrimination which result from them. The validity of such an assumption will indeed be questioned by many readers and even by other contributors in this book. Nevertheless, I prefer to believe that some teachers are beginning to look at themselves and to examine their individual and collective values and attitudes, at least the explicit ones that are visible and easy to get hold of through academic curricula. Those who believe in the 'Treat them all the same', 'They are all children' syndrome often feel proud that they do not operate any kind of conscious discrimination. In practice it often means that children are treated as if they are all 'white' British. It is also used as a reason for not changing the curriculum. But treating the children the same is in no way treating them equally or with the same consideration to their needs as individuals or as members of communities which are significantly different from thier monolingual counterparts.

Whatever the model, be it 'compensatory', 'special needs', 'treat them all the same' or 'curriculum with multicultural trimmings' (for detailed discussion of these, see G. Davies in *Multicultural Teaching*[12]), teachers need to examine the content of what they teach, to analyse the processes they use to teach skills and concepts inherent in their content. Multicultural education is no longer about subjects/activities being tacked on to 'normal' school curricula or introducing a new subject at the expense of other equally important subjects. The quality of education can only be improved by increasing the scope of skills and knowledge that pupils require and not by replacing one area of knowledge and skills with another. The teachers need to ensure a just balance in the curriculum. An important strategy for achieving such a balance is that of 'permeation', whereby a 'child will constantly and throughout his school career come across ideas and images that relate to himself, his family and his culture in a whole variety of contexts'.[13] A culture policy across the curriculum is as important as a language policy across the curriculum.

Focus on process

Since it is relatively easier to focus on the content, the teachers tend to ignore the processes involved. In the words of Alan James,[14] the knowledge and culture transmitted is bound to be reinterpreted and recreated by the next generation. It is the quality of the process of transmission that will determine whether this reinterpretation is creative tending to promote a 'constructive discontent with the system of economic relationships that generate class and racial inequalities or whether it merely recreates those inequalities fostering the destructive discontent which directs the aggression of the majority against innocent minority scapegoats.'

This kind of re-examination is less attractive than innovation in curriculum content. It calls in question our assumptions and expectations, the messages we convey in the process of our teaching. It exposes a hidden curriculum of power, class and racial inequality, not only in the 'traditional' forms and content of education but in much that is thought of as progressive. Perhaps it is not surprising that the attack on the ethnocentric curriculum has been channelled in 'safe directions' mopping-up operations against curricular relics of empire and nostalgic preservation of cultures that are fossilised and trivialised in the process.[15]

These 'mopping-up operations' have continued to provide a smokescreen, and teachers, both radical and liberal, have continued in the belief that they are really doing something good for the educationally disadvantaged children from ethnic minority groups. A recent study of first schools in Bradford[16] has further confirmed the continuation of such apparently interesting and useful but essentially patchy 'mopping-up' operations. There are some excellent examples of multilingual welcome notices found in the entrance of many schools, of using school assemblies to celebrate main religious festivals for a range of faiths, of using common stories from the Koran, the Bible and the Torah on successive days to point out similarities and differences in various religions. Such dramatic and imaginative changes in religious education are, hopefully, intended to help all children to learn and understand more about each other and become better Christians, better Muslims and better Hindus or whatever faith they wish to belong to (also see Wendy Lovett, 'One way of approaching world religions in the primary school').[17]

It is these initiatives, along with school displays, that make up the school's overall ethos and climate. The security, well-being, confidence and identity of all pupils is enhanced by the school's attitude and respect for differences as well as a conscious effort to avoid procedures which may make children uncomfortable. For example, the procedure for providing a choice of meals to accommodate non-vegetarians by simply offering a choice of two main dishes is far more inconspicuous than singling out children as those who require special treatment. Similarly, the choice of a world map, whether it is to indicate origins of children or to study geography, economics or history is important. On the traditional Mercator's projection, India appears to be smaller than Scandinavia although it is in fact three times the size, whereas Peters's projection of the world map is much more accurate where each country is shown according to its actual size, a fact which may not be known to many teachers. Equally important are staff relationships with children and their attitudes and expectations, awareness of factors which promote or undermine children's confidence in the school, experiences of children outside school and their expectations of school.

It is also essential for teachers to be aware of their personal position in race and culture, cultural strengths of their children and perspectives of families to which these children belong. Such an awareness determines decisions about individual teachers' selections of appropriate themes and materials. It also determines selection and grouping of children, their streaming, setting or banding, allocating them to withdrawal groups, examination groups or a special provision group. Notions of inherent ability based on ethnic or cultural diversity can no longer be justified or used as criteria for such selection and grouping. Some people may view this call for self-examination as moralising, but if schools are to eradicate the racism to which Rampton[18] has drawn attention, the staff in these institutions must refuse to collude with social injustices both within and outside their institutions. An awareness of racism in its structural, political dimension is a basic step for teachers who do not wish to perpetuate institutional racism which in its worst form 'allows a white numerical minority in the world material benefits that far outstrip those of the black numerical majority'.[19] A number of people have been experimenting, through Race Awareness workshops, with ways of enabling teachers to examine their collusion with social and educational structures that are racist in their effect. After one such workshop organised for teachers in Bradford,[20] the participants commented: 'It was hard to keep in mind that we were supposed to be inventing. We kept getting pictures of our own experience.' The group worked to a deeper understanding of the school structures that continue, however 'innocently', to promote racism. In Brenda Thomson's words, 'As teachers, we are responsible either for collision with them or collusion by inaction.'[21] The workshop is more fully described in a BBC handbook[22] accompanying the T.V. series on 'Multi-cultural Education'. The same handbook includes a list of 33 ways in which institutional racism operates in our schools.

A whole school policy is probably the best way to ensure a

non-racist selection of content and organisation of the curriculum and resources. This must not only avoid misrepresentation from an early age but also seek to affirm values of all cultures. Such a policy should aim to develop analytical skills and understanding of cross-cultural perspectives and values and ensure a historical perspective that is free from ethnocentric biases. Furthermore, whole areas of curriculum should be open to all children, that is, limited ability should not be used as an excuse to restrict access of certain groups of children to particular subject areas. The following key aims of education have been taken from the policy statements of two first schools in Bradford. School A[23] considers education as a continuous process and is particularly concerned with the all-round development of the individual and with the acquisition of basic skills necessary in an ever-changing world and considers co-operation between the home and the school as vital to the well-being of the child, but also aims towards further integration and interaction of the school and the community it serves. School B[24] believes children must be given the opportunity to develop personally as responsible people and considers it has a duty to help *all* children to learn. 'All children need to be given confidence in their own ability, a confidence which can come from the child's belief that he or she has a rightful place in school.' This school aims to establish for its children a 'caring' community, a secure and stimulating environment, one in which children learn and more importantly develop.

On the surface, both schools seem very keen to create the right kind of environment and to cater for all children equally and consider all-round development of individuals as the primary function of education. But having a policy document is one thing, putting it into practice is quite another. How do these aims translate into action; what is more to the point, how should they translate into action? Who should ensure that actual practices in selection of curriculum content and procedures should in fact be regularly monitored and reviewed?

David Fitch,[25] during a recent study of Bradford first schools, found some useful examples of ways of ensuring policy implementation. One such example was in the form of a series of questions and suggested readings as a basis for head and staff to discuss together their school's policies and practices. This form of staff development is crucial in improving the overall quality of the school's work. But more of that later.

He also found some evidence of steps taken to ensure that all children feel they belong to the school by putting up notices in various community languages and by using various scripts for classroom displays. There are several fascinating examples of turning linguistic and cultural diversity to positive advantage in the classroom. Ray Chatwin[26] recently reported one such example of using Creole constructively in the remedial department of a school in Birmingham where a group of four Afro-Caribbean boys worked without teachers' intervention, discussed and composed stories which they 'audio drafted' with the aid of tape-recorders and eventually produced a text for a play in Creole. The idea was to draw on the boys themselves as a learning resource, to give status to their oral performance and to separate the acts of composition and transcription in the writing process. In addition to legitimising Creole and oral culture in the classroom and providing support and motivation for reading and writing, the transcript provided important clues about how Creole-speakers might be assisted to develop the ability to 'switch' language when appropriate.

Involvement of parents and healthy home–school links are established in some schools through letters and notices sent to parents in their own language. One school in Birmingham[27] has come up with a new way to communicate with some of their parents. They have put together a picture of a typical day in a primary school in the form of a video. This was not seen as a substitute for face-to-face communication with parents but as a way of reaching parents who felt hesitant to visit the school. It was decided to concentrate on those aspects of the school that parents might be least familiar with or most concerned about. The school is 'intending to do different versions of the video with commentary in English, Urdu, Bengali, Punjabi and Gujerati and to use the video at parents' evening and open days but more importantly to lend them to parents free of charge – in much the same way as they hire films from the video hire shops'.[28]

Such schools also have a related but different task of confronting the attitudes of the indigenous community. What has sometimes been referred to as the 'white backlash' may be manifested in less harmful but nevertheless serious ways, such as 'My mum said that I can't do the Indian dancing because it is rubbish.' When she was told that her daughter wouldn't be able to join the maypole dancing either, the parent relented and the girl participated and enjoyed both forms of dancing.

Or in the form of more serious and disturbing incidents such as this:[29]

> a display about India in the hall was ruined last year on polling day by visitors to the school scribbling racist remarks all over

the picture. We had to take it down before the children saw it. The language was so disgusting that we couldn't even use the picture to discuss the incident with the children.

A whole school policy inevitably needs to take into account incidents such as these and evolve a constructive strategy to counteract the damaging effects these can have on the morale of both children and staff. The school needs to be seen not only as a part of the community but also as the community's responsibility. Eventually it is this sense of responsibility which needs to be translated into action to avoid any occurrence or repetition of such incidents.

Staff development as mentioned earlier is another crucial aspect of a whole school policy. To implement this policy staff need to 'question their attitudes, perceptions and beliefs, their teaching styles, professionalism and the very fabric of the structure which determines their value responses.'[30] For changes within the school curriculum to be effective and even possible it is vital that changes are initiated within the staff themselves because any form of curriculum development necessarily involves and requires staff development. This may take the form of sharing knowledge and support using the skills, experience and expertise of staff in a mutually supportive environment referred to as the 'brainstorming technique' by Carl Rogers in 1967 and described more fully by Gerry Davis in chapter 2 in this book. Alternatively this could be in the form of short or long in-service courses. These are in fact found to be quite significant in initiating positive change and were referred to by Fitch[31] as the second most important factor in bringing about change in first schools in Bradford. The same study also includes examples where the seeds of 'multiculturalism' have been sown by a headteacher or on an in-service course or through reading, television, etc., and have grown rapidly, especially if nurtured and supported by colleagues and the school's organisational structure. Alternatively, of course, the same seeds may sometimes fall on stony ground or require massive fertilisation with only little return.

It is this lack of support and enthusiasm from colleagues and the school's organisational structure that disillusions many a caring and dedicated teacher who attends in-service courses. There is no denying that the key agent of change are classroom teachers and the key arena for deliberation and action is the individual school and its classrooms. The Keele report[32] on in-service provision for individual teachers speaks of

The experiences of many of the teachers we have interviewed

> faced with the day to day and minute by minute problems of working in classrooms with children whose cultural, community, intellectual and linguistic situations are diverse and which they only incompletely understand.

As an initial step, teachers might like to consider a series of questions related to their individual classrooms and perhaps to share them with another teacher. An example of a list of such questions can be found in *The Multicultural Curriculum: some guidelines for action.*[33]

As long as the education of minority groups remains exclusively in the hands of white teachers whose attitudes range from those who, while professing interest in combating prejudice, are still able to say, 'I love Little Black Sambo and I haven't a lot of patience with those who argue against golliwogs',[34] i.e. as if they were all white British children, there is very little hope of any real change in our major curriculum objectives or in the processes of implementation of such objectives. Such a change would require teachers to step down from the role of the authority in a classroom to share experiences with students and to allow the children to create their own learning experiences and share their evaluation of these with others. It also requires imagination, particularly sympathetic imagination. It has been suggested that the English education system does little to foster such imagination. Yet it is only this form of imagination that enables us to understand other cultural societies and historical epochs.[35]

> We cannot understand others if we refuse to recognise their identity and respect their individuality but insist on seeing them in our terms. It is only by means of sympathetic imagination that we can cross the space that separates us from other individuals and understand why they view and respond to the world in a certain manner. Without sympathetic imagination we remain prisoners of our own limited worlds and lack the ability to enrich and expand them.

It is not surprising, then, that most teachers educated and trained in such a system find curriculum development as something difficult since it basically questions what they have already set up as appropriate for all our children.

Schools therefore need to stimulate more frequent and active contact with parents and communities and should recognise them for what they are, i.e. 'a powerhouse of richly diverse cultural capital'.[36] The employment of more ethnic minority teachers has been consistently called for by almost everyone who professes to be a multiculturalist, yet relatively little progress has been made in that direction. In addition to acting as positive role models, which may consequently decrease the numbers of ethnic minority children in the 'lower' streams or sets and in special schools, such teachers can work towards providing a just balance in the curriculum – a balance of images that relate to everyone and a balance of life-styles and values that derive from models other than that of dominant culture alone.

But the presence of ethnic minority teachers in itself is not enough. The schools need to create a climate where it is easier to discuss emotive issues such as race, prejudice and stereotyping in a constructive and educational way. Such a climate would encourage a critical examination of the values inherent in the materials presented to our children and more importantly an examination of teachers' attitudes which in spite of their virtues of decency, tolerance and some degree of respect for those different from us, find it difficult to raise themselves to the level of others, thus falling back into the habit of reducing others to the limited proportions of their own linguistic habits and conventions. This is evident in classrooms where teachers do not wish their pupils to speak any language other than English; in fact, in some schools, children still get punished for doing that. By ignoring a child's linguistic resources, the school can and often does reinforce stereotypes by implicitly emphasising the superiority of the dominant culture and rejecting any notion of parity of esteem between English and other linguistic systems. Any school suppressing the pupil's language but taking an interest in his cultural background is bound to be confusing, to say the least, for children who speak languages other than English.

> For the school to ignore the language or treat it as an obstacle to learning while at the same time paying lipservice to multiculturalism is meaningless, for the very language being eliminated is the embodiment of the culture that is allegedly sought to be respected.[37]

Such a school is symptomatic of 'the virtues of decency, tolerance and some degree of respect for others' referred to earlier on. This is to be greatly welcomed. However, in Dr Parekh's words, and I will let him have the last word,[38]

> Tolerance and respect are negative virtues. They stop us from harming others, but they also stop us from appreciating, enjoying, entering into and learning from a dialogue with other

religions, cultures and societies [I would add languages to this list] unless we can enter into the spirit of other societies and cultures, we cannot appreciate their strength. And by failing to appreciate their strength, we fail to appreciate our own weaknesses and limitations.

References

1 DES, *A View of the Curriculum*, HMI Series, 'Matters for Discussion', HMSO, 1980.

2 DES, *The School Curriculum*, Welsh Office, HMSO, 1981.

3 M. Stone, *The Education of the Black Child in Britain: The myth of multiracial education*, Fontana, 1981.

4 R. Willey, Teaching in Multicultural Britain, Schools Council Programme 4, *Individual Pupils*, 1982.

5 Gail Meyers Sharman, 'Multicultural teaching: What is it exactly?', *Multicultural Teaching*, vol. 1, no. 1, 1982.

6 NUT pamphlet, *Multicultural Education in Brent Schools*.

7 *Multicultural Education in the 1980s*, Report of Teachers' Working Party at Birley High School, Manchester, City of Manchester Education Committee, 1980.

8 D. Fitch, 'Multicultural Initiatives' (unpublished study of first schools in Bradford).

9 E. Bolton, Chief HMI, opening address at AMMA Education Conference and published in conference report, 'Positive and Negative Discrimination in Multicultural Britain', 1983.

10 D. Lawton, *Class, Culture and Curriculum*, Routledge & Kegan Paul, 1975.

11 G.V.I. Davies, 'Racism and the School Curriculum, Past and Present', *Multicultural Teaching*, vol. 1, no. 1, 1982.

12 Ibid.

13 Ibid.

14 Alan James, 'Why Language Matters', *NAME Journal Multiracial School*, vol. 5, no. 3, 1977.

15 Ibid.

16 D. Fitch, op. cit.

17 W. Lovett, 'One Way of Approaching World Religions in the Primary School', *Multiethnic Education Review* (Inner London Education Authority), vol. 2, no. 1, winter/spring 1983.

18 A. Rampton (chairman), *West Indian Children in our Schools*, Cmnd 8273, HMSO, June 1981.

19 B. Thompson, 'I am Racism: Multicultural Education and Racism Awareness', *Secondary Education Journal*, vol. 11, no. 3, 1981.

20 J. Twitchin and C. Demuth, *Multicultural Education: Views from the classroom*, BBC, 1981.

21 B. Thompson, op. cit.

22 J. Twitchin, op. cit.
23 Extracted from Aims of Education as in the Handbook of Ryecroft First School, Bradford.
24 Extracted from school policy document of Ravenscliffe First School, Bradford.
25 D. Fitch, op. cit.
26 R. Chatwin, 'Using Creoles Constructively', *Multicultural Education Review* (Birmingham Education Department), no. 1, 1983.
27 Gill Haynes, 'Video for Parents', *Multicultural Education Review*, no. 1, 1983.
28 Ibid.
29 D. Fitch, op. cit.
30 Maureen Matthews, 'The Development of Multiethnic Education at St Veronica's School', *Multiethnic Education Review*, vol. 2, no. 1, 1983.
31 D. Fitch, op. cit.
32 S.J. Eggleston, D.K. Dunn and A. Purewal, *In-service Teacher Education in a Multiracial Society*, Keele University, 1981.
33 J. Lynch, *The Multiracial Curriculum*, Batsford Academic, 1983.
34 D. Fitch, op. cit.
35 B. Parekh, *Exercising the Imagination in Multicultural Education: Views from the classroom*, BBC, 1981.
36 K. Richards, 'Multiethnicity and the School Curriculum', in J. Lynch (ed.), *Teaching in the Multicultural School*, Ward Lock Educational, 1981.
37 R. Ash, 'Mother Tongue Teaching and the Asian Community', seminar paper delivered at NAAY seminar in Leicester. (Revised version published in NAAY Occasional Paper No. 2, 1978.)
38 B. Parekh, op. cit.

Chapter 6

Towards a multicultural curriculum – secondary

Carlton Duncan

It is not generally known that black people have been a feature of British society in substantial numbers since well before 1945. Granville Sharpe in the 1700s estimated that such people numbered 20,000.[1] During the First World War, around 950,000 Indians, together with some 15,000 West Indians, fought on behalf of the mother country. The Second World War attracted even greater numbers. The Indian army supplied around 2 million soldiers and 40,000 West Indians joined forces on behalf of this country. Thus the surge of responses to the invitations to answer Britain's economic needs after 1945 was really nothing new, except that now they came as a free people, and even if at the time their arrival was viewed by themselves as temporary, at least in the short run there was a permanent nature about it.

Indians and West Indians were not the only immigrants to this country. The Jews, the Poles, Italians, Irish and others came too. This fact is sometimes advanced as a reason for not making any special adaptations in order to accommodate the non-white settlers. If the white settlers managed to integrate without any special effort on the part of the host community, so should the others, the argument goes. This argument completely overlooks the impact of colour and associated difficulties. It is one thing to be of a different race but it is quite something else to be visibly so. Nowhere else is this fact more telling than in the performance levels of non-white ethnic minority children in British schools.

Many researchers have considered the problem of under-achievement among ethnic minorities and have concluded that of this there can be no doubt. It is emerging too that a concomitant problem is that of misinformation via the school curriculum to all children, with different effects on them depending on whether they are white or black. These conclusions in any case appear to be reasonable ones to be drawn from one of the most recent educational studies of ethnic minority issues.[2]

But the considerable amount of evidence to the same effect which preceded Rampton appears to substantiate the commonly held view, at least amongst the ethnic minority communities, that Rampton (and the present Swann Inquiry) was totally unnecessary and that such exercises were really deliberate political ploys to buy time on issues which were proving too embarrassing and threatening. Yet one is inclined to believe that if this was the case, and in view of the inner city fires, riots and disturbances which prompted the Scarman inquiries, it was a ghastly political misjudgment which has not yet seen the worst of its repercussions.

Consider for example:

In 1963 a study by Brent LEA found the performance of West Indian children was, on average, much lower than that of white children in reading, arithmetic and spelling.

In 1965 a study carried out by Vernon[3] comparing West Indians in London and Hertfordshire showed similar results.

In 1966 the ILEA researches noted dissatisfaction with the performance of immigrant children as compared with non-immigrant children of the same age within the local authority area.

In 1966 and 1968 Dr Little's studies[4] of reading standards of 9-year-olds in the Inner London Education Authority showed that West Indian children were performing less well at primary school than white children from the same socio-economic backgrounds.

Section 11 of the 1966 Local Government Act provides special funds to Local Authorities (75% of cost) to meet the special needs of ethnic minorities within their areas. Since this source of funds is the only known bottomless pit as far as educational finance is concerned, it seems reasonable to conclude that from early days governments had cause for concern. Indeed, in 1978 a study[5] undertaken in the London Borough of Redbridge corroborated all that had gone before.

But the study which was responsible more than any other for arousing public conscience was that of Bernard Coard. After revealing that a disproportionately large number of West Indian children found their way to schools for the educationally sub-normal he concluded:[6]

> If the children of us immigrants were to get equal educational opportunities then in one generation there would be no large labour pool from under-developed countries, prepared to do

> the menial and unwanted jobs in the economic system, at the lowest wages and in the worst housing; for our children armed with a good education, would demand the jobs and the social status that goes with such jobs – befitting their educational qualifications. This would be a very bad blow to Britain's 'Social Order' with its notions about the right place of the black man in relation to the white man in society.

It was in this climate and around the same period that all three political parties considered the situation serious enough to set up an all-party Select Committee of the House of Commons to investigate issues pertaining to ethnic minorities. They reported[7] in 1977, making eight recommendations pertaining to education. One of these called upon the government of the day to set up 'as a matter of urgency a high level independent Inquiry' to find out why ethnic minorities were underachieving in schools. Hence the Rampton Inquiry (now led by Lord Swann). It should be noted that the Select Committee did not ask us (the author is a member of the inquiry) to find out whether there was underachievement, but *why*.

However, in addition to its brief, Rampton was also able to confirm the problem of underachievement. The Swann Report has similarly confirmed underachievement on a large scale.

Now it would be intellectually dishonest not to mention Dr Driver's report,[8] which appeared to contradict previous findings. His study of five schools revelaed that West Indian pupils, especially girls, did better academically than did their white peers. However Driver himself admitted the following in his report:

(a) 'This group is not meant to be a representative sample upon which nationwide predictions can be made . . .'
(b) He admitted that he was able to go only into those schools which would co-operate.
(c) At times, the relevant records were either missing or non-existent.
(d) The social background of the pupils was outside this terms of reference.
(e) But the admission which for me as an educationist puts to rest Driver's findings was that he did not take account of the effect of organisational, curriculum and staffing situations within the five schools (two in the North, one in the Midlands and two in the Home Counties) from where he drew his population of study. These are the key issues with which one must come to terms before one can have anything

> useful to say about academic achievement, since they are in fact the most important aspects of both the planned and the hidden curriculum. Additionally it must be pointed out that Driver used no control group, and, what is more, his sample was not random in selection.

So, with some justification, Driver's report might be dismissed in preference for the numerous other contrary findings.

Professor Rutter, on the other hand, from various pieces of research, addressed the Swann Committee on 'Growing up in Inner London: Problems and accomplishments'. His evidence pointed to black pupils doing well also. However, it was observed that they needed to stay on in the sixth form longer than their indigenous peers. One might reasonably infer that either there are additional obstacles for black pupils in the system or that they are naturally inferior. But the Jenson/Eysenck positions have been variously discredited since they first appeared. The respectable view now is the IQ tests measure a sample of a child's actual behaviour: what he knows and has learned. Thus the former reference seems the more likely. The case for under-achievement is thus established.

That we mislead our indigenous white pupils there can be no doubt. Evidence of this, surely, might be gleaned from the activities of the National Front. It is known that the real forces behind the Front emanate from fully grown and supposedly responsible people. But the degrading insulting, racist and provocate behaviours are mostly carried out by youngsters many of whom are still at school. Their slogans, actions, etc., are clearly based upon misinformation about their ethnic peers.

In one study carried out on behalf of the Rampton Inquiry the researcher went to an all-white secondary school in a rural area. The following are just a few of mnay quotes taken from 13- and 14-year-olds who admitted that they have never met a black person but that they nevertheless had opinions about them.

> People from the West Indies mainly stay by themselves and don't mix with other people. Most West Indians live around the big cities like Coventry, Birmingham and Wolverhampton. Very few people live in the country. Back in the West Indies they live in shanty towns and eat coconuts all day.

> People from Africa are also black but you do not get many of them immigrating. In their country most of them live in the bush.

> A lot of the time immigrants complain about the way they are treated, the government, money, poor living conditions, etc. If all they can do is complain they shouldn't have come. It was their choice.
>
> I have learnt that a lot of the crime rate is due to the excess immigrants in the country. The immigrants who are mostly unemployed go around in gangs and commit violent crimes.
>
> I have learnt that they are pulling this country down because they all depend on social security.

Many other similar sentiments could be listed here.

One took the view that these views would right themselves with time. But, alas! this is not to be. Extensive travelling of the length and breadth of this country and countless school visits have substantially confirmed that these youngsters later become teachers who then go on to perpetuate the kinds of myths, preconceptions and stereotypes reflected in the quotations given. Teachers very often expressed the views that West Indians are excellent only at sports and dancing but nothing else; that 'they all want to be brain surgeons' in reference to Asian pupils; that West Indian pupils are anti-social, mischievous and loud; that Asian pupils are quiet and well behaved, and similar misinformed and dangerous views. The vicious circle perhaps!

The real difficulty is that, unlike the 13-year-olds, teachers are in a position to effect actions based upon such views. Bernard Coard, it will be recalled, was spurred into writing his book *How the West Indian Child is Made Educationally Sub-normal in the British School System* by the fact of ethnic minority over-representation in ESN schools. There is also considerable evidence (gained during the Rampton/Swann evidence-gathering) to show that ethnic minorities are more likely to find themselves in remedial streams, CSE, as opposed to GCE groups, disruptive units than their indigenous counterparts. Similarly, they tend to suffer exclusions and suspensions at a higher rate. Since teachers are still largely responsible for devising the curriculum in schools, it follows that they are hardly likely to draw up schemes which will stretch their Asian pupils to become brain surgeons, for they start with a doubt in relation to this possibility.

The Rampton/Swann Inquiry often met the reply: 'We do not know how many ethnic minorities are in this school since we do not bother to notice colour. We treat all children alike'; a theme followed by the Tory party during the recent election campaign (June 1983).

Yet, within minutes of this declaration by one headmaster, he was to say that 'the trouble with West Indians is that they have a ghetto-like mentality.' When pressed for an explanation, he swivelled his chair to face a window in his office which overlooked the school's playground. Sure enough he was able to illustrate his meaning by pointing to two groups of West Indian boys in the playground. 'That is what I mean,' he declared. 'They are always together.' We couldn't help noticing that there were also three groups of white boys together. It is significant that the head, only minutes before, appeared to be colour-blind.

Starting where pupils are, is the best way to motivate youngsters. And motivation is the next-door neighbour to achievement, however we define it. To treat all pupils alike must necessarily fall short on this principle. The significant pointers to where the pupils are will necessarily be their cultural, religious, racial and linguistic backrounds. Ignore this and we leave them behind. The Eurocentric educational pork will not be a palatable menu for all. Some will starve. In this respect, nothing is more inequitable than the well-meant but misguided adoption of the 'equal treatment for all' principle. Pupils are not alike.

It is remarkable that this same head wanted to be advised on what to do to get his ethnic minority children out of the remedial and CSE streams where they predominated. The answer might be that he should not treat them all alike.

Having thus established the positions of underachievement and misinformation, the question why this should be the case becomes important.

Several factors contribute to this state of affairs: (a) racism, (b) poor (or no) pre-school provision, (c) inadequate reading and language programmes, (d) the curriculum, (e) biased books and teaching materials, (f) examination constraints (g) poor (or no) school pastoral arrangements, (h) absence of links between the school and the community, (i) disciplinary measures and special techniques and (j) career guidance as given.

Time and space will be given to two of these: racism and the curriculum.

Racism

> . . . racism describes a set of attitudes and behaviour towards people of another race which is based on the belief that races are distinct and can be graded as 'superior' or 'inferior'. A racist is therefore someone who believes that people of a

> particular race, colour, or national origin are inherently inferior, so that their identity, culture, self-esteem, views and feelings are of less value than his or her own and can be disregarded or treated as less important.

This could be either overtly expressed or unintentionally displayed. The result is equally damaging to the recipient. The headmaster who treats all his pupils alike, the teacher who sees West Indians only as good sportsmen, Asians as aspiring too highly, and the like, may be well-meaning intentionally. The result, however, is one of inferior provision for ethnic minorities. This is also a problem of institution . . . institutionalised racism. Take for example a typical instrument of government for a secondary school. Nowhere in them will there be an overt expression of racism directed at ethnic minorities. Yet to put into effect its categories of membership is almost certainly to exclude ethnic minorities. The requirements that local politicians should be in the majority, that there should be academic representation, an industrialist, etc., are effectively closing avenues to ethnic minorities, since these are areas which for similar reasons are largely closed to them. School governors are important people. They are responsible for all the senior appointments who in turn determine what happens in the school.

It is significant that four government reports (Fifth Report from the House of Commons Home Affairs Committee, the Rampton Interim Report, the Scarman Report, and the Thompson Report) all appearing between June 1981 and October 1982, identified racism as at least one major hindrance to equal opportunities for ethnic minorities. The Swann Report also echoed this rather loudly.

The curriculum (planned and hidden)

> Perhaps she could finish her father's unfinished work. He had been interested in savages and backward races. Africa was the best place to find such people . . . Mary would go to Africa. She could go among the wildest savages she could find. She would spend her life studying cannibals.[9]

As teachers, we have the duty and responsibility to be selective and sensitive in our choice of materials for the consumption of young children who are in our care. Presenting the above to any class, let alone a multiracial one, would suggest recklessness at least in the execution of this duty. Yet this is only one of the examples which we found prevalent as we gathered evidence for the Rampton Inquiry. Consider what message was being given to the indigenous white pupils of that classroom. Then consider what message was being taken by the ethnic minorities present.

In view of this, it is not surprising to see in the Education *Guardian*[10] that a black child thought she needed permission to represent herself in one of her own drawings.

> In a first year art class at a South London secondary school the topic was a local street scene. Studying the work of a West Indian girl the art teacher asked: 'Why don't you draw any black people in the picture?' 'Miss, are we allowed to?' came the reply.

This same negative view of oneself was reflected in the black girl's utterance after studying herself in a mirror – 'Ugh, aren't I black?' The author has a personal connection with a similar experience. Soon after he was appointed Deputy Headmaster of the Sidney Stringer School and Community College in Coventry, he had cause to correct and advise a 17-year-old West Indian who was strolling through that vast complex of a place with his arms around his white girl-friend as he demonstrated publicly his obvious affection for her. The advice to this young man was that this kind of behaviour might be more appropriate in private. The young man was most abusive and rude. A white but junior colleague of the author came to his rescue, and the lad with absolute respect for the author's colleague responded. The author went to his office and pondered over the incident. Soon there was a knock on the door. It was this lad again. Only this time he was most humble and apologetic. He had just learned that the author was the new Deputy Headmaster. It was clear that this lad wanted not to conflict with Authority. But his perception of blacks like himself did not extend to the position the author held at the time. In fact he did not perceive much beyond driving or conducting buses or hospital ward-maids as stations for his kind.

The issues arising out of *Red Book One* are not confined to the primary sector in education. A quote from *The Rise of Christian Europe* by Hugh Trevor-Roper (1966) will illustrate. The following is what we found secondary pupils consuming:

> Perhaps in the future there will be some African History to teach. But at present there is none, or very little: there is only the history of Europeans in Africa. The rest is largely darkness . . . and darkness is not a subject for history.

Similar sentiments to those are to be found in standard works of reference which are in use in school today.[11]

> To the conquest of nature through knowledge the contribution made by Asiatics have been negligible and by Africans (Egyptians excluded) non-existent. The printing-press and the telescope, the steam engine, the internal combustion engine and the aeroplane, the telegraph and telephone, wireless broadcasting and the cinematograph, the gramophone and television, together with all the leading discoveries in physiology, the circulation of the blood, the laws of respiration and the like, are the result of researches carried out by white men of European stock.

These references, sometimes with matching illustrations, can have a damaging effect on ethnic minority children, quite apart from presenting an inaccurate picture of the world to all children.

We still teach the different subject areas with a Eurocentric eye. Wilberforce and Lincoln, for example, singlehandedly brought about the emancipation of slaves. At least this is what our children, black and white, understand. No mention is made of the work of black politicians some of whom sacrificed their lives to that end. Telemark (Denmark) Vassey, Nat Turner, Nanny and the Maroons, Harriet Tubman, Sojourner Truth, Frederick Douglas, James Forten and others are either unheard-of or deliberately forgotten. Yet their supreme contribution was necessarily greater than that of Wilberforce and Lincoln.

A simple test for anyone to carry out would be this: Stop any ten school children and query who was Florence Nightingale. Ten out of ten will answer correctly. Our history books, hospital wards, etc., have seen to that. And this is an excellent thing. Children do benefit in terms of motivation from having role-models around. Yet should you ask these same ten youngsters who was Mary Seacole, the answers would be wrong ten times out of ten or thereabouts. Mary Seacole, a born Jamaican, sold all her belongings and travelled to this country with a view to going with Florence Nightingale to the Crimea. The government would not sponsor her. Her colour was an obstacle, then as it had always been. She used what little money she had left to travel there under her own steam. She set up in the more dangerous zones to achieve all that Florence Nightingale accomplished. True, she was honoured by a member of the Royal Family on her return, but silently forgotten thereafter. What equal worth she might be for ethnic minority youngsters? – What better image of black people she could convey to others?

Third World countries are often portrayed as recipients of aid in geography textbooks and lessons. Rarely do we find anything mentioned of the fact that to a considerable extent western civilisation has been in the past, and still today, dependent upon the fruits of the underdeveloped worlds. For example, Bristol and Cardiff are cities whose history should remind us most forcefully of this fact.

In a recent article David Wright criticised the racist and ethnocentric nature of two modern and popular geography textbooks.[12] He concluded his critique thus:

> If teachers with sufficient expertise to be authors of standard textbooks write this insensitive material, what hope is there that other books – and other lessons – are less bad? At a conservative estimate 100,000 pupils have studied *Man and his World*. Some of them are now policemen, teachers, social workers. Others will soon qualify in these fields. What will their attitudes to race be?

Far too often science and mathematics teachers dismiss the multicultural curriculum as a worthy goal but not applicable to their subject areas. These areas are regarded as culture free and neutral in their presentation. In fact, nothing is further from the truth. These areas have as much contribution to make in altering the prejudiced and stereotyped preconceptions held of ethnic minorities as any other subject areas. Every subject taught in schools has a vital contribution to make.

It is difficult to understand why, in a biology lesson being given to mostly black pupils, the teacher insists on illustrating all points with 'blue eyes', 'pink skin', 'blue veins' and 'blonde hair'. Close attention to the language and illustrations used in science lessons will soon put paid to the idea of neutrality. Science teachers wishing to come to terms with the multiracial society in which all pupils are growing up must seek to update the view given of the technology used in the application of science. All pupils must be helped to understand that science is an activity carried on by people everywhere and not solely a matter of research.

Science teachers will need to be much more selective about the types of textbooks and other teaching materials needed in order to avoid the stereotyping images of black people, sadly still commonly portrayed. Science lessons could do much to explode some of the myths popularised about race, genetics and evolution theory. The need for science teachers to realise that science curricula are often culturally biased towards a European/North American viewpoint, ignoring both the current and historical contributions of Africans, Indians, the Chinese and the Arabs, is a strong one. Not many of our pupils, for example, would learn at school that the first successful heart surgeon – Daniel Hale Williams – was a black man.

Ray Hemmings has demonstrated conclusively that the Chinese, the Egyptians, the Asians and others can be called upon to enrich the learning of mathematics.[13] Consider, for example, the Diwali and Holi Festivals. At such times the Sikhs and Hindus would decorate their walls, floors and elsewhere with beautiful geometric illustrations. Is this not a way to link such a vital study more closely with the cultural background of more of our pupils?

Historical mathematics is not an important end in itself. But drawing upon it by way of illustrations at the appropriate times during mathematics lessons enables pupils to get a sounder pespective on the nature of mathematical activity. It could then be realised that this science has developed and is still developing from out of the efforts of various societies to come to terms with some of the numerous problems with which they were faced and are facing. Extending the horizons of the traditional ethnocentric approach to mathematics to include the contributions of different societies, such as their different counting systems, etc., has the following benefits:

(a) ethnic minority children become more knowledgeable about their own cultural background. In this way they are more likely to grant respect and meaning to their origins.
(b) other children are allowed to share in the delights and richness of various other cultures.
(c) the quality of mathematical work will itself be enhanced by drawing upon such cultural diversity.

In other words, it is possible to reflect more positively, for *all pupils*, images of all the peoples of the world. This will necessarily be a benefit for all, for we shall be telling more truths via the curriculum and a few less lies. There is so much to tell in this way. The zero or cypher is a great invention because it is the origin of the denary system. With the zero we can have the binary system, hence computers. Glass-amalgam is from the Middle East. Geometry and other mathematical sciences are from the Egyptians. The magnetic compass and the magnetic needle are from the Chinese. Saltpetre is from the Hindus; it helped in exploding mines, e.g., coal, iron – note the Industrial Revolution.

My call, therefore, is for a balanced, more positive approach to the curriculum for all pupils – particularly in all white schools. I reject Black Studies; I reject the Eurocentric curriculum – all on the same grounds.

Children learn as much, if not more, via the hidden curriculum. How we staff our schools, how we organise our structures, the places we give to ethnic minority teachers in such structures will be important lessons for all our pupils. What kind of message is it that at the time of writing (October 1983) there should be so few black headteachers in the whole of this country? Are ethnic minorities in search of heroes?

A multicultural approach to the curriculum is required.

References

1 G. Sharpe, *The Gentleman's Magazine*, vol. 34, 1764, p. 493.
2 A. Rampton (chairman), *West Indian Children in our Schools*, Cmmd 8273, HMSO, 1981.
3 P. Vernon, *Environmental Handicaps and Intellectual Development*, 1965.
4 A. Little et al., *The Education of Immigrant Pupils in Inner London Primary Schools*, 1968.
5 *Cause for Concern: West Indian pupils in Redbridge*, Black Peoples' Progressive Association and Redbridge Community Relations Council, April 1978.
6 B. Coard, *How the West Indian Child is Made Educationally Subnormal in the British School System*, New Beacon, 1971, p. 35.
7 House of Commons, HC 180-I-III, 1977.
8 G. Driver, *Beyond Underachievement (Case studies of English, West Indians and Asian School Leavers at 16+)*, CRE, 1980.
9 *Reading on Red Book One (an English reader for primary children)*, Oliver & Boyd, 7th ed, 1968.
10 *Guardian*, 2 May 1973.
11 H. Fisher, *History of Europe*, 1945 ed.
12 D. Wright, Lecturer in Education, University of East Anglia, Norwich, 'The Geography of Race', *The Times Educational Supplement*, 15 July 1983, p. 15; books criticised: *Man and his World* by J.A. Dawson and D. Thomas (Nelson, 1975, 7th ed, 1982) and *Elements of Human Geography* by C. Whynne-Hammond (Allen & Unwin, 1979).
13 R. Hemmings, 'Multiethnic Mathematics', *NAME Journal*, vol. 8, no. 3, summer 1980, and vol. 9, no. 1, autumn 1980.

Chapter 7

Approaches to multicultural curriculum – humanities

Sylvia Collicott

'Let the past serve the present' – Mao Tse-Tung

Standing for a moment on a busy street corner need not be an aimless pursuit. Buses, cars and lorries pass. A plane flies overhead. A queue forms outside the local Chinese take-away restaurant. But who's been down that road in the past? Did slow rustic carts pick their way through muddy ruts? Did fast mail-coaches speed past to the next city? Did a monarch pass with Treasury gold slung on the back of a pack-horse? Did a slave pass this way? Were there convicts being transported to America, Africa and Australia? Traders? Soldiers? Sailors? Missionaries? Administrators? It is possible to start a whole history project from a few moments on a busy street corner.

Our links with the past are part of our identity. That includes our family history. It includes the history of the community we live in. It includes understanding the links between this country and the rest of the world. There are a whole series of identities that we need to help children to come to terms with. 'Our links with the past.' What does that 'our' mean? It embraces the experiences of every person living in this country today. The history of the community embraces both the experiences of people who have come into that community as well as people who have always lived there. History has an important part to play in developing personal, local, cultural, religious and national identities.

Few of these objectives can be achieved without a child-centred approach. The classroom must be organised in such a way that all children can work from their own experience and acquire new skills at their own pace. If all the children in the class are given the same piece of work at the same time, not only will little learning take place, because of the mismatch between the work and the skills of many of the children, but the issue of identity cannot be addressed. Each child has a unique family history. Each child must record his own story. That is the starting-point for a spiral curriculum in history. A child should then be able to progress from self-knowledge to an eventual understanding of the international relationships which shape the world we live in.

The theme of Family History can be started in the infant school. It's a wonderful introduction to the subject because it draws on the strength of parental involvement. I attempted such a topic with Middle and Top Infants.[1] Each child was given a big exercise-book. The first page was a personal record of the owner. Every night the child, or I, composed a question on the top of a page. The question was addressed to the parents. Have you been on a steam train? Were you ever a bridesmaid? What was your favourite treat? Every morning a class ritual developed of reading the replies. Self-esteem and mutual respect inevitably followed.

The theme of Moving can also be started with young children. It is possible to draw on the children's own experiences of what it felt like to move house, to go to a new school or to settle into a new neighbourhood.[2] From those discussions I developed a whole-term project on how the Anansi stories travelled from West Africa to the West Indies and into the book corner of our classroom. I asked the question: What do people take with them if they haven't got a suitcase? It's a simple answer . . . their culture. We traced the triangular trade of the Anasi stories: the project included the story of the Oba of Benin, positive images of Africa then and now, basic facts about the middle passage, slavery in the Caribbean and the West Indian islands today. At every stage, through drama and movement, I tried to develop feelings of empathy among the children.

The next step from personal history is into the history of the community around the school. Street writing was the starting point I took for a study of the Past and Present. The object was for children to record the writing around them, not the graffiti, through the medium of their art work and photography.

The children took slide photographs of labels, lettering, notices and traffic signs. The slides, when developed, were then projected on to large sheets of paper and an outline faithfully traced. It is an excellent method of recording detail. The project therefore ncessitated regular class walks around the local streets. Posters, pillar-boxes, price-tags and pub names were all recorded.

Some of the street writing will tell about the past. I asked a group of first-year juniors why a houseless cul-de-sac in

Tottenham was called Factory Lane. They were unable to answer until they had seen the second edition of the Ordnance Survey map of the area, which showed that an India Rubber factory was once on the site. All the children called a local alley Carbuncle Alley. The second edition Ordnance survey map showed Carbuncle Ditch as an open river. The 1619 Dorset Survey Map showed the open river labelled Garbell Ditch. Maps are extremely useful for decoding street names.[3]

Street writing also records the nature of the present community. There was a Kashmiri butchery, a sari shop, a Turkish doner kebab take-away, a Greek taxi advertisement as well as an abundance of English notices. There was the evidence for the diversity of languages within the local community. Links can be made in the classroom between the writing in the community and the many scripts and alphabets world-wide. Chinese calligraphy can be introduced in the infant or junior classroom. The Arabic script can be traced. Children can bring into the classroom personal evidence of the language used at home. The teaching point is that the world holds a great diversity of written languages.[4]

Oral History is increasingly being recognised as a viable source of evidence about the past. The technique of tape-recording old people's memories and transcribing their statements is a natural development from the infant Family History project. Links can be made between school and old people's clubs in the area. The children should draw up a small list of questions they wish to ask. Then comparisons of replies can be made as well as comparisons between the experiences of the elderly and the children.

If your school is in an all-white area, care has to be taken not to draw only on white people's history. Since the early days of trading ships, people have been coming to England from other countries. The evidence will lie in the local Parish Burial and Baptisms Registers and in the Enumerator Schedules of the Census. Check those archives for people coming into the country. The Parish Records will note a negro or a blackamoor, and the Census will show the place of birth. The Oral History will have to be supplemented with a wider evidence.

There are other themes in the local community that a teacher can explore . . . Settlement, Transport, Flowers and Food. What factors, be they environmental or man-made, modelled the growth of the community around the school? Is the area close to a river, a railway-line or an airport? The theme, once examined locally, can be applied to settlements in other parts of the world. Sydney grew on the rim of a large natural harbour, while

Calcutta was a creation of the East India Company. Architecture is an interesting study, too. It can start, with infants, as a topic on shapes. Children will soon spot shapes in buildings.[5] At junior level, a more sophisticated criterion can be used. A series of visual inputs on Greek temples, Islamic domes, Roman arches, European Gothic windows and Dutch gables will help children to decode local housing styles. Local History can be taught through the theme of Transport. Rather than teach the topic in isolation, trace the history of Transport through the lives of local notables: a Roman consul, the Lord of the Manor, an Elizabethan gentlewoman, a Georgian improving farmer or a Victorian lady traveller. How did those people travel? It depends on your notables as to where the theme can develop. The theme can be taken further into an examination of means of transport world-wide.[6] It can also be linked to a study of the local transport system. How many lorries pass in ten minutes? Where did they come from?

The history of flowers in our gardens is the history of many Empires. The Romans brought hyacinths to England, jasmine came with the Moorish invasion of Spain and marigolds came from the Spanish Empire in South America.[7] The same story can be traced in the history of the food we eat: rice puddings from India, potatoes from America and macaroni from Italy.

The history of the community can be consolidated with a display of 'Then and Now' photographs. Old photographs can be ordered from the Local Photographic Archives. Children can then take their own photographs from the same spot. In this way children will realise the ever-changing nature of a community.[8] They will have a common identity.

In selecting the content of the curriculum, teachers must not take an Anglocentric view. Teaching points must be identified and then presented to the children through a variety of experiences. Draw on the history of other countries. Make comparisons between English history and the contemporary events in other countries.[9] As the rulers of Sicily, the Normans were as much a part of Mediterranean culture as they were castle-builders in England. A comparative study can be made, using the evidence of Elizabethan miniature paintings and Moghul miniatures, of Court life in India and Court life in England.[10] 'The Age of Discovery' is a popular classroom topic, but the very title indicates a Eurocentric view. Europeans were not the only explorers. Men like the Muslim Ibn Battuta in the fourteenth century, and Cheng Ho, a Chinese admiral in the fifteenth century, prompt a rewording of the theme, 'The Age of

Encounter' as a more meaningful label.[11]

It is at junior level that many history skills can be taught. The further reading skills are needed before children can locate and abstract information from reference books, so they need to use contents pages and indexes. They need scanning techniques and note-making skills. They need to be able to evaluate material and identify the racism and sexism in books. They need to read with a purpose. A purposeless read is of little educational value. Children can also develop skills of empathy by reading historical novels. Computer skills are gradually being introduced into the history curriculum. Information from the Enumerator Schedules of the Census can be programmed and children can abstract information for given tasks. How many people were born in Scotland? How many children went to school? There are also commercial packs on the market that can help the development of historical concepts.[12]

History should be taught through a whole curriculum approach. A theme, such as the Egyptians, should be at the heart of a class project. Children should learn the theme through stories, poems, movement, music, art and craft, mathematics and science, as well as through the history book. Then children's understanding of history can be flexible and diverse. Historical facts can be fitted into other subject topics as well. 'The Ladies of the Lamp', Mary Seacole and Florence Nightingale, both nurses in the Crimean War, can be brought into a science topic on 'Light'.[13] The story of Luke Howard, the Tottenham man who named our cloud systems as long ago as 1803, can be taught in a topic on 'Weather'.

England has rarely sat in isolation. Its history is one of constant contact with other parts of the world. To understand that history, we need to have a knowledge of the histories of other countries to make comparisons. It is therefore necessary to trace our local–world links and to learn alternative histories. The links between England and other countries were made in a variety of ways; there were links of trade, links of language, links of ideas, links through books and writings and above all links of Empire. Go to the local archives, read the commemorative plaques on the walls of the parish church, search the local history books for evidence of people who travelled and there will be the 'links'. Look for people involved in the East India Company, in the army or navy, owning plantations in the West Indies, or women in the nursing profession. There are the links to a wider world. Is there evidence of black slaves in the Parish Registers? Huguenots? Irish? Imperial troops after the First World War? Such evidence develops a perspective that can illuminate world history and consolidate the concept of historical interdependence.

Can I illustrate how such evidence can be used? I recently held a history session with a group of Top Juniors on the life of Mary Kingsley. I was not prepared just to do a straight biography of that remarkable woman. I offered a series of inputs, thereby hoping to build up a sequence of images that would make Mary's life more meaningful to the children. First I showed a book of Benin bronzes and talked of the Great Empires of West Africa.[14] Then I showed slides about women in Victorian England.[15] Using photographs, books, maps, photostated newspaper articles and Census Returns and finally a letter, I showed the children how I knew that a Nigerian king had lived in Tottenham for five years in the 1850s. Then I told the story of Mary's life and her exploration in West Africa. We finished the session with a brisk walk round to the house where she used to live. I hoped that the children had received a positive image of Africa, a sense of the suppression of women, some basic facts on Mary Kingsley and an understanding of where those 'facts' had come from.

We need constantly to explore the links between people. To understand even a little of the Islamic World is to be able to identify Islamic influences in our own culture. Islam has offered much to European culture: stained glass windows, marbling, carpets, algebra, a number system, to name a few.[16] Similarly China offered the water wheel, the compass, the rudder, paper and porcelain.[17] A brief look at a dictionary is evidence enough of the diverse cultural influences on the English language: shawl from Persian, tea from Chinese, pyjamas from Hindi and cheroot from Tamil. Teachers, therefore, in influencing the curriculum, must inform themselves of other cultures and histories. They then need to re-examine the material that makes up 'the diet of history' for misinterpretation and even falsification. Then it will be possible to teach of England's interdependence with other countries as part of her history. 'Local and national history must be related to a wider context, not only in Europe but in America, Africa and Asia.'[18]

The question of omissions must also be discussed. Who are the people left out of the history books? Women? Black people? Working-class people?[19] It is not enough to identify what is missing, because often the very lack of evidence means that those gaps can never be satisfactorily filled. Children must know why such omissions have occurred. They must understand the racist, sexist and political selections behind the writing and publishing of history books. Then, in the future, there will be a fuller understanding of what constitutes history and what role the historian plays.

I recently gave a series of three papers to secondary teachers entitled 'Forgotten in Haringey History: Women, Africans and Anti-Slavers'. Given the antiquarian approach in local history writing, there are even more omissions than in the writing of national history. Children cannot develop a sense of community history or even make local–world links if the only local history they learn is of a male, white wealthy elite. The paper on Women attempted to trace the wavering story of feminism and women's struggles from Bethsua Makin, the tutor to the children of Charles I, to the Irish wife of an Irish policeman in Hornsey in 1851 to Kate Marsden, the nurse who travelled by horse and sledge to cure lepers in Siberia. The paper on Africans in Haringey began and ended in Nubia; there is an entry in the Tottenham Parish Register of 1611, 'Walter Anberey, the sonne of Nosser Anberey borne in the kingdom of Dungala in Africa was baptised'. The *Illustrated London News* of 6 October 1877 published an article on a public entertainment, 'Animals and Nubians at Alexandra Palace'. The archives at Friends House, Euston, reveal a hotbed of anti-slavery activity around the Tottenham Meeting House in both the eighteenth and nineteenth centuries. The local William Dillwyn brought the anti-slavery campaign from America to London and played a vital role in those early days. The evidence is all there in the local archives.

The theme on the Movement of Peoples should be a constant theme in history teaching. It certainly can be thoroughly examined at secondary level. There seems to be a 'porridge' theory of history that the roads were so bad that nobody ever travelled. The roads of the Silk Route to China were not tarred, but it didn't stop people seeking silks and profits. In 1583 Sir Thomas Wroth called for a traffic census along Enfield Highway: 2,100 horses passed in one morning.[20] People were obviously on the move.

Using evidence from the Enumerator Schedules of the Census, I presented a group of Third Year secondary pupils with evidence of people coming into England. I gave only the Census evidence for discussion. The 1861 Census revealed a family living in Scotland Green: Lydia Collins, daughter of the house, married, aged 20, occupation gold finder/Charles Collins, son-in-law, married, aged 31, occupation gold digger/Lydia Collins, granddaughter, unmarried, aged 10, born Australia, Sydney. I asked the class what story they thought lay behind that entry. The 1861 Census also recorded the family of Michael Rochford living in

Stamford Road. Michael Rochford, head of the family, married, aged 42, occupation market gardener, employing five men and one boy, born Ireland. It was the first business enterprise of what was to become the thriving Rochford's Houseplants. The aim was for the children to tease out the possible stories behind the bald information. If I could, I then told them what I had learnt from other sources. In this way we can stress the mobility of people both at national and international levels.

Migration is a common theme in history. Children need to understand the reasons behind the mass movement of peoples, for those reasons are varied. There is a risk of false comparisons being made if the complicated issues behind the expulsion of the Ugandan Asians or the flight of the Catholic clergy in the French Revolution are not understood. Pupils need skills of empathy and the ability to identify sources of information and their possible bias. Newspapers constantly use the word 'invasion' in an emotive, inaccurate way. Refugees, fleeing from religious or political persecution, have consistently been seen as 'invaders' by the host community. So an understanding of the alienation felt by refugees, or any other newly-arrived minority group, is as pertinent in contemporary society as in the past. The role of the history lesson must include challenging stereotypes. The theme of invasion raises certain fundamental questions. How do people respond to invasion? While some acquiesce, others resist. Cultural identity is suppressed. What is it like to be the conqueror? There is power, riches, a familiar official language, administration, legal system and a new system of land tenure. Invasion implies power and control, so the word used be used carefully.

There is room for a comparison between forced and voluntary movement of peoples. Comparison can also be made between forced movement and resistance. Resistance can be examined, for example, through the action of Queen Nzinga of Angola, who led her peoples to safety in the highlands when Portuguese slaving parties threatened.[21] The movement of Imperial troops in both World Wars were followed by a series of independence movements. Evidence of resistance must be handled with care, for the evidence of the 'oppressors' is more readily accessible and will differ considerably from the evidence of the 'oppressed'.

To achieve an understanding of the wider world, students need to have studied in a some depth a Third World country. Which country may well depend on the local–world links of the district. In Haringey there are strong links with West Africa and Bengal. Other areas will have other 'links'.

History Syllabus D (13–16 Schools Council Project) goes some steps towards a more multicultural approach in the history examination curriculum. The Local History paper is still not seen as a potential for world links. The assessment objectives include learning historical facts, interpreting evidence and constructing and communicating a simple historical argument. The approach is good, but the content still needs broadening. As Nigel File has shown, there are many opportunities in current syllabuses for drawing out world links. However CSE and O level Mode I syllabuses are still predominantly Eurocentric. Many schools use Mode III to escape such limitations.[22]

Chris Power, in his pamphlet *Educational Aims and Objectives for a Multicultural Society*, has set out objectives which are relevant for education in a culturally diverse society.

> To help students to evaluate information and make informed decisions.
>
> To help students to foster the ability to question and argue rationally.
>
> To help students to learn to distinguish between individual, cultural and national identity.
>
> To help students to gain an appreciation of language diversity and to assist the linguistic skills of bilingual literate students.
>
> To help children appreciate human achievements and aspirations.
>
> To help children to understand the world in which they live and the interdependence of individuals, groups and nations.
>
> To help students develop individual self respect and respect for others.
>
> To help pupils develop values and attitudes which support cultural diversity and pluralism as the norm of British Society.
>
> To help students to grapple with the moral dilemmas which they are likely to face in society, e.g. racial prejudice.
>
> To help students acquire the knowledge and skills relevant to life in a fast changing world.

In this chapter I have tried to demonstrate, with specific examples, how these objectives can be achieved in the teaching of history.

Notes and references

1 S. Collicott, 'Families are history', *Child Education*, May 1982.

2 S. Collicott, 'Moving', *Child Education*, December, 1980.
3 Ask about local maps at the Reference Library. Copies can also be ordered from the Maps Room of the British Library.
4 Make a personal collection of different kinds of writing. Postcards of calligraphy can be ordered by post from the British Museum.
5 S. Collicott, 'Out and About', *Child Education*, July 1979.
6 *The Way We Live*, Teachers' notes by Margot Brown and Marieke Clarke, published by Oxfam Educational, Banbury Road, Oxford.
7 John Fisher, *The Origins of Garden Plants*, Constable, 1982.
8 *Kelly's Street Directories* give a valuable record of the residents in the nineteenth century. A comparative study of a row of shops will excite interest.
9 *Illustrated Atlas of the World in the Middle Ages*, Longman, and Colin Platt, *The Atlas of Medieval Man*, Macmillan, 1979.
10 Judith Burdell, Broadsheet, Work in Progress. *Akbar and Elizabeth: Looking at History*, Schools Council Publications, 1983 and Judith Burdell, *Questions about Paintings: Cross-Cultural Themes in History*, a slide/tape pack, Schools Council Publications, 1983.
11 John Milsome, *Ibn Battuta*, Evans English Readers, 1976.
12 *Into the Unknown*, a computer-assisted learning package, simulating a voyage of discovery in the fifteenth century, Tressell Publications, 1983.
13 *The Wonderful Adventures of Mrs Seacole in Many Lands*, Falling Wall Press, 1984.
14 Paula Ben-Amos, *The Art of Benin*, Thames & Hudson, 1980.
15 Carole Adams, *Ordinary Lives*, Virago, 1982.
16 J.R. Hayes (ed), *The Genius of Arab Civilisation*, Routledge & Kegan Paul, 2nd edn 1983.
17 Joseph Needham, *Science and Civilisation in China*, Cambridge University Press, 1954.
18 HM Inspectorate, History, Internal discussion paper; Nigel File, *Assessment in a Multi-cultural Society*, History 16+, Longman for Schools Council, 1983, p. 17.
19 Deirdre Beddoe, *Discovering Women's History*, Pandora Press, 1983; Nigel File and Chris Power, *Black Settlers in Britain, 1555–1958*, Heinemann Educational Books, 1981.
20 Landsdowne Papers, V38 F 89, British Library.
21 David Sweetman, *African Women Leaders*, Heinemann, 1984.
22 Nigel File, *Assessment in a Multi-cultural Society*.

Chapter 8

Arts education as an element of multicultural education

Horace Lashley

During the latter months of 1979 and early 1980 the Commission for Racial Equality (CRE) in conjunction with the Arts Council of Great Britain and Gulbenkian Foundation sponsored a series of five conferences[1] at different venues in England, Scotland and Wales. They focused on 'Arts Education in a Multicultural Society' through the presentation of what was identified as 'good practice' in the different art forms. Each conference presented case studies showing how the various art forms might be used in the classroom.

The series came in the wake of the debate resulting from the publication of *The Arts Britain Ignores* by Naseem Khan,[2] and more particularly the wider curriculum debate on multicultural education.[3] In the foreword to the second edition of Khan's[4] book, she mentioned that since the first publication she had 'been contacted by a range of people – teachers, librarians, administrators of arts centres, organisers of local festivals, members of local authorities, wanting to know what practical steps they themselves could take.' To a large extent we have not moved on significantly. The hindrance to any meaningful advancement has been due much more to the lack of 'know-how' and expertise than an awareness that something has to be done. It, therefore, is intended in this paper to highlight some examples of good practice and focus on some of the wider issues of arts education in a multicultural society. This chapter will not be confined to any one particular stage but will focus more particularly on primary and secondary education.

Music

It has been argued in recent years that music education as practised in British schools is obsolete and to a large extent redundant[5]. This is by no means a blanket accusation, since individual schools have teachers who are forward-looking and prepared to respond to societal changes at any particular point in time. It has also been argued that music teachers are not very cost effective.[6] This is a most unacceptable and unnecessary situation at a time when music is one of the major preoccupations of young people. It plays a central role in their lives since it determines fashion, delineates particular cult groups or followings, acts as a facilitator for cross-cultural contact, and features in many other important facets in their lives and life-styles. Therefore music is of paramount importance in the lives and development of young people in our current society. Popular music makes an enormous contribution to understanding in a multicultural society and forms a major crossroads for the cultures of different societies.[7] Consequently music ought to have a much more important function in education than it has so far done.

It is not intended in this chapter to initiate a major onslaught on music education but to highlight its failure to capitalise on the kinds of issues that would enable it to play a more significant educative function. This concern becomes more acute at a time when education is looking for the kinds of issues and strategies that can help to motivate young people who are becoming increasingly alienated from education and school. It is unfortunate that music as a subject seems to be entrapped in a high culture conception which prevents it from breaking out of an exclusivistic mould.

However, in some schools with significant numbers of ethnic minority children, there are increasing attempts by forward-looking teachers to introduce music curricula which recognise the multiculturality of their classrooms. These developments are sometimes isolated. This isolation often occurs because such worth-while innovation takes place particularly with those pupils who are not entering for examinations. Additionally it happens with classes which are considered to be multicultural purely on the basis of the numbers of ethnic minority children present. The steel band and sitar are seen as West Indian and Asian musical phenomena by schools and have tended to be the main response of music education in multicultural settings. So far we have not had the kinds of explorations in instrument-making, composition, rhythm, tempo and the use of a wider selection of non-European instruments to enrich the musical awareness of all children in schools and more specifically in schools where there are significant numbers of ethnic minorities whose home environments tend to be rich in the arts.

At Handworth Wood Girls' School in Birmingham the music teacher found that the traditional Eurocentric music curriculum was unsuited for the school because of an overwhelming multicultural mix.[8] He however identified two major reasons for this decision. First, he recognised that the children had a very rich musical background of their own which they practised. Second, like their white peers in that environment, their interest in music did not have a European classical or theoretical orientation. He therefore had to develop a curriculum that would utilise the rich musical tradition with which they came and motivate their musical interests sufficiently to introduce aspects of theoretical music education as required for examinations. The major hindrance to most music teachers, however well disposed they might be to change, is the lack of knowledge of musical forms which are not in the classical western European mode. Thus the teacher becomes a prisoner to one tradition of music and the teaching of just that tradition. If, therefore, the teacher is unable to undertake some form of in-service education or does not possess the self-confidence to use the children themselves and the community as a resource, no effective music education will take place in such schools.

Don Gwinnett realised that fact fairly early after his appointment to Handsworth Wood Girls' School. He noted:[9] 'several of our pupils are partially practised exponents of this craft [playing of drums and other Indian temple instruments] and can supply the necessary expertise, that I lack, needed to coach other interested pupils.' They thus supplied the information about where the instruments could be purchased and the basic knowledge of operation. He made contact with the community and was able to acquire further resource in instruments and know-how. By using the community contact approach he was able to meet the needs of Asian children in a way that employed their own musical background and gave credence and status to their culture in the school curriculum.

He used similar strategies for working with the West Indian pupils. Through music he improved their overall motivation in the school environment and additionally gave them an opportunity to express themselves publicly through music. Thus from the small beginnings of a number of church-motivated West Indian girls approaching the school with the request to form a choir, they were able to go on to develop what he now calls, 'black music'. He has subsequently structured it into a formalised musical system. The choir has successfully performed in many churches and concert halls, bringing praise and recognition for the excellent work.

The choir has since made a record 'Break Through'[10] with other gospel groups in Handsworth consisting of former pupils, and choir members, of the school. Don Gwinnett has also moved on to campaign for more relevant and better music teaching for all schools in Birmingham. He has evolved a rather personalised model in which the teacher develops the expertise of management and knowledge by the use of the pupils as a reliable resource. This model can therefore be identified as the teacher/pupil expertise acquisition model.

Mountview High School in Harrow, also with a changed clientèle, recognised the need to utilise the musical traditions which many of the children brought with them. Increasingly many of these children were of an Asian background. For large numbers of these children religion is a major focus of their culture and also a focus of their art forms. Part of the daily ritual of prayer of Hindu and other Asian children with a Hindu-oriented religion consists of singing accompanied by musical instruments. The overall performance is of central importance in their religious worship. Therefore, in many of their homes the harmonium and other Indian musical instruments are common to the household. This cannot be generalised for all the religions to which Asian youngsters in our school belong. However, a disproportionate number of them are from very devout religious backgrounds of which the arts are an important part of the religion. It is not surprising therefore that teachers who have some sensitivity and awareness of the cultures of these youngsters are able to embark on the kinds of curriculum development which would take account of their cultural backgrounds. Additionally, such teachers with this sensitivity also utilise their awareness as an additional form of social contact and motivation of these youngsters.

The foregoing experience was pertinent to the recognition by Mountview School of the need to change its curriculum for the increasing numbers of youngsters entering the school from totally different cultural backgrounds. Likewise it wanted to satisfy the need for a totally multicultural school population where developments would not be exclusive to any one cultural group of the school. The school wanted to accomplish, therefore, two objectives. On the one hand it wanted to develop a curriculum which made music attractive to the vast majority of the children in the school. On the other hand it also wanted to cater for the particular cultural differences which appeared in the school. An additional intention was to stimulate cross-cultural contact among the different cultural groups within the school. The school did not have among its music staff any expertise in Asian or West Indian music forms. It therefore made contact with outside bodies which offered such services. One such organisation was the National Association of Asian Youth (NAAY) based in Southall. It was beginning to develop an interest in curriculum development, particularly in music. It had on its staff a small collection of experts on Asian music. It was also preparing through various forms of funding programmes to 'sell' Asian music to schools, both to those with significant numbers of Asian pupils and other schools with little if any Asian presence but whose interest in multicultural education would have benefited from a diverse musical input.

NAAY was therefore invited to the school to help in setting up the aspects of the curriculum that dealt with Asian music. They provided the teaching expertise necessary to give the subject an authentic framework. The school was rather fortunate that in addition to Asian music and despite the smaller numbers of pupils of West Indian origin on site was a youth worker, Terry Noel,[11] of West Indian origin who himself was an expert in steel band music. Since the school, particularly in its music curriculum, was adopting a multicultural approach he was therefore invited to contribute to the thinking the school was evolving. The steel band was then included as part of the school music timetable. The majority of his pupils were of an indigenous background. At times he had as much as 25% of the entire school population participating in his steel band lessons.

The school intended to use an established examination syllabus which it thought adaptable to the practical multicultural developments that they were introducing in its music curriculum. In so doing, it aimed to use the higher status examination of the two major schools examinations to legitimise its innovation. Thus, they identified a likely GCE syllabus that was thought to be potentially adaptable to their particular innovations. In so doing they had to embark on a campaign to justify the use of musical forms and instruments other than the normal high culture, Western-defined. Thus although they thought they had found a suitably adaptable syllabus they were then faced with a justification more concerned with the use of exotic forms of musical developments and instrumentation than with a demonstration of good adaptive music teaching and innovation. There were also obstacles such as the difficulties in moderating and validating the examination. This introduced a new element in the debate on curriculum and examination reform in a multicultural society. This example clearly demonstrated that the main prestigious examinations in subjects such as music present hindrances which are concerned mainly with exclusivisation and elitism and not with the merits of innovation, particularly multicultural. The more prestigious examinations are therefore used at times to frustrate the attempts to justify and legitimise multicultural curriculum innovations.

The two examples of good practice cited are just the tip of the iceberg. They indicate the two major models of development which are taking place, particularly in multicultural schools. The Harrow model is school-managed with visiting outside experts. Both models have advantages and disadvantages. However, they point to a major gap in teacher education both at the in-service and initial levels. Model-one-type innovation is much harder to cater for in the school examination framework. Model two presents certain difficulties because the classroom teacher is not fully in control of the methodology and knowledge content. However, it has the advantage of opening up the school curriculum to the practising artists and the school.[12] Because of the restrictions imposed by examinations the artists in residence seem more suited to the primary stage and early years of secondary education. It would be useful, however, if school examination boards were to recognise the need to incorporate the work of visiting practitioners of the arts as a major contribution toward making arts examination more realistic.

Some schools in white areas are beginning to use non-European musical forms and instruments. The gamelan and other Eastern musical instruments have been of particular interest. This interest is spurred on through the dedicated work of organisations such as the English Gamelan Society. The campaign of this organisation has taken root through the preparation of teachers with some background knowledge of the instrument in institutions such as Dartington College. A very small number of other music institutions are offering such options. Nicholas Soames in his article in the *Guardian*[13] refers to a number of them where courses are offered in non-European classical forms of music for intending teachers. The part played by music teacher education in hindering a more forward-looking attitude to music teaching cannot be overstressed. Professor Swanwick[14] has categorically asserted that it is unnecessary for music teacher education to attempt to produce performers for the classroom and few teachers of music. If therefore we are to take music teaching in schools beyond the sterility of a Beethovenesque conceptualisation, music colleges and departments preparing teachers must bear in mind the importance of music in the lives of all, and particularly the young. They must see music as a functional factor in our popular cultures. Music is an intrinsic part of our multicultural society. Whether we listen or perform we cannot fail to be affected or influenced by the popular lively interest shown in the music of other societies, and particularly those derived from the mother countries of ethnic minorities in Britain. It therefore behoves schools to play their part in this legitimate happening.

An experience of relevance here, and firmly stuck in my mind, occurred about seven years ago. It happened when I was listening to the BBC Radio Breakfast programme. There was a snippet of West African drumming and children chanting. At the end of the performance the announcer said, 'If you thought that was a group of African children performing' – and I did – 'then you are wrong. It was a group of children from an all-white school in Harlow.' It was my introduction to the work of Felix Cobson,[15] a Ghanaian who was the Arts Director at a secondary school in Harlow. I have subsequently followed Felix's career with great interest. Many of those children he had introduced to West African music and dance are still associated with him. Two points are relevant in my reminiscences. First, he showed that, with expertise, children in an all-white school would easily respond and see relevance in such activities. Second, he was introducing an alternative music, art, and dance curriculum at a time when even schools with a very high percentage of Afro-Caribbean children did not feel confident enough to do so despite an increasing multicultural awareness. Felix has now gone on to make this expertise available to all by developing the Aklowa project. This project is part of a growing number of specialist groups who can supply schools with the expertise they lack to provide music, dance and art of non-European cultures, and therefore feature prominently in the second model I referred to earlier.

Drama

Drama is increasingly an activity of some importance in the school curriculum at all levels. Additionally it is often used as a tool of psychosocial analysis and therapy. It is therefore no longer the presentation of the traditional school play at a particular time of year. It is no longer the unspecified curricular activity in which a small number of highly selected children would work with an enthusiastic teacher to present a formal production which ignored other dramatic talent among significant parts of the school population that were left out for a variety of reasons which had nothing to do with drama potential. It has become an effective analytical instrument of self-image and group relationship. In some schools, drama has become highly specialised. It is sometimes used with difficult youngsters to help them to analyse their behaviour, hoping that through the analysis they would embark on self-corrective measures. Psycho-drama, as it is called, is increasingly used in schools with large-scale difficulties, social and otherwise. Much of what can be called modern school drama is less production-oriented but much more analytical; it is used to draw out societal issues and bring real-life behaviour under the microscope, virtually in an instant. The audience become the participants and the participants become the audience, thus having a kind of total observation and total participation. In many such issues it is used to examine identity, self-esteem and self-confidence.[16]

The use of community languages is one of the major issues drama can highlight in multicultural schools. Thus the Bullock Report[17] noted: 'drama has an obvious and substantial contribution to make to the development of children's language, and possibilities in this respect have yet to be fully explored.' Here I shall not be looking at dialect and community languages as a separate issue. However, at this point, it is useful to draw the attention of the reader to the part played by language in building self-identity and self-esteem. The Bullock Report indicated that to disregard the language of the child in any way is like disregarding the child itself.

The middle-class culture and language of education and schooling in many ways disregard the language of children from cultural backgrounds other than that of the school. In so doing, the language of the school, which children are supposed to acquire, plays a role in alienating many of these youngsters. One can find that there have been attempts in schools to use drama to repair such damage by permitting youngsters to act out their real-life situations in their own community language and cultural context. Through such exercises the children perceive the school as able to respect and accept their language and cultural background. It is unfortunate that other subjects do not as readily present such opportunities. Psycho-drama exercises[18] in particular have been shown to produce (1) improvement in language performance, (2) improved confidence in forming social relationships, and (3) improved school performance. Such benefits have been noted in schools with greatest social needs. The exercises should therefore be expanded, developed and made a more integral part of drama education. Many schools are already exploiting psycho-drama to the benefit of ethnic minority youngsters and disadvantaged white working-class youngsters as well. This, however, needs to be expanded and introduced into other schools that can benefit.

Some years ago I visited a large secondary school in Hertfordshire well away, as it were, from the beaten track of visible multiculturality/multiracial presence. The school was undertaking a project on 'American Life Today'. It incorporated aspects of language work focusing on black American literature and drama. The life of Martin Luther King formed the main theme of the drama work. Although this project was being specifically run for pupils who were doing a Certificate of Extended Education (CEE), the project had a visible effect on the rest of the school. It impinged on other departments, and different age groups also paid some attention to the project, which in some ways was all-pervasive. The project, therefore, drew attention to race relations as well as British multiculturality. It questioned the racial stereotypes and assumptions of youngsters who are in a totally all-white area, oblivious of the fact that Britain is multiracial, since most of them have very little contact, if any, with their fellow peers who are black. This project was run by a group of teachers who were conscious of the need for factual and reliable information about black people and race relations to combat the increasing influence of racists among local school pupils.

Many youngsters of ethnic minority backgrounds have as part of their culture very ancient traditions and rituals which are dramatised: some are annual festivals and other forms of celebrations or observances. Some are retained as folk stories which have been transmitted from generation to generation, in some cases for thousands of years. The Ramayana is one such dramatic tradition which has been passed on for many centuries and has during that time retained an authenticity in its content and form. This is a particular aspect in the culture of Asian children of Hindu background. Children of West Indian background have also brought with them the African-inherited traditional stories which can be dramatised. The most famous of this particular tradition are the 'Nancy' stories, more commonly called the Anansi stories. These and other African traditional tales provide a base for folk tale drama with children of a Caribbean background. The present back-to-Africa movement by black youth is pertinent to the social historical experience they share as well as a symbolic reversion to their African ancestry. This offers them pride of person in what they consider to be a hostile environment.

Among Chinese children there are similar folk tales which depict many of their ancient customs and traditions. Within their community there is a rich tradition of folk lore which can be drawn on when doing drama work with ethnic minorities in general, and Chinese children in particular. In many of these cases there can be use of the mother language. One can also explore the use of the original language which would give youngsters a feeling of security. The school can thus demonstrate its ability to accept and respect the traditions and cultural heritage of a multicultural Britain and the world. In some schools traditional folk drama and stories have been used and in some cases adapted to the current situation in which many of ethnic minority youngsters find themselves. This has been done in particular with the Anansi stories, the Aklowa education project and other Afro-Caribbean Education Theatre projects. The Aklowa version was used during the pantomime season, and gave black youngsters an opportunity to see something of their own traditions as contributing to the wider pantomime tradition that is so much part of British culture.[19]

The kinds of developments and innovations that can be undertaken in drama need a more exhaustive discussion than can be undertaken here. However, it should be noted, first, that there is a great deal of scope and potential in developing multicultural drama. Second, ethnic minority youngsters can benefit positively by being introduced to a drama which utilises their own traditional and ancestral culture. Third, drama may be used as a vehicle for language, both by introducing community languages and by providing for children from non-English-speaking backgrounds additional language exercises through drama as a strategy in ESL teaching and language exploration.[20]

Visual arts

The visual art forms, in many respects, ought to have presented the least challenge to teachers in a multicultural society, because in many ways they have always had elements of multiculturality. However, this phenomenon has seldom been acknowledged. On the one hand many of those involved in art are not themselves aware of the multicultural origins of various initiatives, techniques and forms that have influenced art development. Second, cultural imperialism always conveyed an impression that whatever cultural knowledge exists in the metropolis is of itself entirely part and parcel of the cultural reality and development of the metropolis. In this way, through ignorance on the one hand, and arrogance on the other, the influences of many of the world's cultures have not rightly been acknowledged in visual arts development in Europe as in other forms. In education there has therefore been an unrecognised practice of art forms of other cultures. They have become traditional practice and form part of the regular activities in visual arts teaching. Multicultural art forms have been more commonly utilised in primary schools than in secondary schools. The restrictions in secondary schools have invariably been caused by examinations. Activities such as batik painting, tie and dye, vegetable printing and dyeing and many other activities of a visual arts nature have had their origins in cultures outside Europe. For this reason I have always seen art as a natural jumping-off point for multicultural education practice. At least, if not the jumping-off point, an integral part of demonstrating how knowledge has been evolved from an interdependence of cultures. Unfortunately, however, this has not been the case.

When I visit schools I generally look for visual pointers to the kind of multicultural development taking place. The art work on display is generally a good initial pointer. In many schools, one finds, despite the high proportion or any proportion whatsoever, of ethnic minorities, that the art work seldom reflects such multiracial/multicultural mix. It is most surprising that this often happens in schools which profess multicultural, and anti-racist policies. This is unfortunate for a number of reasons. Firstly, it shows the extent of insensitivity in an area which is particularly alive with interest among the ethnic minority youngsters. Secondly, it indicates a neglect for the cultural origins of the peoples, and thirdly, it is an important barometer of the actual kind of ideological underpinning of multiculturalism adopted by that school. The art work of a school can therefore indicate the extent of sincerity of a multicultural policy by reflecting the cultures and colours of the children that comprise the school. The more usual pattern of art work found in most schools, and this includes those that profess multiculturalism, more rightly indicate policies which are purely and simply integrationist.

From a multi-cultural perspective, the recent HMI Report[21] on art in secondary schools is very disappointing. First, it did not see fit to take as one of its examples a school with a multicultural intake of any substantial quantity. Second, it did not seem to think fit to draw out any discussion as to how what was observed related to the needs of a multicultural Britain. It is unfortunate that such an important document at this crucial point in our educational development saw fit to miss this important issue. Although I do not want to dwell on the point, however, it appears rather curious that despite continual DES reassurances of being in a multicultural society, important curriculum reports such as this ignore the multicultural nature of Britain. An omission of this magnitude further emphasises the marginality of multicultural education. It also gives evidence to the many critics of multicultural education who are unable to see the underpinning need for a multicultural policy throughout education as being healthy and necessary in the wake of the current significant changes taking place in our society. It must be emphasised, therefore, that change does not necessarily mean undermining the quality of education or excellence in standards. However, the omission to highlight the multicultural needs by explicit national policy only serves to ignore the significant developments that have taken place and the contributions made to this society by the new and equally valid cultural and art forms that now actively abound in our society. What is also not realised is that such exclusions indicate to children from ethnic minority backgrounds that their cultures and art forms are not seen as valid and acceptable by the school culture. This therefore ultimately contributes to further alienation and underachievement on the part of many ethnic minority youngsters who assume a posture of rejection by the education system.

One of the better examples I have witnessed in art teaching in a multicultural society was at the Birley High School in Manchester. The school implemented an explicit multicultural policy and attempted to permeate the entire curriculum with aspects of multiculturalism, so that art education became part and parcel of the wider multicultural education thinking. It was not surprising therefore to see that the art work on the walls had multicultural themes whether they were still life compositions or environmental reproductions. Here one saw a deliberate attempt to use art as a means of getting youngsters to accept themselves as they are, racially and culturally.

Some schools in Leicester have prided themselves in their attempt to introduce into the art curriculum elements of multiculturalism. This enthusiasm can probably be attributed to the influence of the work of Professor Brian Allison at Leicester Polytechnic. Allison[22] argues that 'one of the prime areas of concern in a responsible curriculum for art education is that of providing and developing appreciation, understanding, knowledge and experience of the art form of different cultures.' His institution provides postgraduate courses which expose large numbers of art teachers to the challenges of a multicultural society. He suggests that, 'because of predispositions originating in both art teachers' own backgrounds and theories of child art, the narrowness of concerns characteristic of much present art teaching leads to a neglect of the cultural area of the art education curriculum.' His department is one of the few in Britain that has seriously attempted to look at need of art education for a multicultural society.

For significant numbers of ethnic minority youngsters, art serves specific functions in their daily lives. Religion provides an important source of this particular phenomenon. Children of Hindu, Chinese, Sikh, Muslim and Buddhist background have very strong traditional artistic activities and artefacts involved with the practices and festivals of their religions. They celebrate festivals throughout the year which draw upon art in many different ways. These celebrations can therefore be used in many instances as a source of art work in the classroom. In these circumstances, unlike what we are normally accustomed to in European societies, art is not a practice or an activity which is totally separate from normal community life. For these children art is a community activity which generally serves a functional purpose. This does not in any way mean that art within these societies does not have its own particular kinds of fine art forms. However, art is a popular activity in the form of craft which a large part of the community subscribes to and which is functional in many aspects of cultural activities.

It is unfortunate that art history in particular has tended not to give sufficient opportunity for those interested and from other cultural backgrounds to explore the wealth of art contributions from Asia, the Orient and Africa. The contributions made by many of these societies, not only in painting and drawing styles and architecture, are enormous, and the opportunity ought to be provided to study the development of cross-cultural influences and put it in the right context in the overall historical development of art. Sculpture in many of these countries has also been of particular importance and influential on the modern schools of Western sculpture. The origin, historical importance and development of this influence are yet to be explored.

Makonde sculpture in particular has had an enormous effect on many of the developments that have taken place in Western sculpture in the twentieth century. The Mitla paintings of India have also influenced some of the modern schools of painting in Europe. Finger paintings and other similar forms of art technique from China and Japan have also played important roles in the development of modern Western schools of art and in many cases earlier than the present century. These issues have yet to be explored fully and placed in their right context for the effect they have had on art development in the West.[24]

Dance

In recent years dance has been introduced more readily into the school curriculum. A major aspect in the development and evolution of dance movement education has been the influence of other cultures.[25] Despite folk and classical dance having been considered as more fundamental to the creative arts initially, in curriculum development terms, dance movement evolved as part of the provision and thinking of physical education.[26] This conflict is now being resolved by curricular development in dance movement in its own right and the preparation of dance teachers as part of the strategy of professionalising and legitimising dance education. Although much of the provision of teaching expertise to date has been either postgraduate or elements of PE teacher preparation, more recently main subject dance courses are being introduced in the Bachelor of Education programme in many colleges and departments of education. Many schools in their attempt to utilise and cater for the multicultural mix of their school have imported visiting dance teachers from other cultures. Asian classical dancers such as Pratap and Praba Praval, and Alpana Sengupta are increasingly used by schools to teach Indian classical and folk dance. Asian cultural and community organisations also provide suitable dancers for schools and organise courses for school teachers to learn some of the rudiments and techniques of Asian dance to introduce in their normal school dance curriculum.

The Ekome dance group from Bristol has made a major contribution to multicultural dance in schools. They have concentrated on developing the educational potential of West African and Afro-Caribbean dance. They have also expanded their work to include the music, drumming and art of West Africa. The Aklowa Centre has also contributed to developments in this area. It not only takes its activities to schools, but also provides residential in-service training for teachers, students and groups of young people. There are other educational projects such as the African Arts in Education project, providing expertise in dance of other cultures to schools by use of the artist in residence model. In addition they also use a model of rudimentary expertise initiation through in-service and short courses. In this way teachers learn the rudiments of the art form so that they themselves can introduce it in their schools.

In recent years, increasing numbers of black youth are themselves organising dance groups. This is very often the result of exposure to the kinds of projects earlier outlined as well as an increasing popular interest in dance. The use of the abundance of creative talent possessed by many black youth is on occasions used as a political weapon to combat racism. Black youth have always been credited by schools as being rhythmic and natural dancers, but despite this assumption they have been overlooked when schools organise dance as part of their formal exhibitive presentations. Schools, as well as ballet companies, have also been reluctant to bring to the attention of these 'natural movers' the career potential of dance. However, through youth clubs and the voluntary youth organisations, many of these youngsters have gone on to have their dance potential recognised and gained professional training at schools such as the Laban Centre and The Place. They are also increasingly being found among the membership of the smaller modern ballet dance companies.

Increasingly it is argued that there is a rich oral tradition and written literature among ethnic minorities which have been ignored by schools. This has contributed to the feeling of alienation that the Bullock Report[27] has indicated as tantamount to rejection of these communities by the school system. It is therefore somewhat encouraging to see the developments that have taken place in this area recently. Many projects have sprung up focusing on story-telling based on ethnic minority folk lore. The ones I refer to would not be a complete list. The stories are being recorded in three different ways: (1) cassette tapes, (2) video tapes, and (3) written books. In some cases they are done by professional ethnic minority artists and in others by community people – e.g. grandparents and other older members of the communities. A good example of this kind of project is being undertaken by Jennie Ingham at Middlesex Polytechnic. The project aims to collect folk tales from a variety of cultural groups, mainly in the boroughs through which the polytechnic spreads, Enfield, Haringey and Barnet. The groups include Asians, Greek and Turkish Cypriots. The stories collected are being prepared for publication in English as well as in the mother tongues, and schools from infants through to secondary are being used. Jennie Ingham has found the project so successful in its collection of stories that she has suggested the need for a Community Folk-lore Centre in London.

In conclusion it must be admitted that we have come a long way, but the ultimate objective, to ensure that multiculturalism permeates the whole curriculum, is still far off. In art education in particular the progress has been somewhat slower, and I would argue that this is a result of the poor multiculturality in main subject areas of the teacher education curriculum. While schools continue to rely on the visiting/out-of-school expertise model, the multicultural arts will continue to be poorly developed. Schools must realise that 'it is important to see the arts, not as separate and different from children's other experience inside and outside schools, but as emerging from them and as providing a means of enriching and making sense of them.' The multicultural nature of British society fits in particularly well with this notion. The fact is that even in areas where there are no ethnic minority populations, young people are influenced by the cultural variety in which they are immersed and are consequently employing fashion, music, literature and other art forms independent of the schools' influences. It is not enough for the schools to continue to ignore these phenomena and important documents of the arts, to refer to multicultural education only incidentally, if at all. It must form a major item on the agenda.

References

1 CRE, *Arts Education in a Multi-cultural Society*, report of five Regional Conferences. CRE, London, 1981.
2 Naseem Khan, *The Arts Britain Ignores: The arts of ethnic minorities in Britain*, CRE, London, 1978.
3 See CRE, *Local Authorities and the Education Implications of Section 71 of the Race Relations Act 1976*, CRE, London, 1981.
4 Khan, op. cit.
5 See the article by Nicholas Goames, 'Missing the Boogie Beat', Education *Guardian*, 6 September 1983 p. 11. In this article he discusses with Professor Keith Swanwick the need to modernise music teaching.
6 Claudia Clark, 'British music education and Europe', *J. NAIEA*, no. 12, spring 1981, p. 21–2. See also Prof. Keith Swanwick's comments in Nicholas Goames's article.

7 G. Vulliamy and Ed Lee, *Pop, Rock and Ethnic Music in School*, Cambridge University Press, 1982.
8 Donald Gwinnett, 'Music in a Multi-cultural School', *Music Teacher*, vol. 58, no. 9, 1979, pp. 13–15.
9 Ibid.
10 Handsworth Break Through, Gospel Power in Music Break Through/ Sound Advice, 67 Newhall Street, Birmingham B3 1NU.
11 Terry Noel, *The Steelband from Bamboo to Pan*, Commonwealth Institute, 1976.
12 See Arts Council of Great Britain, *The Arts Council and Education: A consultative document*, Arts Council of Great Britain, 1981.
13 Soames, op. cit.
14 Professor Swanwick is referred to in Nicholas Goames, op. cit.
15 Felix Cobson has, in recent years, left full-time teaching in order to devote his entire energies to developing the Aklowa Centre. At the Centre he has a model West African village which is used as a teaching resource.
16 Arnold Matthew, *Advisory Approaches to Multi-cultural Education*, Runnymede Trust, 1981.
17 Bullock Report, *A Language for Life*, HMSO, 1975.
18 Ted Hazelton, Betty Price and George Brown, 'Psychodrama Creative Movement and Remedial Arts for Children with Special Educational Needs', *AEP Journal*, vol. 5, no. 1, summer 1979.
19 Christopher Bagley and Bernard Coard, 'Cultural Knowledge and Rejection of Ethnic Identity in West Indian children in London', in *Race and Education Across Cultures*, ed. Gajendra K. Verma and Christopher Bagley, Heinemann Educational, London, 1975.
20 See some of the works done by black psychologists such as William H. Grier and Price M. Cobbs, *Black Rage*, Cape, 1969 and Franz Fanon, *Black Skins, White Masks*, Penguin, 1967.
21 HMI, *Art in Secondary Education: 11–16*, HMSO, 1983.
22 Brian Allison, 'Art Education and the Teaching about the Arts of Asia, Africa and Latin America', *CRE Educational Journal*, vol. 111, no. 3, July 1981.
23 Horace Lashley, 'Arts Education, The Curriculum and the Multi-Cultural Society', in Malcolm Rose ed., *The Arts and Personal Growth*, Pergamon Press, 1980.
24 Calouste Gulbenkian Foundation, *Dance Education and Training in Britain*, 1980.
25 Mary Clarke and Clement Crisp, *The History of Dance*, Orbis Publishing, 1980.
26 Janet Adshead, 'The Validation of Courses in Dance', *J. of Further and Higher Education*, (NATFHE), vol. 6, no. 1, spring 1982.
27 Bullock Report, op. cit.

Chapter 9

A second language or language for learning

Ranjit Arora

The teaching of English as a second language (ESL) in schools has had a history of conflicting arguments, interesting innovations and some very positive methodological changes. To understand the present situation, it is necessary to consider the past and the wider educational context which has a bearing on it.

Until quite recently, approaches to ESL work have been strongly influenced by methods developed to teach English as a foreign language to older learners. These methods placed much emphasis on drills, exercises and remedial programmes that focus on language in abstraction. The prescriptive nature of such methods and the demands they made on the teacher's time fostered the belief that ESL work could be tackled only by the specialist ESL teacher working with small groups of children.

Such an approach does not fit comfortably into current notions of learning and teaching in the primary school, nor does it sufficiently equip ESL learners in the secondary school to benefit from normal schooling. In prescribing what language is to be taught, it has ignored what children bring to the learning task and the choices they make about how and what they want to learn. Furthermore, the location and organisation of language provision did not measure up to the demand. The language centres, reception centres, withdrawal groups, peripatetic advisory teachers and English language services all contributed to provide special and concentrated teaching of English as a second language in small groups, varying in size from four or five to fifteen. Whatever the pattern of provision, the main aim was to give pupils sufficient English to enable them to join normal schools as quickly as possible. The success of such special provision depended very much on the close and constant liaison of language teachers with the subject teachers and the class teachers and on the continuity of learning experiences provided by them. One of the important disadvantages of language centres and withdrawal groups was that ESL children were being taught away from those English-speakers who provide the most powerful models, i.e. their peer group. Peer-group interaction is an important element in any learning situation, but its particular strengths in a classroom with ESL learners cannot be over-emphasised.

The separation of second-language learners from the main-stream classroom cannot easily be justified on educational grounds, since in practice it leads to both their curriculum and language learning being impoverished.[1]

> Common sense would suggest that the best arrangement is usually one where the immigrant children are not cut off from the social and educational life of a normal school. The money spent on transporting children to other schools or centres, or peripatetic teachers from school to school, might sometimes be much better allocated to the appointment of full-time language experts to the schools where the children are on roll.

However, it is not enough to put ESL learners in mainstream classes or to put ESL staff in schools where these learners are. In the first instance, where one hopes that children will pick up both the language and the subject of various curriculum areas, it is quite possible for individual children to remain unnoticed for a long period and not learn anything. To quote Daphne Brown:[2]

> There was no time to try and understand what they were endeavouring to communicate to me in their own language, and both boys were thrust into the classroom activities with little thought as to whether they understood what was happening around them. If they were occupied and appeared to be happy they were left alone, while I concentrated on the children who could easily tell me what they wanted, and who responded quickly to my suggestions and requests.

To take up the second point mentioned above regarding ESL staff in normal schools, it is important to establish a way of working whereby the ESL teacher had to be seen as equal to the mainstream teacher. Otherwise, a group of ESL learners in a mainstream classroom could still remain an entirely separate group with their teacher being seen as a 'second-rate' teacher helping the 'second-rate' learners.

What is required is a model that is flexible and more sensitive to the learners' needs, a model that helps teachers to identify individual difficulties and decide how best to intervene and support language learning within a mainstream classroom. Such a model should necessarily aim towards genuine language use to achieve a particular objective. Whatever the objective, whether it is to interact with native speakers of English or to benefit from classroom instruction in a specialised language class or mainstream school learning, the emphasis needs to be not on what knowledge of language children can acquire but on what they can do with the language.

Since ESL learners need linguistic help not only in an English lesson but right across the curriculum, it is only reasonable to suggest that all subject teachers need to be much more aware of the language demands their particular subject makes on pupils. The notion of language across the curriculum takes on a broader significance in this context and makes it possible for subject teachers to see the importance of their role in this co-operative venture. The Bullock Report has also pointed out the need for such a flexible co-operative system within the school, where the role of language teacher is seen to be as one of a 'consultant and adviser across the curriculum, rather than of a teacher confined to a single room'.

Clearly, a first step in this direction is to convince subject teachers that even the most practical subjects require the pupil to be able to follow verbal instructions and explanations, that all pupils need the language to ask for advice, information, assistance and that the pupils will only learn to the extent that they can follow the language of the teacher or the book.[3]

> Failure to understand information, explanation or instructions provided by the teacher need not always be put down to perversity or lack of intelligence on the part of the pupil. The reason may be a linguistic one.

The reason may also have something to do with how actively the pupil is expected to use language in learning and whether a teacher encourages verbal interaction as a necessary part of the learning process or not. Indeed, one of the central recommendations of the Bullock Report is based on this notion of 'language permeating all other learning activities'. 'For language to play its full role as a means of learning, the teacher must create in the classroom an environment which encourages a wide range of language uses.' This wide range of language uses does not necessarily mean all possible uses of language. There is a difference between creating a model to account for all possible uses of language and selecting those uses which deserve closer attention to make learning at school possible. It is also important to remember that cognitive development is part of the learning process, and since language and cognition are interdependent, any model of language development would necessarily incorporate cognitive development.

Hilary Hester's curriculum development project (SLIPP) is one such example. This project includes exploration of ways of supporting children, within the primary classroom, who are learning English as their second language. Some of the activities and approaches developed through the SLIPP project are:[4]

* supporting a child's learning of English through his or her involvement in learning tasks;
* building on a child's willingness and ability to draw meaning from the context he/she is working in, providing maximum visual support, to aid his/her understanding, and by providing clear models for ways of working;
* mixed groups of children learning English and competent speakers of English working together on an appropriate learning activity, so that children learning English are given opportunities to learn language through interaction with their peers;
* accepting the need to reduce the range of language a child is exposed to in the early stages of learning English, but approaching this through the phasing of learning tasks, rather than the grading of linguistic items;
* concentrating on those curriculum areas where:
  (a) the range of language used normally by speakers of English is more predictable because of the nature of the tasks or activities they are involved in,
  (b) the repetition of a process leads to the repeated use of certain language, e.g.
    – in repeating sequence stories,
    – turn-taking games and activities,
    – investigations in maths and science,
    – the making of charts etc., to record the result of investigations,
  (c) material and apparatus normally used provide powerful visual support for understanding.
* providing opportunities within the classroom for supportive listening activities on tape recorders and language masters related to on-going classroom work.

The above activities and approaches are far more acceptable to and feasible for the primary school teacher who, by virtue of his/her training and experience, is likely to think in terms of integrated, rather than subject orientated, work. However, in the secondary school, all subject teachers need to be aware of:[5]

(i) the linguistic processes by which their pupils acquire information and understanding and the implications for the teacher's own use of language;
(ii) the reading demands of their own subjects, and ways in which the pupils can be helped to meet them.

The principles which underlie the ECHE (Ealing College of Higher Education) approach to language across the curriculum are largely based on these recommendations. Their first concern was the language demands made by teachers and materials on children of *all* language backgrounds. This meant that children may have been born in this country and acquired a degree of fluency in English, but were still technically non-native speakers of English and, therefore, described as ESL learners. The objectives of ESL teachers in such situations are the same as that of any teacher responsible for language development or communication skills work in any secondary school. However, ESL teachers, because of their training and exprience, may have a better understanding of the role of language in schools, and may well be better equipped with teaching strategies.

The ECHE materials design and methodology were, therefore, skill-based and comprised the following principles:[6]

- that the language children use in their school work can be fairly rigorously described in linguistic terms;
- that the learning activities in which they engage can be analysed and broken down into constituent skills, and that if a child is deficient in his ability to carry out these activities, he can only be helped by a teacher who is prepared to examine these constituent skills and give practice in them;
- that it should not be too difficult for subject teachers to incorporate a basic understanding of the broader principles of school language use into the procedures they normally adopt in the classroom and the materials they normally use.

A framework for observation based on a questionnaire in *Language Across the Curriculum*[7] was adopted to produce language profiles of French, geography, history, home economics, needlecraft and physics lessons in a local secondary school. This framework is a useful checklist to determine the language demands of subject areas and includes questions related to four language skills. This can also be useful in analysing the linguistic content of each subject area (see Figure 9.2, on p. 113)

Some middle school teachers would perhaps argue that it is all very well for secondary schools, where the language demands of a specified task can be analysed and met by paying attention to areas of difficulty. Some would also suggest that language work in infant schools is part of an integrated day, and that teachers do not need to be concerned with individual subjects at that level. The underlying concern of these teachers is perhaps justified to some extent, especially where no ESL teachers are provided in the school. However, the situation is not entirely without hope. Topic/project work in middle schools has long been an accepted and valued strategy for learning and teaching. Language plays a crucial role in every stage of the project from preliminary consultation to development, through to its final presentation and follow-up activities. The key word for its success is 'collaboration': collaboration with the teachers of various subject areas, as well as with the ESL specialist; collaboration between students and teachers; and collaboration between students themselves.

The important underlying considerations for such a model include:

1 an understanding of how the contextualisation of language practice operates;
2 a knowledge of the language linked features of any educational task;
3 some idea of the kind of support that can be offered at different points in a framework of an educational task.

It is, perhaps, appropriate at this stage to describe one example of such work undertaken by the BEd students at Bradford College, training to be teachers in multiracial first and middle schools. The project was a part of the course work and was designed for their second school experience period (five mornings). The general theme suggested was 'Shops and Markets', but students were expected to develop it in different ways appropriate to the various age groups of the children involved, and the various teaching situations. All the students were, however, expected to design an integrated project to cover curriculum areas such as history, environmental studies, RE and art. The intention was to select and organise appropriate activities for the learning to take place, and to allow to emerge from such activities the language functions necessary for understanding and exploring the topic. It was also intended to choose, for the benefit of ESL learners, language items and language skills which would enable them to perform those functions. The role of the student-teacher was to be one of a consultant, a participant-observer, a sharer of joint interests and an empathetic listener, who would also provide explicit assistance in the development of expressive oral communication skills and the written conventions. Needless to say, each student designed the project with a different focus. Everyone started with a visit to the local supermarket or the local wholesale market, but beyond that, each project had a character of its own. Some focused on the countries of origin of various types of grain, some explored the history of local shops and development of supermarkets, while others concentrated on scientific aspects of food production. (For examples see Plates 9.1–4.)

Figure 9.1 shows one example of the project design, depicting some of the curriculum areas. The language activities and skills

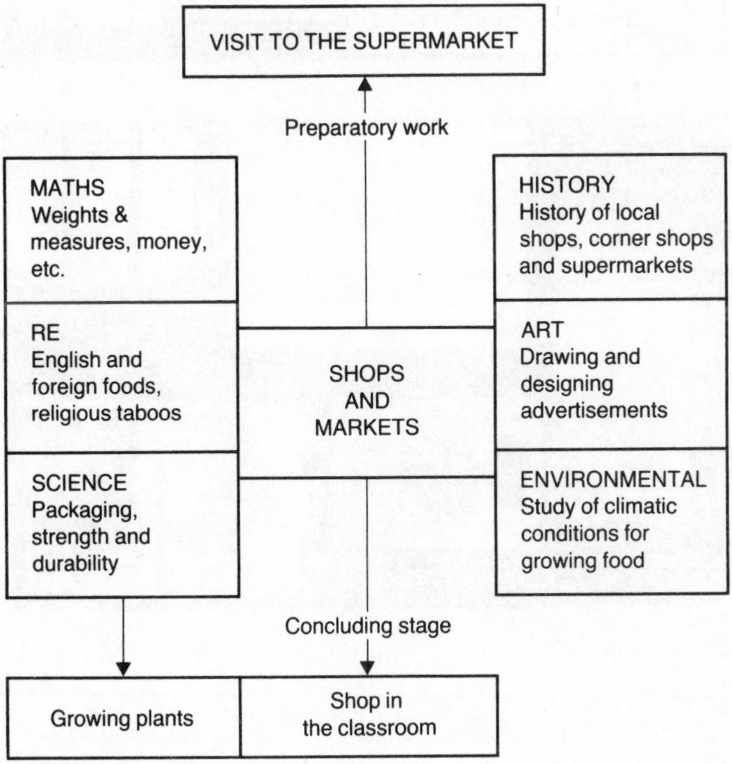

Figure 9.1

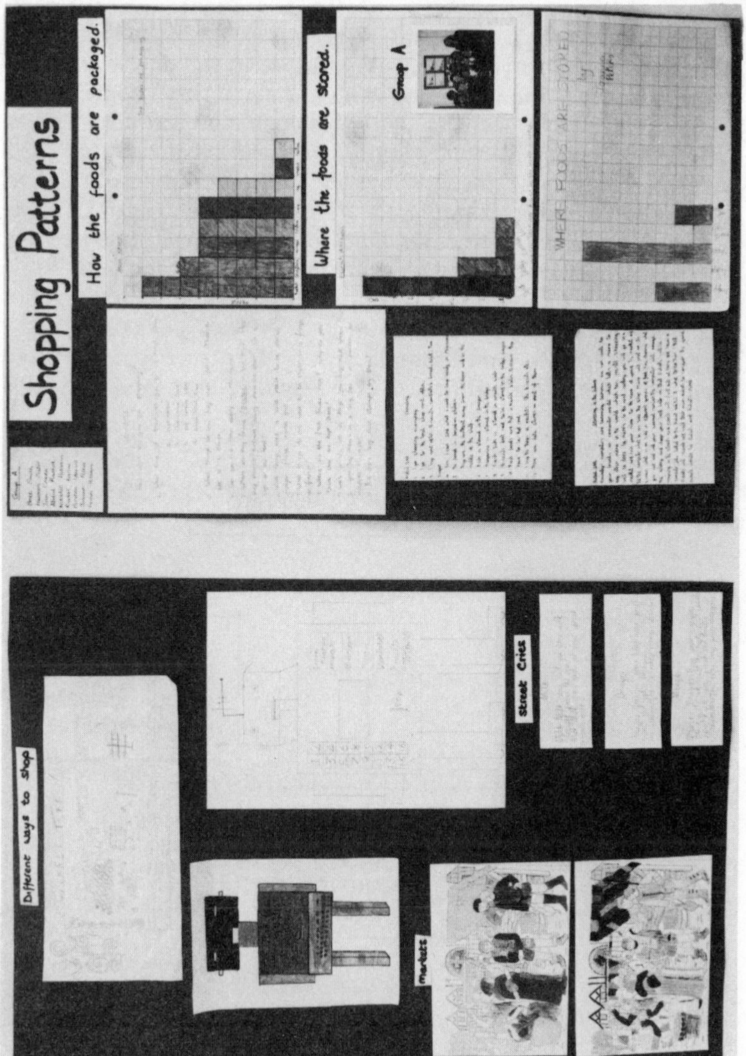
Shopping Patterns
How the foods are packaged.
Where the foods are stored.
Group A
WHERE FOODS ARE STORED
Different ways to shop
Street Cries
markets

Plate 9.1

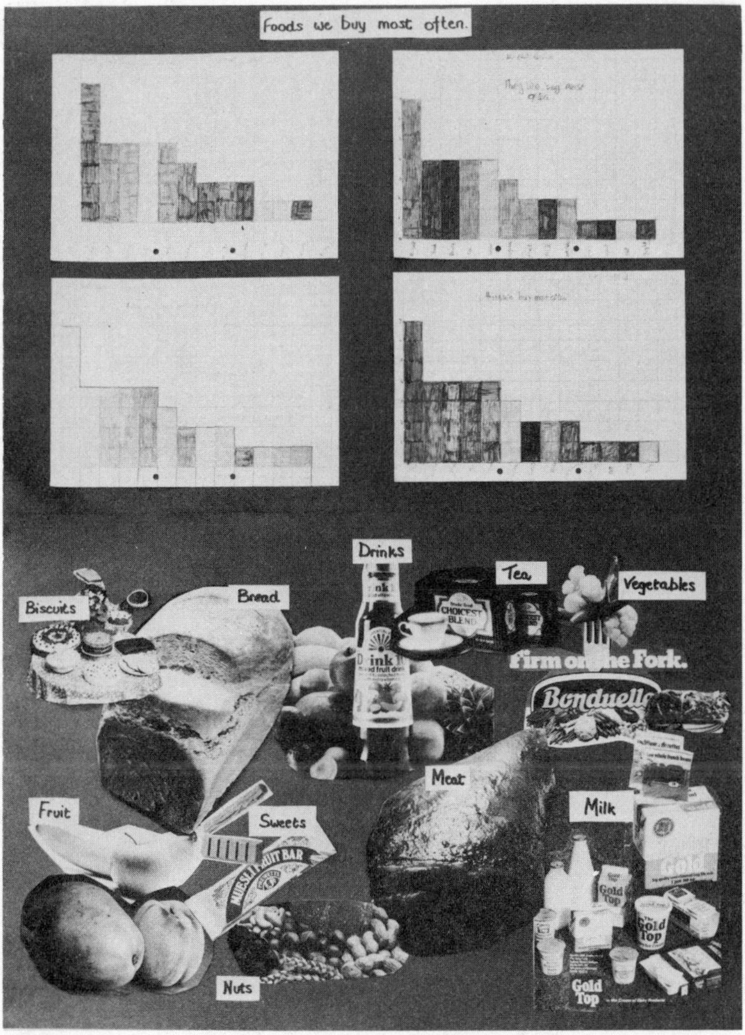
Foods we buy most often.
Drinks
Tea
Vegetables
Biscuits
Bread
Meat
Milk
Fruit
Sweets
Nuts
Gold Top

Plate 9.2

USES OF RICE
Tilda
BASMATI
RICE TERRACES
VESTA
PADDY FIELDS
WHERE RICE GROWS

Plate 9.3

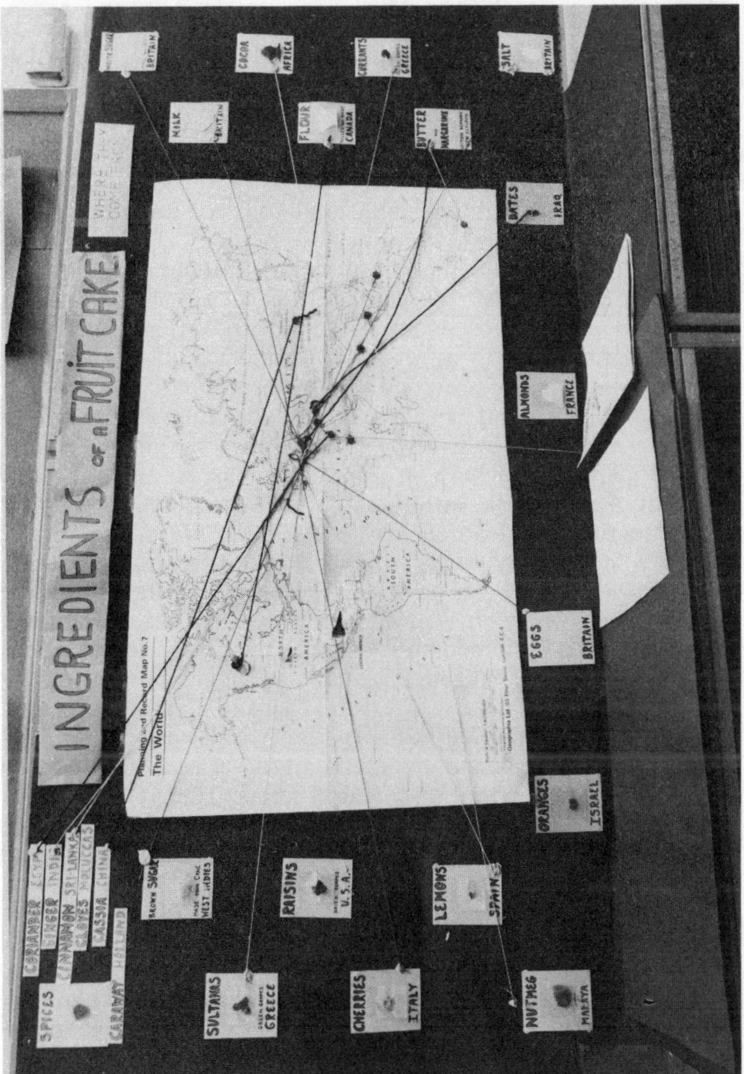
INGREDIENTS OF A FRUITCAKE
SPICES
CORIANDER
GINGER INDIA
CINNAMON SRI LANKA
CLOVES MOLUCCAS
CASSIA CHINA
CARAWAY HOLLAND
SULTANAS GREECE
CHERRIES ITALY
NUTMEG MALAYA
BROWN SUGAR WEST INDIES
RAISINS U.S.A.
LEMONS SPAIN
ORANGES ISRAEL
EGGS BRITAIN
ALMONDS FRANCE
DATES IRAQ
SALT BRITAIN
BUTTER MARGARINE
CURRANTS GREECE
FLOUR CANADA
COCOA AFRICA
MILK BRITAIN
Planning and Record Map No.7
The World
SOUTH AMERICA

Plate 9.4

associated with each one of these areas will make specific demands on ESL learners. For example, in the case of environmental studies, it will be necessary for children to be able to *read* the various food wrappers to locate the country of origin. A discussion about why a particular type of food was not grown in this country would involve children in *talking* to each other and to the teacher.

Finding out about the climatic conditions required for certain types of food would involve further explorations, discussions and recording of findings. Some of this work will require skills to use textbooks from the library and some of it will involve asking questions and perhaps experimenting with various plants. In short, the children will be required to understand the teacher's use of language; to respond to it or express difficulty in understanding it; find specific information from texts and to present information in writing so that others can understand it. ECHE materials include a good example of the language demands of a specific history talk. The important thing, with regard to the ESL learners, is to locate the areas of language difficulty and identify points within a framework where meaningful language support can be offered. A suggested framework for locating such points is shown in Table 9.1. This framework includes only a limited number of interest areas, activities and situations and the language skills associated with them. By support, I do not mean that ESL learners should be given a simplified text which does not include specialised terms or long sentences. The language requirements of certain activities do require a certain amount of technical terms. These terms should be made more meaningful by focusing on the process of learning and teaching, by using and building on what is known and familiar, to explain what is new. Familiar words used in a special way, e.g. series, energy, balance, also need to be looked at in more than one context so that meanings acquired in a different context are not considered unimportant.

Equally important in locating points of support is the teachers' repertoire of skills in giving instructions, reading aloud, explaining a process; in talking to and discussing with individuals, small groups or the whole class; in asking open-ended questions, giving children opportunities to talk and keeping a balance between teacher-talk and pupil-talk. An excellent check list by Douglas Barnes is included in *Language Across the Curriculum*.[8]

THEME/TOPIC
e.g. spring

Possible interest areas, activities and situations

Environmental studies	*Geography*	*Science*	*Art*	*Maths*
Park, garden playground	Recording weather info., city and country situation	Planting seeds, bulbs, observing animals' & birds' life-cycles	Drawing and painting, collecting leaves & flowers for collage	Sequence of time, counting nos of trees & plants required for seeds to germinate

LISTENING	*Skills required include*: understanding teacher's instructions and use of specialised vocabulary used by the teacher; evidence of pupil difficulties in tasks related to listening, e.g. summary, note-taking, etc.
SPEAKING	*Skills required include*: asking questions, expressing opinions, participating in pair work, group work or class discussions; describing objects, events and people, responding to different types of teacher-talk, expressing difficulty
READING	*Skills required include*: note-taking, use of index, sub-titles, summaries, skimming for general content, scanning for specific purposes, understanding *specialised vocabulary* as well as *special uses of language*, e.g. consequently, therefore, thus, furthermore, etc.
WRITING	*Skills required include*: interpreting teacher's guidelines, comments and corrections; note-taking, listing facts, sequencing; punctuation and spelling; understanding charts/graphs/posters; presenting information in graphs and tables

Figure 9.2

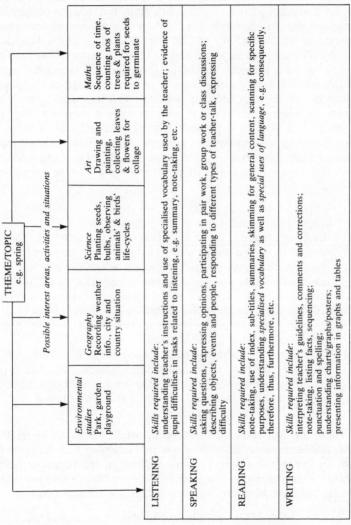

Concluding comments

To conclude, ESL teaching is best done through fully integrated project work where language development equals language use within a normal school learning situation, but where appropriate language support through intervention is available as and when necessary. Such teaching should aim towards genuine language use by focusing on meaning rather than on correct forms. The target for ESL learners should be language which enables them to interact with native speakers without any disadvantage, and language which equips them with the learning strategies. The extent to which ESL teachers have already moved out of their conventional 'broom cupboard' can be measured by numerous initiatives, up and down the country, which have made labels such as 'language in use', 'language for life' and 'language for learning' more meaningful than ever before. These initiatives include:

(a) ESL teachers and subject teachers, together, analysing the language demands of specific educational tasks;
(b) teacher-to-teacher exercises to examine the textbooks for opaque language use as well as for racist and sexist bias;
(c) ESL teachers working with subject teachers during their lessons to identify areas of language difficulties for ESL learners;
(d) ESL teachers assisting class teachers or subject teachers in rewriting their worksheets and adapting texts to make them more accessible to ESL learners;
(e) ESL teachers, with their colleagues' co-operation, compiling language skill profiles for individual children. For example, a reading profile would include the purposes for which the reading is done, the kind of reading involved and the reading level of the materials.

These are just some of the ways in which subject teachers and ESL teachers are collaborating towards enabling ESL learners to achieve genuine learning of content through the language being learnt. Unfortunately, such collaboration does not yet exist among teachers in a variety of language teaching situations.[9]

> We talk, for example, about second and foreign language teaching techniques, but it might be both more effective, and less repressive, to relate all language work together, and to think about an overall language teaching strategy in which mother-tongue maintenance, second language acquisition, and

the teaching of foreign languages such as French, to all students, can be seen as part of an integrated policy, in which bilingualism is seen as an advantage, rather than a disadvantage. Such a view would have major implications for our relations with parents, with speakers of minority languages, and with our status as teachers.

The message is clearly for everyone concerned with and involved in the making of a school's language policy. If language development of all our children is the prime concern, if phrases such as 'language for learning', 'language across the curriculum', 'language in use' and 'language for life' have to be credible, then the language policy of all our schools has to be comprehensive enough to embrace language use in all possible contexts, including the teaching of modern European and minority community languages as and when appropriate.

References

1 A. Bullock, *A Language for Life* (Bullock Report), HMSO, 1975, 20: 10.
2 D. Brown, *From Mother-Tongue to English*, Cambridge University Press, 1979.
3 *Education Digest*, 20 July 1973.
4 SLIPP, *Language in the Multi-Ethnic Primary School* (videos available through Central Film Library, Government Building, Bromyard Avenue, Acton, London).
5 Bullock Report, Recommendation 138.
6 ECHE, *Language Across the Curriculum* (report available from Ealing College of Higher Education, St Mary's Road, Ealing, London W5).
7 M. Marland (ed.), *Language Across the Curriculum*, Heinemann, 1977.
8 Ibid., p. 174.
9 Chris Brumfit, RSA Day Conference Report on TESL in Multicultural Schools, 1980.

Further sources

D. Barnes, *From Communication to Curriculum*, Penguin,
D. Barnes and F. Todd, *Communication and Learning in Small Groups*, Routledge & Kegan Paul, 1977.
I. Robertson, *Language Across the Curriculum*, Schools Council Project, Methuen Educational, 1980.
M. Torbe, *Language Policies in Action* (Language Across the Cur-

riculum in some Secondary Schools), Ward Lock Educational, 1980.
Clive Sutton, *Communicating in the Classroom* (a guide for subject teachers on the more effective use of reading, writing and talk).
NATE, *Language Across the Curriculum* (guidelines for schools), Ward Lock Educational.
J. Levine, *Developing Pedagogies for Multi-lingual Classes,* NATE Journal.

Chapter 10

Multicultural approach to mathematics

Derek Dyson

Aims

Mathematics is a powerful tool of technology and commerce and therefore teaching this subject has always had major social implications. Developments in multicultural education have placed greater focus on the social responsibility of the mathematics teacher, for now it may be seen that the way in which mathematics is taught has a direct effect on the attitudes of all people.

The multicultural approach to mathematics may be justified by the following:

1 it enables ethnic minority children to see themselves in a more positive way;
2 it enables indigenous white children to see their ethnic minority peers in a more positive light;
3 it encourages greater harmony amongst the races;
4 it contributes to the concept of equality in education;
5 it provides new ways of approaching mathematics;
6 it encourages better academic performance amongst children, in particular ethnic minorities whose performances tend, at present, to be lower than those of their white peers.[1]

If mathematics teachers recognise the contributions of other cultures to mathematics in their lessons they will play their part in fostering the acceptance of different cultures and contributing to greater equality in education. By using a child's culture as the context for mathematics we may also enhance his or her self-esteem, which is vital to academic performance.

A problem that besets most teachers who wish to modify their teaching in this direction is the generation of ideas. Asking ethnic minority pupils what they would like or what they think should be taught seldom yields any useful suggestions. Hence the mathematics teacher will need other ways of generating ideas. Mathematics is a multicultural product but it does not follow that by simply teaching mathematics the purpose of multicultural education is being fulfilled. This aim can be achieved only by informing the pupils of the various cultural contributions to the subject. A good starting-point in the search for ideas is the aim of cultural parity. To recognise the contributions of other cultures would suggest that the history of mathematics should be examined as a source of ideas. There are other avenues of approach for pursuing the objective of parity. In fact any idea that implicitly recognises the presence and worth of children from other cultures would be of great help. If this is not done, we are effectively saying to such pupils that their presence is not recognised.

For convenience, topics for our consideration in mathematics can be grouped into three categories:

1 those which give some acknowledgment to the presence of people of different cultures rather than recognise different cultural contributions;

2 those which directly recognise the contribution of other cultures within our society, an important source of ideas being the history of mathematics;

3 those which recognise the contribution of other cultures which are not represented in the society in which the pupil lives. For the subject to be taught using the multicultural approach and also to avoid ignoring large sections of mathematical history it is necessary to do this, although some teachers may argue that this offers no assistance to the objective of harmony between the cultures in our society. How relevant, for example, are the works of a German mathematician to our considerations? It can be argued that even by taking this approach the objective of encouraging harmonious relations in society is being achieved. A person who is educated to appreciate the contributions of one culture is more likely to show appreciation of yet other cultures. This is the purpose of multicultural education. To exclude any culture would be inconsistent with the altruistic objectives of the founders of the multicultural education movement.

Departmental strategy

To alter the whole approach of a mathematics department is a task requiring considerable effort and obviously the support of each member. It is more effective to operate on a departmental level rather than individually. In the author's school (Wyke Manor Upper),[2] Carlton Duncan, the Headmaster, encouraged the setting up of multicultural working parties in each faculty. The individual subject areas within a faculty have a representative on the working party. Sharing ideas is facilitated by discussion at meetings specially designated for this purpose. The initial value of these meetings is often that vague ideas are replaced by more consolidated thoughts. It is well to remember that there are no real experts in this field and that a new objectivity is being forged. A primary requirement is the drawing up or modification of objectives. Schemes of work require modifying and necessary inclusions may need to be made, remembering, of course, that the purpose is not to alter the actual mathematics covered. Initially additions to schemes of work will be experimental, as certain ideas may well prove impractical.

One approach is to start a collection of worksheets dealing with particular topics in a multicultural way. The collection should be a joint effort. It does not matter if there is duplication of syllabus items as long as this leads to a variety of methods. This can be viewed as a first step in the permeation of the multicultural approach into the conventional teaching practices. As material then builds up and as topics are found to be successful or not, so the schemes of work can be amended. Under the pressure of a normal teaching load the amount of material ready to hand is of importance to the teacher. Any valuable experience should be recorded, and making worksheets is one way of doing this.

A good aim is for each classroom to have some multicultural wallcharts. The Diwali and Hindu patterns discussed in this article have been found very useful. Many of the wallcharts available on the market are not intentionally multicultural but have a lot of value for this purpose.

Another important requirement is to build up a departmental library of reference books and books on the history of mathematics to aid the preparation of multicultural lessons. Useful articles should also be filed.

Ideas from geography

Geography lends itself most readily to multicultural analysis and the mathematics teacher might well find useful aids from geography textbooks. Problems on times in different parts of the world as related to the lines of longitude are an example of this. Obviously a knowledge of angles is required. The possibilities for graphical work displaying data in the form of bar charts or pie charts are endless (e.g. relative rainfall or wheat or rice production of different countries). A valuable suggestion is to compare our statistics with those of the Third World. Comparing the areas of different countries by means of a bar chart is also a useful addition to work on area. As the areas concerned are very large, the pupils could cut squares of coloured paper to represent a convenient number of square units of area. Each square would be part of a component of a bar chart which could then be used as a wall display.

Work on scale in mathematics could make use of maps of different countries. Pupils would measure the distances on maps using lengths of cotton or by breaking routes into small straight-line segments. The measurement may then be read off on a scale or multiplied by the scale factor. The reference to different countries is a vehicle for recognition. A project could be to determine the length of the longest river of a country or the distance of a route taken by someone visiting the country. Maps which are divided into provinces may be used to explore the minimum number of colours required to shade in each province so that none of the abutting boundaries has the same colour on either side. The choice of maps need not be confined to political boundaries but could indicate the flora, geology or type of region, i.e. tundra, grassland, etc.

Related to geography, of course, is travel and commerce between countries. Perhaps of relevance to pupils would be problems related to sending letters or parcels abroad to a relative or friend. The details of this could be acquired from the post office and suitable worksheets based on this information could be made. Pupils in many schools do individual projects on this sort of information as this is a more interesting way of learning mathematics for any pupil. Prices by airmail can be compared with those of postage by other means, and the advantages in terms of times of delivery may be considered. Journeys abroad are also a source of problems and worksheets, and when the pupils deal with the information direct, for example from a holiday brochure, this can be a valuable experience for them.

The exchange-rates of different currencies that one sees displayed in the front window of banks can also provide data for problems or worksheets. Exchange of currencies is a common enough syllabus item, which has some multicultural value. For many pupils there is nothing wrong with doing ordinary monetary calculations with foreign money with work ranging from simple addition to percentages. In many cases this may help to bring out the common sense of the arithmetic.

The foregoing discussion suggests the following ideas for worksheets or projects:

(a) bar and pie charts on data of different countries;
(b) area project;
(c) scale work (maps of relevant countries);
(d) the four-colour problem in different contexts;
(e) letters or parcels abroad;
(f) journeys abroad;
(g) foreign exchange

Using what may be described as the geographical approach yields ideas that correspond to category (1) above, which emphasises acknowledgment of the presence of pupils from particular cultures.

Mathematics and art

It is fortunate that art, an important part of most cultures, has common ground with mathematics. This gives valuable opportunities for investigation. Even in the decorative art of neolithic man such important geometrical properties as congruence, symmetry and similarity were used. Another example of where artists or designers have been unintentionally mathematical in their efforts to create some work of great beauty is the Parthenon. The proportions of this piece of architecture are almost equal to the golden ratio, well known to mathematicians. This and similar observations may be explained by the aesthetic appeal of shapes in this ratio. A great deal of mathematics involves things that have the quality of pattern not only visually but in algebraic sequences, number systems, etc. It is sometimes said that mathematics is the study of pattern. The fact that art deals frequently with patterns must partly explain this convergence between the two subjects.

Teachers are becoming more aware that the study of spatial problems is very important in mathematics lessons as people

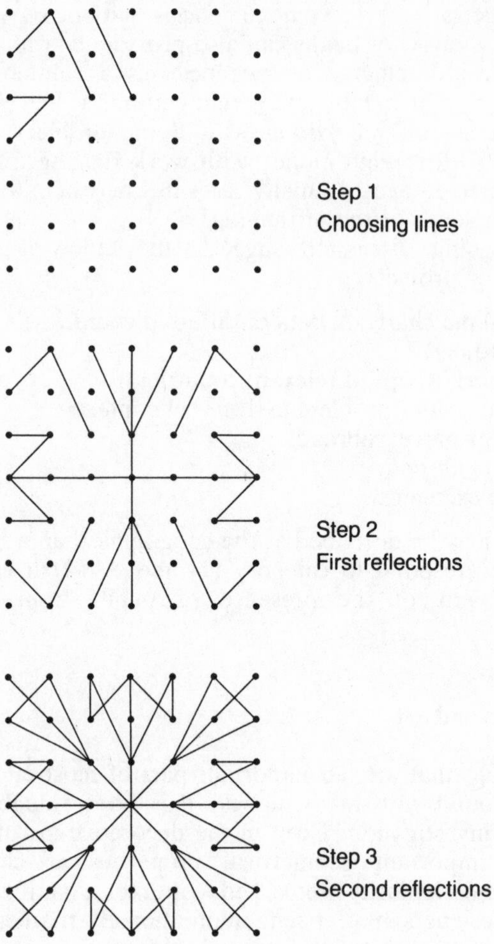

Figure 10.1

encounter these as often as numerical work in everyday life. Spatial awareness is vital in our understanding of our environment and in mathematics generally. Hence such work as making tessellations is easy to justify. The Rangoli patterns described by Hemmings are an excellent example of spatial work drawn from a cultural context.[3] These designs are used by Hindu families as decorations during the Diwali celebrations. The most frequent method of drawing these is to use a square grid of dots.

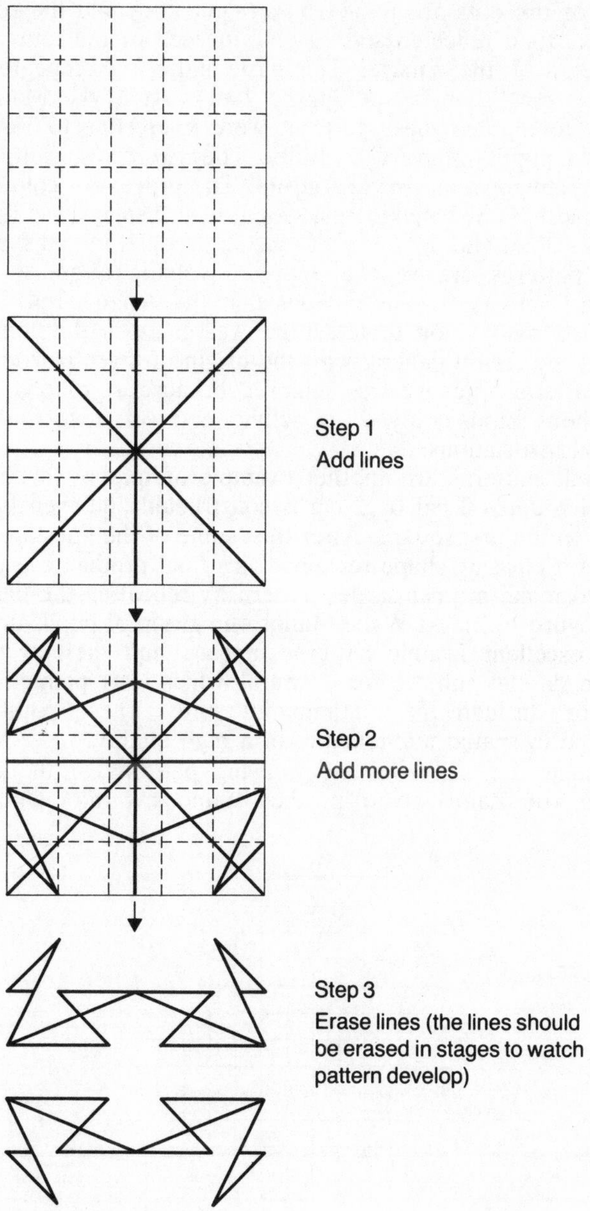
Step 1
Add lines
Step 2
Add more lines
Step 3
Erase lines (the lines should be erased in stages to watch pattern develop)

Figure 10.2

Some of the dots are joined by straight lines and the resulting figure is then reflected successively in each of the four axes of symmetry of the square. The basic pattern is repeated thus creating new shapes (see Figure 10.1). At Wyke Manor the author found that these patterns were interesting to 13- to 15-year-old pupils of average ability. They were also suitable for pupils younger than this age group. The process of colouring in these patterns and making classroom wall displays was found to be enjoyable, and as a way of teaching reflection and symmetry these patterns are very effective, involving a great deal of practical activity. It was obvious that the Asian pupils appreciated the recognition their culture was given in the concluding part of the lesson dealing with the origin of these patterns. The multicultural objective was achieved because a group of mainly indigenous pupils enjoyed this activity and were conscious of the cultural associations.

Islamic patterns are another example of spatial work. First a grid of squares 2 cm by 2 cm is constructed and then lines are added to the first square. After this, some of the lines are erased so that a pleasing shape remains. This final product can then be used to make a much larger pattern by repeating the basic unit (see Figure 10.2). At Wyke Manor one group of pupils produced some excellent Islamic patterns in class and these were then chosen as the subject for a mural which was painted in the corridor through the mathematics suite. These pupils were involved in spatial mathematics of a high quality.

Designs derived from the weaving patterns of the Bakuba people (of Zaire), who produce famous raffia velours and

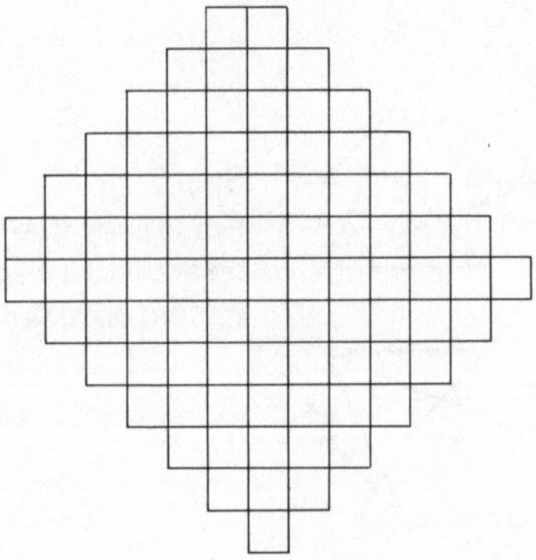

Figure 10.3

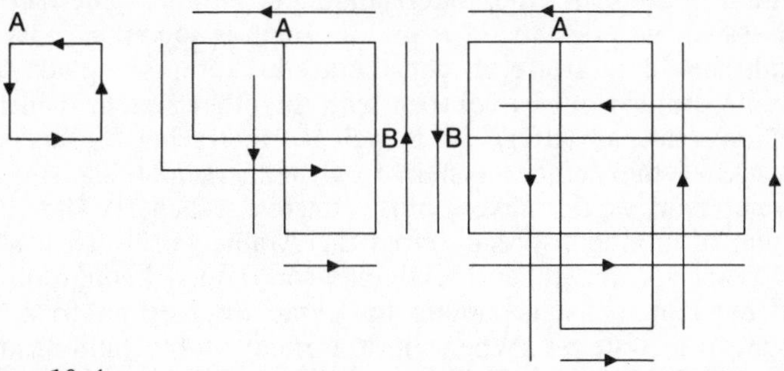

Figure 10.4

embroidered cloths, are an example of network patterns.[4] A Belgian anthropologist noted how boys could trace designs such as the one in Figure 10.3 without lifting their finger or tracing over a line already drawn. This seemingly impossible task can be accomplished with the aid of network theory. The process may be broken down into simpler stages (see Figure 10.4) with the starting- and finishing-points indicated at the two odd nodes. A group of pupils at Wyke Manor were asked to practise this on graph paper and to find methods of drawing similar networks of any size. In the practice networks it was noted that the number of small squares is the same sequence as that of the triangular numbers: 1, 3, 6. Also the number of squares in each column gives each counting number, though with even numbers and odd numbers down opposite sides (see Figure 10.5). The whole exercise is relevant to the teaching of networks in topology.

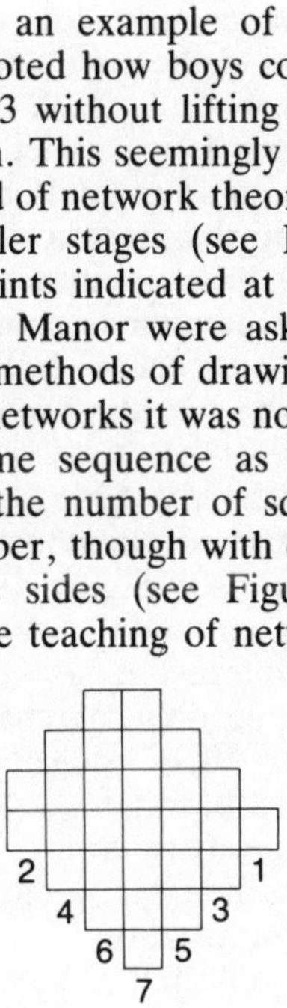

Figure 10.5

History of mathematics

In examining the history of mathematics, the study of various number systems is of considerable importance both for multicultural reasons and the understanding of number. The fact that our system was developed mainly in India is something that our pupils should be aware of, and the useful features of place value may be brought out by contrast with the other systems which do not have this advantage. It is well worth tracing the historical passage of the number system to Britain. A map showing this development would make a most effective wallchart. The Hindu system of numbers spread across the Arabic world. Then about 700 years ago an Italian merchant's son named Leonardo, who had lived many years among the Arabs in North Africa, was taught the system.[5] When he returned to his homeland he introduced the system to his countrymen. From Italy the system eventually spread to Britain. A contribution of this importance to the subject of mathematics must not go unrecognised.

It may also be related to the pupils how at first there were only nine symbols: 1, 2, 3, 4, 5, 6, 7, 8, 9, and the numbers were written in columns when being added. The Hindus noted that with careful writing the columns could be omitted. The possibility of confusion gave rise to the invention of zero. Such numbers as 073, 730 could now be written without cause for doubt.

The details of various number systems provide the raw material for some interesting worksheets. It has been noted by some teachers that pupils often find the use of different symbols quite fascinating.

Rod numerals, used by the Chinese thousands of years ago, consisted of short pieces of bamboo placed on boards. The symbols are as follows: (see Figure 10.6). Forty-two would be written 𝍬𝍡 that is 40 and 2. Another example is 𝍰𝍡 representing 82. An interesting aspect of this system is that multiplying by 10 may be done by changing the position of the rods. In multiplying 3 by 10, 𝍢 is changed to 𝍫. In multiplying 8 by 10, 𝍧 representing 8 becomes 𝍰 which is 80. Hundreds are represented in the same way as units (𝍠, 𝍡, 𝍢 etc.) and thousands in the same way as tens (𝍩, 𝍪, 𝍫 etc.). Various questions may be set on this sort of information.

When writing was established, the system shown in Figure 10.7 was adopted. These numbers were written from the top downwards. The number 697 would be written as shown in Figure 10.8.

Interesting worksheets may be written on the Mayan and Ancient Egyptian systems. The Mayan system, thought to have been in use in Central America in about 3000 BC, is as shown in Figure 10.9. After 19, the system employs levels. The top level shows the number of twenties and the lower level shows the

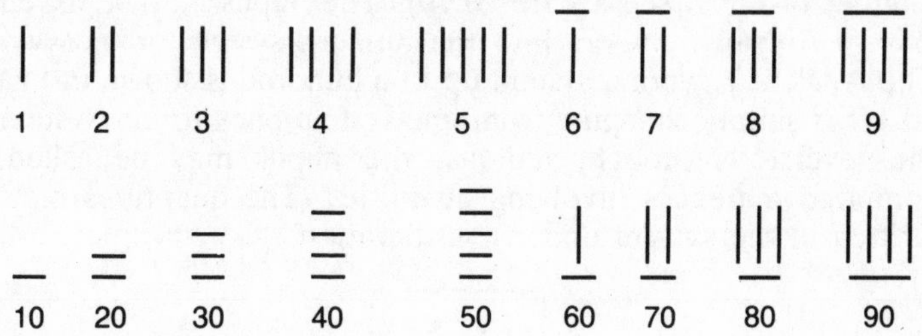

Figure 10.6

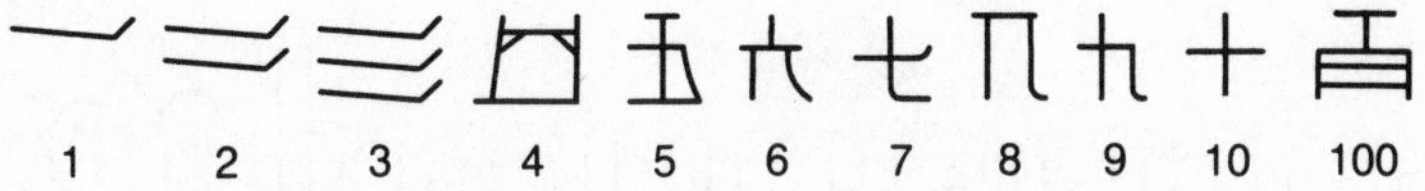

Figure 10.7

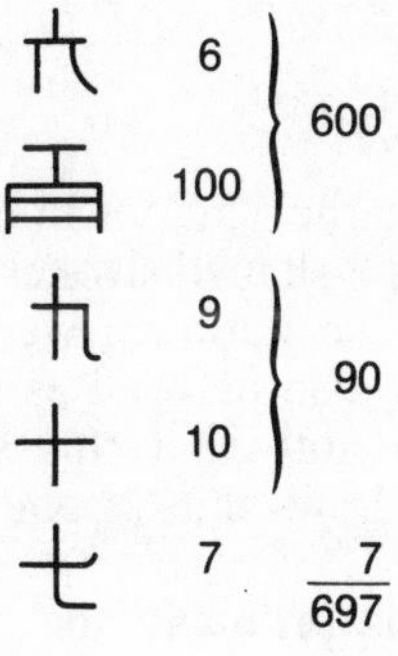

Figure 10.8

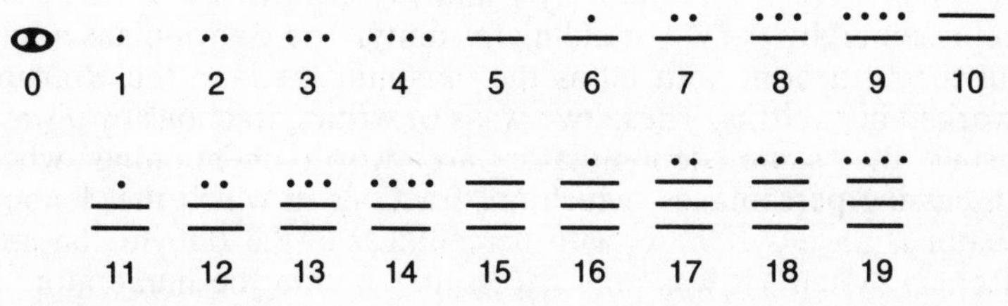

Figure 10.9

number of ones (see Figure 10.10). The pupils may be asked to change Mayan numbers into the modern system or vice versa. The Ancient Egyptian system up to a hundred is shown in Figure 10.11. If simply changing from one system back to our system or the reverse is thought tedious, the pupils may be asked to complete sentences involving quantities. The quantities may be written in the system under consideration.

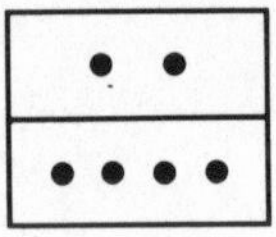

Figure 10.10

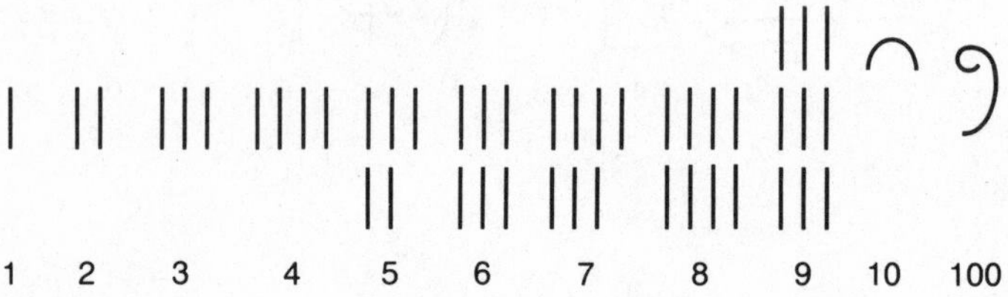

Figure 10.11

The Babylonians made their figures in damp clay by means of a piece of wood. The wedge-shaped strokes of the writing is known as cuneiform (cuneus is the Latin for wedge) (see Figure 10.12).

Roman numerals may also be used as material for worksheets and it is interesting to note that this system, along with the Chinese rod numerals, shows that at one time five was the basis for counting.

The Rhind Papyrus is probably the oldest book on mathematics in the world and was written approximately 3,500 years ago by the Egyptian priest Ahmes. In this work all fractions were written with unity as the numerator with the exception of ½ and ⅔, which were represented by [and ⌒ respectivaly. ⅝ would be represented by [⌒, ○ standing for unity. The Babylonians wrote all their fractions with 60 as the denominator, and the Romans worked in twelfths. These two ways of writing fractions by always using the same denominator are worth mentioning when discussing percentages, which are fractions in which the denominator is always 100. As with percentages in the Babylonian and Roman system, it was only necessary to write the numerator.

When teaching decimals it is worth while discussing Stevins

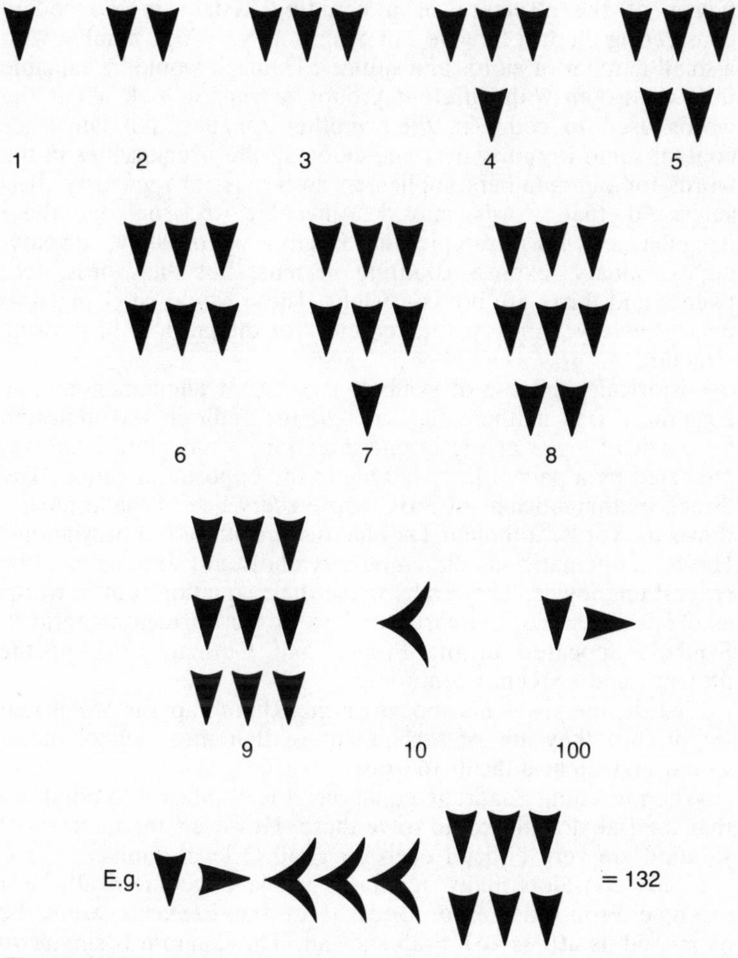

Figure 10.12

notation and comparing it with that used today. For example 256.25 would be written 256 ⓪2 ① 5 ②. Other earlier methods may be pointed out: i.e. 3′6″ representing 3 tenths and 6 hundredths and 2562′5″ representing 256 $^2/_{10}$ $^5/_{100}$. These rather cumbersome methods were replaced by the following: 53⌊$\frac{4}{5}$63 or 53$\underline{263}$ or 53.263.

While on the subject of number it is worth making a digression which is not historical. Many people are not really aware of the power of the structure of a counting system in use today, considering the fact that we can count to a very high number with a small number of words and suffices. Hence it would be valuable in a classroom with different groups present to talk about the words used to count in their mother tongues. All languages contain some irregularities, and studying the irregularities in the words for our numbers implies an awareness of regularity. It is suggested that words may be invented to iron out these irregularities. For example the English words sixty, seventy, eighty, ninety, express counting in tens, but the words, ten, twenty and thirty are not consistent. These would be changed to one-ty, two-ty, three-ty, four-ty, etc., for the purpose of showing structure.

Historically the use of symbols is a recent phenomenon. The Egyptians used mathematical ideograms: addition was indicated by a pair of legs walking in one direction, while subtraction was indicated by a pair of legs walking in the opposite direction. The Greek mathematicians of 3 BC wrote every line of the argument down in words, although Diophantus introduced abbreviations. Hindu mathematicians did employ symbols and sometimes using several unknowns. The Arabs wrote their equations out in words as did Italians (i.e. Leonardo of Pisa in the thirteenth century). Symbols appeared in the French and German work of the fifteenth and sixteenth centuries.

First degree problems appear on the Rhind Papyrus of Ancient Egypt, but they are of such a nature that most school pupils would find them difficult to grasp.

When teaching quadratic equations it is of interest to point out that the Babylonians could solve these. However, the methods of solution are very difficult even for good O level pupils.

Euclid considers many quadratic problems geometrically. For example Proposition 1 of Book II of the *Elements* would be expressed as $a(b+c+d) = ab+ac+ad$. The diagram is similar to that in Figure 10.3. Most teachers have probably used this as a teaching aid. Proposition 2 could be written in algebraic terms as follows: $(b+c)^2 = (b+c)b + (b+c)c$. The diagram is shown in Figure 10.14. Again, this is probably a common teaching aid.

Relevant to quadratics and second degree problems in general are square root calculations. The Babylonians used tables of upper bounds for this purpose. A method of finding the square root which was known to the Greek, Hindu, Arab and Byzantine scholars is explained in Heron's *Metrica*. The method is sufficiently simple to be of interest to pupils in upper school provided they have achieved a fairly high standard of numeracy.

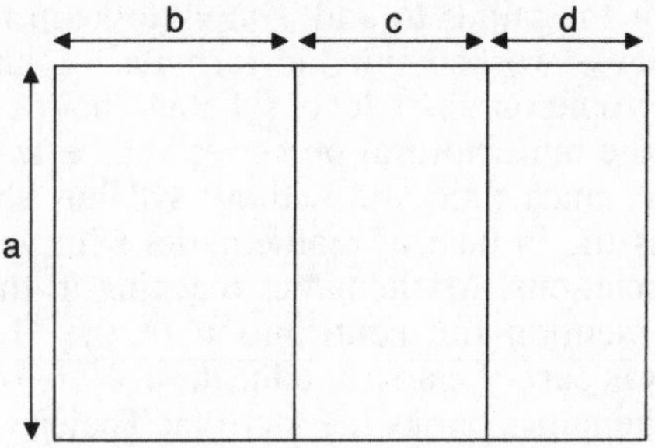

Figure 10.13

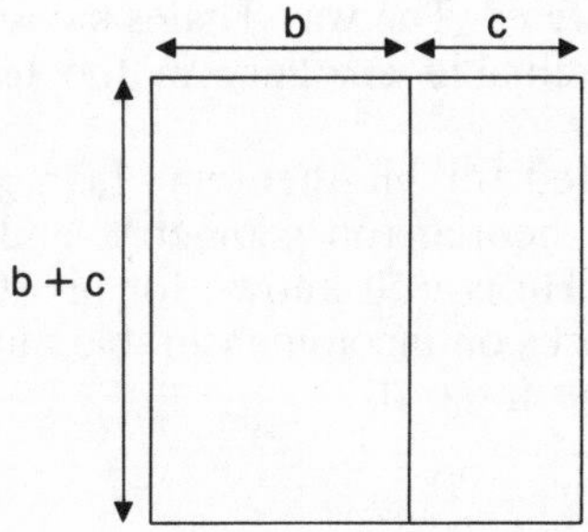

Figure 10.14

Suppose we wish to find $\sqrt{(132)}$. Then we use the next number of known square root, in this case 144. Now $\sqrt{(144)} = 12$ and 132 is divided by 12 giving 11. 11 is added to 12 and the result is halved giving $^{23}/_{2} = 11\frac{1}{2}$. Now $(11\frac{1}{2})^2 = 132\frac{1}{4}$ so there is a difference of $\frac{1}{4}$. If a difference of less than $\frac{1}{4}$ is required, the process is repeated, this time starting with $132\frac{1}{4}$ instead of 144.

Some of the examples on the history of algebra do raise the question of ability. Perhaps the suggestion of introducing multicultural mathematics at advanced level will provoke some anxiety among teachers, especially in view of the difficulties of teaching a syllabus with a restricted amount of time available. If it were to be tackled, the best approach would be to use the multicultural approach in such a way that it reinforces the subject under study. When teaching arithmetical progressions in pure mathematics it is worth relating the story of how Gauss, at the age of ten, derived a method for finding arithmetic sums. His teacher, knowing a formula for the answer, would set long strings of numbers for the pupils to add, simply to keep them occupied. The young Gauss worked out the formula for himself. If, with each separate topic on an A level syllabus, points of interest are sought after, the multicultural objective will be achieved without consuming too much time and without syllabus changes.

Geometry is the branch of mathematics with very well known historical associations. Mathematics teaching in the past has not neglected to mention the contribution of the Greeks, perhaps because this was part of classical education. Very often, however, in school mathematics books the fact that Thales was responsible for the theorems stating that opposite angles are equal, the angles in a semicircle are 90° and that the two angles in an isosceles triangle are equal is not mentioned, although these topics are important syllabus items. The way Thales measured the height of the pyramid is a valuable auxiliary in the teaching of similar triangles.

Pythagoras is noted for his theorem. In fact it was probably one of the earliest theorems in geometry, and was known long before Pythagoras. He is well known for his study of space and number, and his works on incommensurable number and number in music are of great interest.

Language

There may be less of an inclination among mathematics teachers to study the role of language in education than there will be among teachers of the more literary subjects. Indeed, to many mathematics undergraduates, language in education may, for various reasons, be thought an incompatible subject to be incorporated in a mathematics/education degree. The actual language that teachers use in explaining their subject has important pedagogical implications[6]. Also the language used in textbooks is frequently remote from the pupils' own personal language, and hence a block to learning.[7] Such considerations apply to children of indigenous and minority backgrounds. The mathematics teacher should have a sympathetic attitude to any difficulties pupils may have and an appreciation that the language of both the pupils and teacher very much determine the response of pupils to lessons.

It is very important that mathematics teachers become more aware of the language they use to teach their subject and its implications for the pupils. Discussion between mathematics and English teachers about pupils with any kind of language problem or aspect of language (whether this be related to ethnic origin or otherwise) may be very useful.

Conclusion

The purpose of this article is to assist a teacher who is about to start teaching mathematics, using the multicultural approach, by suggesting ideas that have been applied by the author at Wyke Manor School. These ideas are intended to provide a new and flexible approach to mathematics which may be expanded upon by the teacher in the classroom to further multicultural objectives.

The author has found it helpful in developing the sense of worth that ethnic minority pupils feel about themselves and their cultures, to mention the specific contributions of their cultures to the wider field of mathematics. For example, by mentioning the fact that the Hindus used symbols in algebra when later civilisations did not, the teacher can highlight the real importance of the culture to the later development of mathematics. Besides promoting a greater confidence of ethnic minority pupils in the subject, the teacher is also opening the eyes of indigenous white children to the value of their ethnic minority peers.

The development of the number system through various cultures has been found not only to promote the ideals of multicultural education but also to reinforce the specific mathematics content being taught. Teaching by this method has been found to be more beneficial to the pupils who were able to see the reason why place value is important in mathematics. Not only did this assist the acquisition of mathematical skills of all pupils and help them to remember place value, but it also promoted interest in the subject in that the majority of pupils found working with different symbols extremely fascinating.

The author found the geographical approach to mathematics to be more meaningful to ethnic minority pupils as it directly acknowledged their presence. The use of maps of different countries associated with the ethnic origins of those present offered an alternative approach to teaching scale and enabled pupils to view mathematics as being particularly relevant to them. The rangoli patterns and other artistic approaches also promoted greater personal participation in class activities and broadened the scope and interest of indigenous white pupils. They are especially useful in view of the greater emphasis now placed on space in mathematics and they provide new ways of teaching certain geometrical concepts.

It is now hoped that other teachers will use and expand these ideas for the combined benefit of ethnic minority and indigenous white children. The mutual respect which can be gained by both parties in the study of multicultural aspects of mathematics is of great benefit to racial harmony and must not be undervalued. Finally, the real increase in interest in mathematics shown by ethnic minority pupils, where multicultural methods were employed, should be seen as the basis for the promotion of greater academic performance.

References

1 A. Rampton (chairman), *West Indian Children in our Schools*, Cmnd 8273, HMSO, June 1984.
2 Wyke Manor Upper School, Wilson Road, Wyke, Bradford, West Yorkshire.
3 R. Hemmings, 'Multiethnic Mathematics', *NAME*, vol. 8, no. 3, 1980, p. 3.
4 C. Zaslavsky, 'African Network Patterns', *Mathematical Teaching*, no. 73, 1975, p. 12.
5 S.E. Williams, *Stories of Mathematics*, Evans, 1965, p. 15.
6 D. Barnes, J. Britton and H. Rosen, *Language, the Learner and the School*, Penguin, 1976, p. 74.
7 A. Cashdan and E. Grugeon (eds), for the Open University, *Language in Education*, Routledge & Kegan Paul, 1972, p. 119.

Further reading

Bridges, F.F. and Wright, T.F., *Mathematics in the Making*, Cassell, 1967.
Dedron, P. and Itard, J., *Mathematics and Mathematicians*, vol. 1, Transworld Publishers, 1974.
Dedron, P. and Itard, J., *Mathematics and Mathematicians*, vol. 2, Transworld Publishers, 1974.
Delaney, K. and Dichmont, J., 'Do-it-yourself Islamic Patterns', *Mathematical Teaching*, no. 86, March 1979.
Gowar, N., *An Invitation to Mathematics*, Oxford University Press, 1979.

Chapter 11

Science education for a multicultural society

Sue Watts

'What is an experienced science teacher doing working for the ILEA's multiethnic inspectorate?'

When colleagues and acquaintances in science education circles ask me about what I am doing these days, they are usually surprised and sceptical. What is 'multicultural science'? What do you actually do if you attempt to develop science curricula for a multicultural society? In this chapter I shall attempt to develop some of the issues which science teachers need to consider and to make some suggestions about ways in which the science curriculum could be developed to make it part of a more appropriate education for pupils in this multicultural society. Many ideas will be familiar to active science teachers, although perhaps with some different emphases. I am not suggesting a few minor changes or a short section added on. We need to rethink science education with, among others, a multicultural perspective.

Multicultural education has had its critics,[1] many of them. I do not intend to justify or defend but to state my position. We live in a racist society. For me a multicultural approach must be anti-racist; we must develop an education which works against the racism which exists in our society: a racism which our virtually all white, Anglo-centric curriculum currently perpetuates, even if unintentionally. Science teachers, like all others, need to consider their own position. We cannot hide behind excuses; our subject is not neutral or culture-free. We are involved in the education of all children and I believe that we should be working towards a more equal society than exists at present.

Science teachers, like all others, are strongly influenced by their own education. We can attribute many of our ideas of what our own subject area is about to the way or ways it was presented to us as students – at school, college or university.

What is science?

I recently came across a quotation from the American physicist Richard Feynman – 'Science is the belief in the ignorance of experts.' This appeals to me, as it seems to be the opposite of what we present to children in schools. Try asking some of the children you teach what they think science is. You may get some surprising answers. These are a few of the responses from some 11- and 12-year-olds from two London schools.

'Science is about discovering things.'

'Science is about what scientists have found out.'

'Science is what scientists know is right.'

'Science is what's in science books.'

This raises many questions for science teachers which are directly relevant when we consider education for a multicultural society. One of the results of European colonialism and imperialism has been the suppression of the culture, including the sciences, of other peoples. This has led to the impression that there is only science as it has developed in Western Europe and North America. This, in turn, leads to the view of 'European science' as a neutral, culture-free body of knowledge. This is certainly the impression of science that I received from my own journey through the education system towards a degree in chemistry.

When we try to set up situations in the school laboratory for pupils to make their own observations and investigations, they usually insist that their teacher knows the 'right' answer. Problem-solving in school science tends to be the pupils trying to solve the problem of what their teacher wants them to find. I have frequently been asked 'Miss, is this right?', 'What should have happened?' and similar questions. This is a common experience for science teachers.

I have moved directly from science and pupils' view of what it is, to what goes on in school science lessons. We need to provide all pupils with different experiences in school science; they should experience science as a process. Science is about being curious, asking questions, exploring, investigating, observing. Investigations are followed by explanations about observations and events. There are many sorts of explanations, but not all are scientific. Explanations which are scientific have to have supporting evidence and be tested to determine whether they are valid. Science is a human activity and, as such, is part of culture. How can we present this picture of science to our pupils? It must be possible to show that science is an activity carried out by people everywhere; it is not just for 'experts' wearing white coats and working in laboratories.

We tend to have the view of a scientist as an expert who has a particular body of knowledge and who uses that knowledge to solve a range of problems. However, these experts tend to ignore problems not seen to be within their area. The work of the expert, or in this case the scientist, is therefore outside the usual problems of everyday life. To become a scientist is to be induced into this body of knowledge, which is separate from everyday life.

You may well be wondering what this has to do with the consideration of science education for a multicultural society. Let us consider how the content of science courses and syllabi is selected. Although it is not always stated as being so, one of the main criteria for selection of content is what will be required for the next course at a higher level. Thus even the structure of so-called integrated science courses tends to be dominated by the traditional academic disciplines. If we do not manage to break away from this pattern, we shall not change the image of science as an area for the experts and one which takes place only in a European/North American setting.

In order to consider what the implications are for the science classroom, we have to go back to our view of what science is. How can we present science as the sorts of processes described above? We shall, of course, need content, but we must think much more carefully about our criteria for the selection of this content. There is obviously much more scope for change and development in primary schools and the lower part of secondary schools. There are two areas to consider. The first is what can be done in areas where content is not dictated to us by external agencies like examination boards – that would be to at least the end of the second year of secondary education. The second is what influence we can have on examination boards and the like as ordinary secondary school teachers.

There is plenty of opportunity in lower school science for a change at least in emphasis. There should be scope for individual pupils to experience science for themselves; they should be able to be curious, to ask their own questions, to explore, to investigate, to observe. They can be encouraged to develop explanations about observations and events and to test their explanations. There are a number of things which can be done to attempt to show science as a human cultural activity. In addition to encouraging children to ask their own questions and to develop and test their own explanations, we should provide them with more examples of people in various parts of the world solving problems and being 'scientific'. A useful source of information for science teachers trying to develop materials giving these sorts of examples is the Third World Science Project.

The units from this project were put together by a team at the University College of North Wales, Bangor, led by Professor Iolo Wynn Williams. Details of the Units and how they may be obtained are given at the end of this chapter.[2] I shall also say more in a later section about using this resource.

We must also consider what teaching style and strategies are appropriate for this type of approach. Teachers have to see themselves as facilitators, not as the source of all the 'right' answers. It will not be effective if, whatever changes are made, it is obvious to the children that their teacher knows all the answers before they begin to do experiments, develop and test explanations, etc. We must be able to say 'I don't know, how could we find out?' and really mean it.

The way science is currently taught tends to emphasise the achievement of white male scientists in Europe and North America. This implies, even if not directly, the inferiority of black people and women, and encourages white racism.[3] We rarely do anything to show that modern science is the product of the thinking and achievements of all peoples of the world. A stronger historical perspective to science teaching could show that new developments have arisen in response to the problem-solving activities of different peoples at various times. The achievements of black and women scientists are never mentioned.

There is another point to be made before we leave this area of the nature of science and its implications for science teaching in our multicultural society. This is one of the contributions that science can make to anti-racist teaching and approaches. Scientific explanations and statements have to be supported by suitable evidence and have to be testable and reproducible. A respect for the need for evidence is lacking in much literature from extreme racist groups. Thus the experience of the processes of science in a real and meaningful way and their application throughout life can contribute to an overall anti-racist approach. It is possible to challenge various stereotypes and assumptions through some activities in science.

Language

There have been many studies on issues of language in science education.[4] I do not, therefore, intend to develop this section in great depth.

The discussion developed in the previous section applies to teachers in all schools, those with representatives from a variety of ethnic, cultural and linguistic groups and those where the population is all white, or virtually so. There are, of course, some issues in the area of language which have to be considered by those of us who teach in multilingual, multicultural schools.

There are many examples of effective co-operation between teachers of science and English as a second language. These range from teaching to joint preparation of learning materials. School science tends to use specialist accommodation and equipment. If bilingual pupils are kept separate for their tuition, they will miss the experience of their peers. Thus the effect of their exclusion from science lessons can be more divisive than from some others. Science teachers in these schools, therefore, must make every effort to develop strategies to involve their bilingual pupils in the mainstream of science classes, whatever their stage of learning English.

Many science teachers have in their minds a model of what good written science is. We tend to make the demands of the public examination system an excuse for insisting on the use of certain forms. We need to concentrate more on thinking of children's work as pieces of communication, and should assess their effectiveness with this in mind. We also need to consider whether the writing that children do in science can contribute to their learning of science. If we are talking about experiencing science, then the traditional formal report of an experiment will probably not be an appropriate form for written work.

Practical aspects of science lessons give ideal opportunities for pupils to work in a collaborative way. We need to work out strategies that will facilitate this collaborative learning. This is especially useful for those who are in the early stages of learning English.

It is easier than many of us would suppose to alienate a group of children from science through language. 'I don't understand!' might not actually mean that the science is not understood; it might be a problem of understanding the language structures and form of the teacher or the learning materials. It is so easy to build barriers with the teacher and 'science' on one side and the pupils on the other.

An investigation into language issues in the multicultural classroom can offer a way into considering the curriculum and the ways in which it could be developed. In one school we began by looking at language – the curriculum in action. We made plenty of use of tape-recorders, made some transcripts and interviewed small groups of children about their views on language and learning in science. From what we learned, we had a very strong base on which to build the curriculum work which followed.

Science teachers in a multilingual school can make some moves in the encouragement of the languages of their bilingual pupils. There are schools where the laboratory safety rules are available in the major languages of the pupils. It is also an interesting task to label cupboards used for storage of apparatus, etc., in all of these languages. Although only a small point, it will add to ideas that science is not just the activity of Western European peoples. It is also an excellent way of involving bilingual pupils in their science lessons and in the work of the science department. It will indicate that the department recognises and values the bilingualism of some of its pupils.

Resources

Book and worksheet type of resources for teaching science are many. There have been a number of studies that have shown the gender bias of most science books.[5] If you begin to consider the race bias of most science texts and worksheets, it will not take you long to realise that this is even more obvious. If any black people are shown at all, they will probably have some sort of disease: protein deficiency, leprosy, rickets, etc. They may be shown with a white male 'expert' explaining something to them about health or agriculture; they may be shown with some sort of 'primitive' device for irrigation or ploughing. But they will probably not appear at all. The message about who does science is very clear from the majority of the printed resources available for the use of science teachers.

A very few published schemes and books now do make an attempt to reflect our multicultural society, but there is virtually nothing available which illustrates science as a universal human activity carried out by people everywhere.

Teachers who are involved in curriculum change for a multicultural society are therefore usually involved in making their own learning materials. There are a number of sources of help for those undertaking this task, but it is still very time-consuming. The Third World Science Project has been mentioned already.[6] This is a rich source of information for science teachers writing their own materials. The units are not suitable for direct use with school pupils. At one school we have made readers for various first and second year topics. We used units from Third World Science as our main source of information. The titles currently available are:

Carrying Loads on Heads	Housing
Charcoal	Iron Smelting
Clay Pots	Methane Digestors
Dental Care	Natural Dyes
Distillation	Plants and Medicine
Energy Convertors	Salt
Fermentation	Soap

You can see that there is much which fits in directly to many existing science courses.

There are also other materials which should be considered by science teachers trying to widen the perspectives of their courses. Look at materials produced under the heading of 'development education'. There are many science teachers who had found useful materials at the Centre for World Development Education or through their local development eduation centres.

Most of us use textbooks of some kind of another. We must now look more critically when assessing books for use as class sets or reference books. Since the ideal book is unlikely to be available, you will have to write it yourself or make do with what there is. I give some guidelines for looking at biology books, but many of the points made apply to other science books as well.

Bias in biology textbooks

Some points to look for:

1 Skin and temperature control –
   Does the book mention changes in skin colour?
   Vasodilation – skin goes pink;
   Vasoconstriction – skin goes pale or slightly blue.

2 Balanced diet –
   Does the book suggest what the components of a balanced diet should be? Is it either stated or implied that a balanced (and therefore healthy) diet should contain meat and/or milk? Are other sources of protein mentioned?

3 Food (related to 2) –

Food values and nutritional information – for which foods are data given? Which foods are included and which are omitted? which protein sources are mentioned? Are sources of vitamins and minerals given which occur in a wide variety of diets?

4 Variation –
Are examples chosen that could divide a multiracial class into 'racial groups'? Could it be inferred that the only variations which occur in the human species are those which can divide into so-called racial groups (e.g. hair type, skin colour, eye colour)?

5 Genetics –
Is human heredity considered? If so, which characteristics are mentioned? What sorts of examples are used? Could pupils get unintentional messages about human inheritance from these examples?

6 Evolution –
How is evolution treated? How much attention is given to the evolution of the human species? Especially, what are the illustrations of modern 'man' and earlier forms like? Is the most highly developed person a white European male? Is Darwinian evolution presented as 'true' or an explanation possible, given the fossil evidence available?

7 Poverty and disease –
How are these topics treated? What image is given of black people in the illustrations used? Do white people ever suffer from deficiency diseases now?
What are the implications of images of other parts of the world? Do they give a realistic and balanced view of the lives and surroundings of people in other parts of the world?

8 Is there any information given about the history of science? If so, is it implied that only Western European people (men?) have made contributions to this history?

It is more difficult to give criteria to look for in physics and chemistry books. However, these are some points to consider:

(a) Are black people shown as normal people, or as having various diseases, or not at all?
(b) Do you get the impression that only Western Europe and North America are scientifically and technologically advanced?
(c) What about the history of science? See the 'bias in biology' textbooks section above.

If you are unable to find suitable texts you will have to choose whatever you consider to be the best available. However, you can try to counter some of the bias by providing supplementary resources, e.g. posters, and also by discussion of the bias in the books with your pupils.

Anti-racist approaches to science teaching

One of the contributions of science teaching to a whole-school anti-racist approach has already been mentioned. Experiencing science as opposed to just learning some of the scientific body of knowledge should give our pupils an appreciation of the need for testable evidence when making statements, etc. It was also suggested that science education should aim to make the pupils sceptical and to require evidence. Science teachers can use this to challenge some areas of stereotyping.

Classification of living organisms appears in nearly all lower school science courses. It is also a topic that occurs at later stages in biology courses. Classification is an important skill in science as a way of organising what is known. However, classification of people is not the same as many other forms. People cannot be divided into races in the same way as vertebrates can be divided into mammals, birds, reptiles, fish and amphibians. Race is not a biological classification, although it is used to group people for a variety of reasons and it has many social, economic and political implications. In our multiracial, multicultural society, implications that grouping people in this way is scientific is divisive and racist. Descriptions in biology books of the 'races of man' based on investigations of blood-groups are either extremely simplified or do not reflect the nature of our society now, as they tend to ignore the effects of the world-wide movement of peoples in the past few hundred years. Teachers wishing to read more about race and biology can consult the references given at the end of the chapter.[7] It would be helpful if examination boards were to give careful consideration to this area. Meanwhile we all have a responsibility to make ourselves familiar with the information and to begin to develop effective teaching strategies in this area.

It is more positive to consider the diversity and variation of living organisms. The variation within a species is well demonstrated in human beings. Most science courses include measurement of some of the factors which vary between people: height, hand-span, etc. Skin colour is merely one example of continuous variation, and there are many others. Any feature which varies continuously is not suitable for the purposes of dividing into groups.

Explanations of the variation of the pigmentation of skin which merely involve adaptations to different environments are not adequate. The adaptation of living organisms to their environment shows a great deal of variation. Statements that black people are adapted to life in a hot, sunny climate do not explain how white people have managed to survive for a very long time in Africa. These simplistic explanations also ignore the social, political and economic factors that cause people to move from one area to another. They are, therefore, inadequate and can lead to racist responses – 'If they're adapted to living in Africa, why don't they go back there?' Science teachers cannot ignore the effects of European imperialism and colonialism any more than can teachers of any other subject.

Some content issues in science education

Although I began by emphasising the consideration of science as a process to be experienced by our pupils, there are issues raised by some of the content frequently found in science courses.

Conflicts with religious belief

Some of the content of science courses or practical work undertaken can cause problems to some of the students in a multi-faith classroom. This is nothing new, but we must be sensitive to these issues so that we do not cause conflicts and difficulties for any of our students. It is obviously not possible for me to provide a complete list, but I give a few examples of the sort of thing I am referring to. Muslims do not only not eat pork, they should not even touch meat from a pig. It is therefore unacceptable to use bacon or pork luncheon meat for food tests.

Many faiths do not accept Darwinian evolution. Even if we do not teach directly about evolution, many of the ideas which do come into our courses are based on it. We should never present theories and explanations as 'truth', but as what they are, explanations based on the evidence available. There is not necessarily always only one explanation or answer. Evolution, especially, cannot be demonstrated experimentally; we should just present it as one explanation derived from some of the fossil evidence found. Science lessons do not have to be about belief or faith; that is another area of experience.

Genetics and evolution

Our teaching of genetics and evolution is very white-centred. Biology books are still being published which use the inheritance of eye colour as the main or only example in human inheritance.[8] This is hardly relevant to our black students. Diagrams of evolutionary trees of mammals show white males as the highest and most developed form; earlier forms of man are often shown in a way that makes them appear to be black. We should choose examples of inheritance which are meaningful to our students. This will probably mean discussion of the inheritance of skin colour. In addition to the consideration given to the issue of evolution in the previous section, we should always ensure that there is no implication that white people are more highly developed than black people.

Health education

There is a significant amount of health education in many science courses. In addition to taking especial care that any illustrations used are representative of our multicultural society, we must ensure that we do not imply that the only healthy and balanced life-style is that of the white, middle-class, two-parent family.

Another very important area is that of nutrition. We must provide nutritional information on a much wider range of foodstuffs than has previously been the practice. We must also show that a wide range of diets are adequate nutritionally, and that it is not necessary to eat meat to be healthy.

Sex education, or teaching about human reproduction, is an area which always demands extreme sensitivity from teachers. In a multicultural multi-faith school this is even more important. Science departments should be open and should encourage parents to come into school to see any learning materials and to hear about what will be taught. Interpreters should be available if this would be appropriate. Contact with local religious leaders might also be of help in allaying fears and worries of parents. However, if after all this has been done, parents of, for example, Muslim pupils still wish to withdraw their children from these lessons, their rights must be respected.

It has not been possible in the space available to raise all the issues and suggest classroom practices which would be more appropriate than many that are currently used. Science education has not received as much attention as some other areas of the curriculum. It is up to us as science teachers to take on all these issues and to develop science education for a multicultural society which has a firmly anti-racist stance.

The views and opinions expressed are those of the author. I would, however, like to acknowledge the value of many discussions with colleagues, especially the other members of my team and the group of science teachers from some ILEA schools with whom I have worked. My thanks are particularly due to the staff of the science department at Catford County School, south-east London. My final thanks are to the many children who have always made me think about what I do as a science teacher and how it is done, without whom there would be no point in this sort of discussion.

Notes and references

1 For example M. Stone, *The Education of the Black Child in Britain*, Fontana, 1981.
2 The Third World Science Project, available from Centre For World Development Education, 128 Buckingham Palace Road, London SW1W 9SH, price £2 per unit.
3 For example M.D. Robson and A.G. Morgan, *Biology Today*, Macmillan, 1980, pp. 162–3.
4 For example, B. Prest (ed.), *Language in Science*, Association for Science Education, 1980.
5 For example G. Walford, 'Sex Bias in Physics Textbooks', *School Science Review*, vol. 62, 1980, pp. 220–7.
6 Third World Science Project, op. cit.
7 Some suggested reading for teachers about biology and race: NUT, *Race, Education, Intelligence*, National Union of Teachers 1978; S.J. Gould, 'Why We Should not Name Human Races: A biological view', in *Ever Since Darwin*, Penguin, 1980, pp. 231–6; J. Tierney, 'Race, Colonialism and Migration', in J. Tierney (ed.), *Race, Migration and Schooling*, Holt Education, 1982; C. Husband, ' "Race", the continuity of a concept', introduction to C. Husband (ed.), *'Race' in Britain: Continuity and change*, Hutchinson, 1982.
8 For example M.D. Robson and A.G. Morgan, *Human Biology Today*, Macmillan, 1982, p. 144.

Chapter 12

Resources for multicultural education (Where to find them and how to choose them)

Gillian Klein

Resources for education in a multicultural society are of essentially two kinds:

those used in the classroom
those used by and for teachers.

Historically, teachers in search of good practice in multicultural education have begun in the classroom: teachers of infants and lower juniors often with picture and story books, middle and upper school teachers with a discrete area of the curriculum. Queries that flooded the Centre for Urban Educational Studies Library in the mid-1970s were of the 'Are there any Turkish folk tales?' or 'Do you have anything on Toussaint L'Ouverture . . . Harriet Tubman . . . Mary Seacole?' kind. Or even the pursuit of resources with which to teach 'black studies'.

And those kinds of searches still continue, but are more likely now to come from isolated teachers in all-white schools. While it is unsurprising that such teachers are finding the resources that exist, or existed, in their schools totally inadequate, such an approach is as likely as not to lead to tokenism. Introducing a home economics topic on Indian food or a unit on steel bands in music can, as Maureen Stone[1] has shown, be divisive and even damaging, particularly to black children, if it is done as an adjunct or, worse yet, as an option to the conventional curriculum.

Before selecting the resources that will allow them to develop the curriculum appropriate to a multicultural society, teachers need to think about what they are trying to do. Who is the curriculum going to be for? Why are these new topics being considered for teaching? Are you sufficiently informed to be able to teach the topic confidently?

Essentially, what are the aims and objectives of any new initiatives? Are they part of an overall re-evaluation of the school's curriculum? Are they one aspect of an overall commitment to anti-racist teaching? Are they a response to demand, overt or covert, from the pupils?

So while resources are essential to the development of new curriculum initiatives, they cannot in themselves teach the pupils. The teacher has to understand thoroughly not only the resources, but the principles behind the development of the curriculum.

Where anti-racist, multicultural education is the reason for a new curriculum initiative, it is essential that the teacher understand that, too. This means becoming informed about the issues. One would hope that support will be forthcoming, from within the school and/or from in-service courses, but even so, becoming informed does mean: Teacher, teach thyself. Look at and discuss relevant videos like ALTARF's *Racism: the 4th R*,[2] read the currently significant and some of the background books.

Resources for teachers

The Schools Council found it useful in its last gasp to update their 1981 publication *Resources for Multicultural Education: an introduction*.[3] Although one of the nine sections does look at potential curriculum materials, the book is mainly intended as an information guide for teachers to develop their own knowledge and their attitudes. List 1, 'The context; multicultural Britain', is consciously designed for a chiefly white audience, who need to know more about the backgrounds, cultures and experience of the children in their classrooms. More important, they need to know something about the experiences beyond school of their black pupils, most of whom are born in Britain. Realities of prejudice and discrimination are statistically recorded by the Runnymede Trust[4] and other bodies; some of the causes are documented by writers like A. Sivanandan in *A Different Hunger*;[5] how it must *feel* is expressed in work like Amrit Wilson's *Finding a Voice*,[6] the LMSA video, *Motherland*,[7] AFFOR's anthology *Talking Chalk*.[8] List 2 takes the issues into the classroom. Ever since Bernard Coard's critique of British education in 1971,[9] writers like Dhondy, Stone and Mullard[10] have analysed the failure of our schools to educate against racism and adequately for a multicultural society. Of current interest are David Milner's *Children and Race: Ten years on*[11] and James Lynch's *Multicultural Curriculum*,[12] but a book which should be required reading for all teachers is that edited by John Tierney, *Race, Migration and Schooling*.[13]

There are even resources on how to develop a multicultural approach in areas of the curriculum. Significant among these is another series of Schools Council publications on *Assessment in a Multicultural Society at 16+*.[14] These will be the last publications to offer that logical link between examinations and curriculum that the Schools Council has always been about. At the time of writing, the titles published are *English*, *History*, *Religious Studies* and *Community Languages*. Other subject areas, it is hoped, will follow. The same authors have taken their thinking into a book edited by two officers of the Schools Council, Alma Craft and Geoff Bardell, *Curriculum Opportunities in a Multicultural Society*.[15] The contributors include Ray Hemmings on mathematics, David Hicks on geography, John Broadbent on modern languages, Nigel File on history, and Jack Dobbs and Frances Shepherd on music. But science, arts and RE, social sciences and PE are all represented, and the approach throughout is essentially practical.

Equally practical is a six-page 'Contemporary Affairs Briefing' which I prepared on *Race Relations in the School Curriculum*.[16] While I am ambivalent about the value, except in certain very aware schools (which may not need such a curriculum module anyway!) of teaching this as a specific curriculum area, I am also made constantly aware in my information work that teachers are taking this on. Research such as the body of work under the NARTAR programme[17] has shown that such strategies may even be counterproductive. I urge teachers, before making such attempts, to familiarise themselves with the book edited by Laurence Stenhouse and his team, *Teaching about Race Relations: problems and effects*.[18] Further exploration of the rationale can be found in a paper by Dave Dunn entitled *Race education*,[19] published in 1981 and in the CAB already described, which also analyses seventy-one potential sources for learning about race relations and racism in Britain.

To return to the Schools Council bibliography, and to an issue already touched upon tangentially, namely teachers' attitudes, List 5, 'Reading for Pleasure' suggests a rather different category of resources for teachers. Unlike all the informative resources I have mentioned, which may certainly affect teachers' attitudes obliquely, this list is designed to affect them directly, but in an unthreatening, even enjoyable, way. It lists and briefly describes about thirty of the hundreds of novels which can offer insights and understandings of other lives, other lands. The best novels permit the reader to see the world through the eyes of someone else (in this case, mostly, through the eyes of black characters) – in the very best, the reader 'isn't quite the same person' after reading it. Selection was of readable, generally paperback, novels set in Africa, the Americas or Asia. And the selection was personal, though not only of books which have made a lasting impact on *me*. It includes classics like Wright, Achebe, Rao and more recent works by such as Desai and Rushdie, Soyinka and Thelwell.

More structured initiatives in changing teachers' attitudes with regard to race are part of many current INSET initiatives. Race Awareness programmes are increasingly featured; one published report is available from the NUT.[20] Self-evaluation on the part of teachers is an even slower but potentially even more effective strategy; James Lynch and his colleagues have recorded such a programme being run in Sunderland.[21]

Direct guidance on all aspects of anti-racist and multicultural education is available also in numerous of the LEA Policy Documents (currently around thirty) on multicultural education, and in the carefully itemised papers from ILEA. Professional bodies such as the NUT[22] and AMMA[23] also provide guidance and information, but what this body of resources does most valuably is to shift the emphasis of multicultural education away from the individual responsibility of each practitioner into a part of the appropriate professionalism of all those involved in educating children and young people for today's Britain and today's world.

Resources for use in schools

Deliberately, this second main category, the resources that are used with pupils and students, is not headed 'Resources for the classroom'. There is no denying that it is classroom materials that send teachers off on their odysseys of searching, but it is essential to keep in view also the hidden curriculum. Nothing exemplifies and illustrates better the hidden curriculum than the resources that exist in the school, be they in classroom cupboards, stock cupboards, library shelves or corridors. The overall parameters of knowledge deemed worthy of imparting and learning are demonstrably reflected by the books and materials in use in the school. It is still all too easy for the prevailing message to be that only European history and languages are worth knowing, only white men have performed heroic deeds and pushed back the frontiers of knowledge, only the traditional Anglocentric curricula will qualify pupils for further education or future employment.

The school library, in its fiction and its information provision, is ideally placed to display and promote materials that support knowledge systems other than the traditional English, and to present a view of the world that is not Anglocentric but 'multi'-centric, or even global. And there is no lack of materials which will beam this message loud and clear, even to the most casual browser. Posters, shelf-labels in relevant languages, community notices and publications recognise the relevance of knowledge held by the community to the learning within the school.

For those children who read for private enjoyment, fiction can extend their views and insights. Again, there is a growing body of appropriate material coming from both mainstream and alternative presses. Books which reflect our multicultural society, which explore issues of racism at a pain-dulling distance; books which in their literary merit contribute also to the rich heritage of English literature for children. In some all-white regions, printed resources may be the only medium through which another generation of British children can be made aware that they are in fact part of a multicultural society. It is important that this happens, or educators will be seriously misleading their pupils.

With so much around, how does one choose? Here there is a real difficulty: teachers who have spent their time and their energy in the classroom would, experience shows, welcome having the selection done for them. But this cannot be, especially at a time of such financial stringency in which no school can afford to spend their money on mistakes. So ordering straight from catalogues is out. And ordering from lists not much better. In the end, selection depends on two things: (1) the clientele, i.e. who the book is for and how it will be used, and (2) the educational aims and objectives of the school. If the latter should include an anti-racist and multicultural objective, then purchasing racist books is also unacceptable.

What *can* be offered to teachers is guidance and support. A collection of initially selected materials, as provided at multicultural resource centres of LEAs, or in general consultative collections of Schools Library Service, is the important initial step. Also important is expertise at the centres: a librarian or teacher who can match the most appropriate materials to the specific curricular needs. Failing that, a system of (sensitive) reviews of each book, as is provided in Leicestershire and Nottinghamshire.[24] Lists are useful in providing bibliographic information to facilitate ordering, but can be no more than guides; in the end the materials themselves must be handled and evaluated before purchase.

Guidance is available also in the form of published criteria for selection and studies of the forms of racism in children's books. Of the latter, Bob Dixon's *Catching them Young*,[25] S. Zimet's *Print and Prejudice*[26] and the WCC's *Slant of the Pen*[27] are still relevant, and most current (1984) is *Reading into Racism*.[28] Each of these identifies forms that racism can take in children's books. Specific curricular areas have been analysed in depth, such as the work of Dave Hicks[29] and Dawn Gill[30] in geography.

Criteria, too, are abundantly available. The World Council of Churches has produced the most comprehensive and detailed, and these are published in *The Slant of the Pen*. Others have focused more closely on the potential impact that books may have on children, and are useful as starting-points for discussion and thought. Best of all are the initiatives set up to consider children's books and develop criteria for one's own use: Bedford used this approach in the 1970s in a NAME working party[31] that included teachers and librarians, and Dudley[32] found a similar exercise equally productive in 1983.

The Schools Council has kindly given permission for the criteria I prepared for *Resources for Multicultural Education* (op. cit.) to be reprinted here. They are not intended as definitive; what they attempt to do is to set criteria by which one selects materials in schools in the context of children's experience of reading and their *use* of books in schools.

Books in schools – what to look for

Neither reading nor writing takes place in a cultural vacuum. All authors bring to their work their own values and attitudes; all readers relate to what they read in the light of their own perceptions.

Each early reading experience validates the printed word, be it 'Butcher' on a carcass-filled shop window or the 'Way Out' sign that brings us up from the underground. It is some years before children learn to question the truth of what they read, and even then they are unlikely to identify and challenge biases which do not immediately threaten them, unless they are actively encouraged to do so.

Consider the role of print in shaping children's attitudes towards the world and relate it to the multicultural society into which they are growing up. The population of Britain has changed radically in the past forty years: books have changed little. There is much greater cultural diversity in customs, languages, religious beliefs, skin colours and life-styles, and yet the view of many is of one cultural norm and one way of looking at the world; and prejudice and discrimination remain a reality.

Consider next children's reading matter in relation to children in the UK and their wide range of life-styles and experiences. Many children see cultural diversity all around them but find little confirmation of it in what they read. Children from ethnic minorities in Britain need to see their culture accurately portrayed and their existence acknowledged in the books they encounter. Children in areas still predominantly white and monocultural are likely to accept without question exclusively monocentric portrayals of other lands and racial stereotypes in books.

All these children are growing up into a multicultural society and a shrinking and interdependent world. We who bring them into contact with books have a responsibility to ensure that those books offer not outdated and biased views but accuracy and a multicultural perspective on the world and the people in it.

Practically any book can be used in the classroom: what matters is *how* it is used. Teachers need to be aware that they automatically endorse the books they use with their own authority and approval – unless they say otherwise. Challenging prejudice and stereotyping as they arise in a book has been found effective in encouraging children to question and explore the issues in a controlled situation. The teacher, however, needs sensitivity, both to the messages in the book and to the children in the class, and needs also their confidence in him or her. When the book being used is clearly biased, it is advisable to offer as well a publication with an alternative view.

Children studying on their own will accept the messages of the resources as part of the knowledge they are seeking; there is no one to challenge bias when it occurs or to provide another view. Nor is there when children are reading for pleasure. And this is when they are at their most unquestioningly receptive, having selected the book for themselves and entered the one-to-one communication with the author.

Fiction and fantasy can have a profound impact upon children. They can help children to make sense of the world and provide an avenue through which they can explore their own fears and aspirations. Fiction confirms the child's sense of self, offering characters who are – in some way – as they see themselves to be, or wish to be. At the most direct level, black teenagers are noted reading avidly from black authors, reassured to find their own experiences and feelings confirmed in literature. But identification is seldom so clear-cut for the reader, nor need authors necessarily write only from their own ethnic and cultural experience.

Fiction has the power to transport us through space and through time. It can extend our thinking and understanding far beyond the limits of our own experience. If, through their reading, children are led 'behind the eyes' of characters from cultures and backgrounds other than their own, characters who are emphatically and vividly portrayed, they learn that there is more than one way in which to regard their fellow beings.

In the Schools Council project, Children's Reading Habits (10–15), Frank Whitehead[33] and his team researching into children's responses to fiction found that while children recognise a narrative as 'only a story', they accept the judgments and attitudes of the author, and it is these which leave a 'residue' in the child's mind. Values and attitudes about themselves and others, and about their own and other cultures, are part of this 'residue' that builds up – and remains – in children's minds.

Criteria for selecting classroom materials

Select books which aim at a world view. Avoid books which equate the white man with 'civilisation', those with patriarchal or white philanthropical approaches to other peoples, or which reduce all non-Western societies to the exotic, the primitive or the quaint. These views may be evident in both what is said and what is *not* said: omissions can be equally damaging.

The rest of the criteria follow from this reassessment of viewpoint and attitude. Children need:

Books that are factually accurate and up to date – the maps and illustrations as well as the text.

Books which present peoples with a variety of attributes, whether of personal characteristics or life-styles; not those where whole cultural groups or individuals are portrayed as stereotypes ('the attribution of supposed characteristics of the whole group to all its members', David Milner, 1975, *Children and Race*).[11]

Books which use language with care: do Africans live in homes or in huts; are they ruled by kings or by chiefs; do they 'jabber and shriek'; do they speak a language or merely a dialect; are whole peoples ever described as 'childlike' or 'savage'?

Books that give students information about a variety of cultures and societies, showing their effectiveness and achievements, whether historic or present-day. *Discovering Africa's Past* by Basil Davidson (Longman, 1978), for example, clearly illustrates that there were important and stable civilisations in Africa long before it was 'discovered' by the Europeans.

Books that could equally well be used 'in an all-black classroom and an all-white classroom', and those which 'would not give pain to even one black child' (from Rae Alexander, in *Interracial Books for Children*, autumn 1970).

Books which show children of different cultures and races carrying out the activities illustrated, be it in mathematics, design and technology, the sciences, music, etc.

Some criteria in specific curriculum areas

Teachers of world studies and economics can be guided by the publication of the World Studies Project and a paper by David Hicks, *Images of the World* (available from the London University Institute of Education). Each culture has its own values, and it is by these that it should be judged. 'Poverty' should not be defined as merely a lack of Western goods. The reasons for the poverty of certain nations should be set in the historical and political context.

Science teachers should be on guard against any assumption in textbooks that it is scientifically viable to classify people in terms of race. This type of classification can lead to the implication that one 'race' is biologically superior to others. See: *Race, Intelligence and IQ*, a booklet from the National Union of Teachers (list 6) and *Bias in Biology Books: Some points to look for* by Sue Watts (from Room 465, County Hall, London SE1).

Many religious education teachers acknowledge a special responsibility to avoid the approach that there is only one true doctrine. RE teachers are well placed to demonstrate that all religions provide a moral and social framework. The article by W. Owen Cole in *Education 3–13* (autumn 1981) recommends some useful resources.

Teachers of English could consider their classroom books in terms of the fiction criteria outlined under personal reading. One possible approach is to consider the recommended syllabuses suggested by Scilla Alvarado (in no. 3 of the *English Magazine*) representing Afro-Caribbean, Asian and black American authors at all levels up to GCE A level.

Reading schemes need scrutiny. If they show only white middle-class girls (helping mum) and white middle-class boys (kicking footballs) they are likely to be quite irrelevant to many of the children in the class.

Criteria for selecting fiction and other private reading material

Aim for a book stock which offers to children and young people:

A balanced view of the world, seen from many different perspectives.

Books which relate experiences common to children of all ethnic groups and in which they can all share, for example, the wobbling of that first baby tooth in *Berron's Tooth* by Joan Solomon (Hamish Hamilton, 1978).

Books among which children from the variety of ethnic groups represented in Britain today can find characters which will confirm their own sense of self and enhance their self-esteem; in which ethnic minority characters have important social roles; where adults are seen to be supportive in family relationships and to hold positions of responsibility, doctors as well as orderlies; where ethnic minority children are seen to make their own decisions.

Books which communicate vividly and perceptively how it feels to be a member of another ethnic or cultural group.

Books in which ethnic minority characters do not have to justify their blackness to the white characters (or readers) by being unbelievably good, or brave, or strong.

Books in which illustrations of ethnic minority characters are accurate and avoid caricature by using sensitive artists or photographs of real individuals.

Books which accurately reflect the population of Britain – so that those with an urban setting show not just a 'token black' (prevalent in publications of the 1970s), but represent cities and towns as truly multicultural – for example, Methuen's 'Terraced House' series or *Mother Goose Comes to Cable Street* by Rosemary Stones and Andrew Mann (Kestrel, 1978).

Books in which language does not evoke stereotypes (avoid books in which 'savages' 'jabber and yowl' or the 'brown boy's eyes roll'); in which dialect is used appropriately – to extend expression and contribute to children's respect for one another's speech – as in James Berry's or Linton Kwese

Johnson's poems, Charles Keeping's *Cockney Ding-dong* (Kestrel, 1975), C. Everard Palmer's *Baba and Mr Big* (Collins, 1976).

The book stock should also include folk tales which can bridge cultures, and books written by young people themselves, from a variety of cultures.

Keeping informed

With an understanding of the issues involved in multicultural education, and the ability to select materials appropriate to an anti-racist approach to education, all that remains for teachers to do in terms of resources is to keep informed about new publications and developments. This, too, takes time. Time, I would argue, best spent by information officers and librarians who should then disseminate relevant information. But this happens seldom within the structure of education authorities. At present it appears that the bigger the LEA, the more people there are each independently and energetically discovering each new wheel, if not actually inventing it.

Outside organisations are of most help: again, these are listed in the Schools Council Resources book. Ethnic minority and specialist bookshops offer an invaluable service, providing expertise as well as materials, and teachers and librarians should make certain that they have access to funds when visiting these shops or the specialist exhibitions at which they are represented, so that they can go ahead and buy the appropriate materials then and there.

As a last resort, there are the lists themselves. As well as those mentioned, there are some fairly detailed bibliographies (see List 4, Schools Council) and the current, selective lists which are of most immediate value such as AFFOR's *Issues and Resources*[34] and ACER's excellent *Resources and Information Guide*.[35] Selective fiction lists appear from time to time from public library services or in periodicals: the most useful at present is Judith Elkin's series in 'Books for Keeps'[36] through 1983.

In a field in which all practitioners, as well as the pupils, are learning constantly, most books are of short-lived value, or become historic shrines to an outdated approach. Periodicals are more appropriate for disseminating new information promptly.

Encouragingly, more general educational journals are presenting articles on research, theory and practice in multicultural education, e.g. the NUT journals, *Primary Education Review* and *Secondary Education Journal*;[37] *Education 3–13*;[38] even *The Times Educational Supplement*. The issues permeate the thinking in others, such as *Contemporary Issues in Geography Education*,[39] the *English Magazine*,[40] *Teaching London Kids*,[41] *World Studies Journal*.[42] Views are offered in *Race and Class*[43] and *Race Today*,[44] *Mukhti*,[45] *Roots*,[46] which contribute vastly to the educational debate,.

Then there are the specialist journals: the *Journal of Multilingual and Multicultural Development*.[48] The NAME[49] journal is helpful on theory, and reports current developments, and the CRE publishes *Education*.[50] *Multicultural Teaching for Practitioners in School and Community*[51] provides a platform for records of good practice and extensive reviews and reports. It also offers an annual abstracted index. And a wide range of journal articles can be located through *Multicultural Education Abstracts*.[52]

It may still take some effort, but matters are improving. Not only are there an increasing number of appropriate materials of high standard, but there are more information services – though these are all partial and therefore none is wholly adequate – about them.

In the end, though, resources are only as good as the way in which they are used. And this comes down to a matter of approach. To quote my conclusion to an article in *The Times Educational Supplement* of 6 May 1983:

> Teachers need to understand that there is a great range of knowledge that is of value to children in our schools today – which includes languages, customs and religions, arts and music, and techniques of problem-solving. This inevitably calls on a multitude of materials. Any and all that extend children's parameters of knowledge and understanding in this way, are resources for multicultural education.

References and notes

1 Maureen Stone, *The Education of the Black Child in Britain*, Fontana, 1981.
2 ALTARF, *Racism: the 4th R*, All London Teachers against Racism and Fascism.
3 Schools Council, *Resources for Multicultural Education: An introduction*, Longmans Resources Unit, Tanner Row, York, 1981 (rev. ed., 1984).

4 Runnymede Trust and Radical Statistics Race Group, *Britain's Black Population*, Heinemann Education, 1980.

5 A. Sivanandan, *A Different Hunger*, Pluto, 1982.

6 Amrit Wilson, *Finding a Voice: Asian women in Britain*, Virago, 1978.

7 ILEA, *Motherland* (available outside ILEA from Chalfont Films).

8 AFFOR, *Talking Chalk*, 1982 (from 1 Finch Road, Lozells, Birmingham).

9 Bernard Coard, *How the West Indian Child is Made Educationally Sub-normal in the British School System*, New Beacon, 1971.

10 Farrukh Dhondy, *The Black Explosion in British Schools*, *Race Today* Publications, 1982 (see ref. 44); Mullard, in Tierney cited in n. 13, and in *Racism in Society*, V, *Schools, History Policy and Practice*, 1980 (from CME, London Institute of Education, 20 Bedford Way, WC1).

11 David Milner, *Children and Race: Ten years on*, Ward Lock Education, 1982.

12 James Lynch, *Multicultural Curriculum*, Batsford, 1983.

13 John Tierney (ed), *Race, Migration and Schooling*, Holt, 1982.

14 Schools Council, *Assessment in a Multicultural Society at 16+* (obtainable from Longmans Resources Unit, Tanner Row, York).

15 A. Craft and G. Bardell (eds), *Curriculum Opportunities in a Multicultural Society*, Harper & Row, 1984.

16 Gillian Klein, *Race Relations in the School Curriculum: Rationale and resources*, CAB, 1983 (from Centre for Contemporary Studies, Ingersoll House, 202 New North Road, London N1).

17 NARTAR, *Teaching about Race Relations*, 1979 (NARTAR is based at University of East Anglia, Norwich NR4 7TJ).

18 Lawrence Stenhouse (ed.), *Teaching about Race Relations: Problems and effects*, Routledge & Kegan Paul, 1982.

19 Dave Dunn, *Race Education*, 1982 (paper from Community Education Development Centre, Briton Road, Coventry CV2 4LF).

20 NUT, *Race Awareness Workshop Report*, 1983 (from NUT, Hamilton House, Mabledon Place, London WC1).

21 C. Biott, J. Lynch and W. Robertson, 'Teacher Training Report', *Multicultural Teaching*, vol. 2, no. 3, summer 1984.

22 NUT, *Combating Racism in Schools*, 1981 (see n. 20).

23 AMMA, *Our Multicultural Society: The educational response*, 1983 (free from 29 Gordon Square, London WC1).

24 Central Library Serviecs, Thames Tower, Leicester; Central Library, Nottingham.

25 Bob Dixon, *Catching them Young*, Pluto Press, 1977.

26 Sarah G. Zimet, *Print and Prejudice*, Hodder, 1976.

27 Roy Preiswerk (ed.), *The Slant of the Pen*, World Council of Churches, 1980.

28 Gillian Klein, *Reading into Racism: Bias in children's literature and learning materials*, Routledge & Kegan Paul, 1984.

29 D. Hicks, *Bias in Geography Books*, Institute of Education (see n.

10); *Minorities*, Heinemann Education, 1981.
30 Dawn Gill, 'Assessment in Geography for a Multicultural Society', *Multicultural Teaching*, vol. 1, no. 2, spring 1983.
31 *Promoting Multi-ethnic Education through Learning Materials*, EL&RC, Acacia Road, Bedford.
32 Dudley NAME, c/o Blowers Green Primary School, Blowers Green Road, Dudley.
33 Frank Whitehead et al., *Children and their Books*, Macmillan, 1977.
34 AFFOR, *Issues and Resources* (see n. 8).
35 ACER, *Resources and Information Guide*, 1983 (ACER, c/o CLR, 275 Kennington Road, London SE11 5QZ).
36 Judith Elkin, Lifeline Two – series of six titles in 'Books for Keeps', starting Jan./Feb. 1983, ending Nov./Dec. 1983.
37 NUT, *Primary Education Review* and *Secondary Education Journal*.
38 *Education 3–13*, Nafferton, Driffield, North Humberside.
39 *Contemporary Issues in Geography Education* (from Francis Slater at Institute of Education, see n. 10).
40 *English Magazine* (from ILEA English Centre, Ebury Bridge, Sutherland Street, London SW1).
41 *Teaching London Kids*, 20 Durham Road, London SW20 0TW.
42 *World Studies Journal* (WSTTC, University of York, York YO1 5DD).
43 *Race and Class* (Institute of Race Relations, 247 Pentonville Road, London N1).
44 *Race Today* (165 Railton Road, London SE24).
45 *Mukti* (213 Eversholt Street, London NW1; available in Hindi, Punjabi, Gujerati, Bengali, Urdu, English).
46 *Roots* (Roots of Culture Foundation, 3 Knowles Close, Halstead, Essex).
47 *New Community* (from CRE, Elliott House, Allington Street, London SW1).
48 *Journal of Multilingual and Multicultural Development*, quarterly, TIETO, Clevedon, Avon.
49 *New Approaches in Multiracial Education* (NAME).
50 CRE, *Education* (free from CRE, see n. 47).
51 *Multicultural Teaching: To combat racism in school and community* (Trentham Books, 30 Wenger Crescent, Trentham, Stoke-on-Trent, ST4 8LE).
52 *Multicultural Education Abstracts* (Carfax, Haddon House, Dorchester-on-Thames, Oxon.).

Chapter 13

Initial teacher training

(A case study of a decade of change in Bradford)

Ranjit Arora

While the history of its component units spans a century, Bradford and Ilkley Community College itself was only formed in 1982 as a result of a merger between Bradford College and Ilkley College. These two institutions, independently of each other, had already gone through a series of mergers in the last ten years. In 1973 Bradford College of Art and Bradford Technical College merged to form briefly Bradford College of Art and Technology.

During the 'rationalisation' of teacher education in 1975 Bradford College of Art and Technology merged with Margaret McMillan College of Education and later Bingley College of Education merged with Ilkley College. Each had developed pioneering work in a range of quite distinctive fields, which include Bingley in middle years schooling; Ilkley in home economics and community education and Margaret McMillan in early years schooling. Both Bradford and Ilkley colleges made a special feature of inter-professional training. Ilkley established a major reputation in the field of youth and community work and Bradford in the field of multicultural education. The common ground of responding to the needs of a multiracial, multicultural community has provided a suitable context in which the new college has established a corporate identity for its present flourishing teacher training programme.

The academic policy of the new College, defined by the Academic Board and fully underwritten by the Governing Body, has a commitment 'to offer comprehensive and non-divisive further and continuing education responsive to the identified needs of its community and the other communities and subgroups that comprise it'.[1] Such a commitment is fully reflected in the College's comprehensive nature, its responsive curriculum, the community context in which it operates and in its contribution to the economic prosperity and the quality of life of the district it serves. The College has at present over 12,000 students attending both full-time and part-time courses and a teaching staff of nearly 539 full-time and 616 part-time lecturers.[2]

The context of Bradford is multicultural, multiracial and multilingual and is characterised by a tradition of hosting immigrant communities. By the 1970s there had been four major movements of ethnic groups into Bradford. The Irish between 1800 and 1860, German merchants and East European Jews between 1870 and 1910, East Europeans recruited from refugee camps during the 1940s and groups from the West Indies, from India and largely from Pakistan moved into the centre of Bradford between 1950 and 1971.[3] At present all of Bradford's thirty wards have people from different races and different cultures. The 1981 census shows the total number of Bradfordians born outside the UK was 44,993, 17,668 of them in Pakistan and 12,784 in the New Commonwealth.[4] This means that one in every ten Bradfordians was born outside the UK. A similar number were born in this country but have parental origins in another, whether in Europe, Asia, the Caribbean or elsewhere. It is also significant that nearly half of Bradford's black population, whether born in the UK or outside it, are under 16.

However, the issues of multiculturalism confronted by the schools of Bradford today are somewhat different from those identified by ethnic, cultural and religious differences of the new migrant groups of the 1960s and 1970s. The earlier models of simplistic assimilation and even 'integration' through the establishment of language centres for English language teaching, and of 'busing' out of children to avoid those in immigrant areas becoming segregated, have proved to be inappropriate, foolish and perhaps even dangerous.[5] Public pressures from community groups and politically active educators have identified the education system as an instrument in the reduction of social inequality thus increasing the accountability of schools. This chapter examines an institutional response to these processes.

Towards a policy for teacher education for a multicultural society

Teacher training institutions in Britain have in the main been slow to respond to the changing needs of our schools. It is only recently that, partly due to institutional pressures from the Department of Education and Science (DES), the Council for National Academic Awards and the race relations lobby that colleges are now more prepared to accept that some changes are desirable and possible.

Any attempt to show one of the ways that an institution can devise and implement an effective policy for teacher education is likely to include a consideration of effective management and training processes, underlying assumptions of such processes and factors which will affect its success or failure. One of the dangers of abstract descriptions such as the present case study is that they give an impressive appearance of coherence and integration to a set of activities which are at best isolated from each other and at worst in direct conflict. However, it is hoped that this attempt will at least identify the best, albeit diverse, elements that make up its truly multicultural comprehensive provision and make reference to those elements of implementational difficulty that are clearly identifiable.

Consistent with its designation as a community college and in line with its academic policy, Bradford College[6] has had a declared commitment to multicultural education and an ethos conducive to implementing that philosophy. The general complexion of the total College educational programme was responsive to the community's social, cultural, environmental and industrial needs. In response to the Committee of Inquiry into the education of children from minority groups, the Academic Board of Bradford College made reference to its

- courses as preparation for people who are going to live and work in an urban, industrial, multicultural society.
- specific support courses to make the major provision of the College's programme both accessible and acceptable to members of ethnic minority groups.
- resources to the development of specific courses aimed at members of ethnic minority groups.
- programmes of multicultural studies for all students irrespective of origin, to appreciate the pluralist nature of the present British society and to understand the salient elements that make up the diversity of its constituent cultures.

Among other things it also made reference to its Multicultural Education Unit, the Access Unit and to its Open Access policy, to its Student Services and its Staffing Policy. The overall approach suggested a rather wide-ranging institutional commitment to multiculturalism. It also suggests an ethos of 'permeation' which has high significance for the institution's teacher education programmes which are intended for students preparing to teach children between the ages of 3 and 13. It is this wide-ranging commitment to multiculturalism and its specific implementation in teacher training programmes[7] that this chapter will attempt to describe.

As far back as 1966 the Margaret McMillan College of Education in Bradford offered 'conversion' courses for Asian teachers. The purpose of these courses was to enable graduates with overseas qualifications to gain an entry into the teaching profession. The course did not necessarily fulfil the students expectations of advancing their teaching careers or of gaining entry into it.

This DES-sponsored retraining course lasted four terms and was intended for immigrant teachers (not teachers of immigrants). To be admitted to a course, candidates had to obtain recognition of their entitlement to qualified teacher status from the DES. At the time of admission they were given aptitude tests designed to assess the personality of the applicant and his suitability for the course. The candidates were continuously assessed throughout the course on all three components, i.e. English, social studies and language, and language and education. The English language component was primarily intended to diagnose language difficulties and to measure the candidates' linguistic progress in spoken and written English. The social studies and language component was intended to give an introduction to manners, behaviour and customs in a variety of contexts in contemporary Britain, whereas the language and education component involved a practical study of the language used by teachers and pupils in the classroom in several different kinds of activity. At the end of the course it proved very difficult to place many of the students in schools in Bradford. The amount of improvement effected in the candidates' English was not found to be satisfactory and the course did not provide continuity of experience in a single school as the teaching practice was organised on a termly basis. The comments of the candidates on the course ranged from:[8]

> 'No incentive, no freedom of thought or expression, we are forced to do unwanted things as barking like a dog in the class. Lost the fluency and self-confidence'

to

> 'This course has been of great help to me. I am improving, or rather have improved my English and have now a better understanding of the educational system. I write this because I didn't know anything about the classroom situation here. Now,

to some extent, I know it from bottom to top.'

The normal teacher training courses in the same institution, however, continued without any attempt to make them more accessible or acceptable to students from ethnic minority groups. The general conditions for the award of an Initial Teacher Training qualification were as laid out in the University of Leeds Institute of Education handbook. The content of these courses included:[9]

(a) a study of the principles and practice of education with the usual content, i.e. study of child development, the growth of personality, children as members of the family and society, the child in school and a study of the growth of educational thought and practice and health and physical education;
(b) choice of one main curriculum area;
(c) supporting studies:
 (i) to complement the main course of study to enable the student to specialise in the teaching of a certain discipline or to gain competence in the teaching of a discipline other than the main course;
 (ii) to study areas of general, cultural significance and importance which add to the background knowledge essential to a teacher;
 (iii) to investigate problems which develop awareness, concern and sympathetic understanding of local and world difficulties.

In practice it meant that there was a 15-hour elective on multicultural education. But there were some opportunities within supporting studies to take up special curriculum interests which might be relevant to teaching in multicultural schools. Opportunities were also available to develop the linguistic and cultural awareness of children of immigrant families attending primary schools in Bradford. But there was no attempt to include in the training the skills and knowledge required to develop materials and approaches appropriate for the needs of children for whom English was not a first language.

The cutback in teacher training numbers led to the School of Education being merged with the School of Adult and Community Education which helped the opening up of teacher education to the community context.[10]

It allowed the professional bases of courses for teachers in urban multicultural schools to interact with a major commit-

> ment to meeting the social and community needs of ethnic minorities and certain disadvantaged groups in ways designed to generate greater community autonomy and individual independence.

Although the School of Education committed for preparing students 'for schools as they really are' saw its primary task as establishing professional credibility, the School of Adult and Community Education in their wish to be responsive to the community 'as it really is' saw its concern as to dissolve 'artificial barriers that tend to fragment certain experiences.'[11]

Thus, although the formation of the School of Community and Teaching Studies was intended to facilitate an increased interaction between staff concerned with the professional training of teachers and those developing contacts with both ethnic minority groups and with other community groups defined by shared interests, cultures or experiences, such interaction was not without problems. It had to be argued that genuine community education must be initiated from a community base however diverse its different groups may be. Despite the different values and interests of its subgroups it is the nature of that community which should shape the College curriculum so that it can be seen to reflect the key values of the community. To design courses of teacher education which could prepare teachers to implement such a curriculum and to respond to the contradictions and conflicts inherent in the concept of community education was no mean task.

The ensuing dialogue led the College to formulate a policy for teacher education that kept the exploration of this dilemma between 'community activists' and 'professional educators', with their respective weaknesses and strengths, in the forefront of its thinking. It recognised that any policy for teacher education in a community college must provide a bridge between the immediate and local concerns of community groups and the wider political, social and educational perspectives of society. Community responsiveness, a vocational orientation and a practical emphasis on the educational theory in teacher education courses were already firmly established as necessary in response to its location. Conventional views of teaching related strongly to issues of control, the value of certain forms of knowledge and the need for certain kinds of organisation were certainly in conflict with community values in a variety of subtle ways that can affect the classroom decision-making process. It was therefore important that teacher education should be designed so as to raise teachers' consciousness in social interaction within and outside the classroom and to incorporate community awarenesss in their thinking. It was also acknowledged that such awareness can be translated into action only by equipping teachers to operate in much more open systems that are sensitive and responsive to community needs and by reflecting the community commitment in its selection of knowledge, in its structures and practices, in its relationship with its practice schools and in the philosophy that shapes these elements. When this was considered in the context of multicultural commitments, several problematic issues emerged, thus heightening the dilemma even further. The schools did not always share the College's assumptions and beliefs, and indeed racist attitudes in some schools prevented them from participating in the process of teacher training. In turn, the College did not always state its position on multicultural education or demonstrate its implications to students on practice or the schools who received them. The staff on these courses were not always convinced that multicultural focus was in the best interests of the students or the schools. The guiding assumptions of multicultural processes of teacher training at Bradford College were clearly spelt out by Ken Polk[12] at the IMTEC seminar in 1979. These will be discussed later on in this chapter. It was against a background of a network of dilemmas that the teacher education programme had to establish professional credibility for its students in schools 'as they really are'. The College, determined to articulate a policy for teacher education that was genuinely responsive to the needs of multiethnic communities, laid down the following criteria. It had:[13]

(a) to be community informed and responsive to community defined needs;
(b) to ensure the interaction of community values with those of wider social organisations;
(c) to equip all members of the community including those from subgroups, both to play a full role in their own community and to achieve fully within the majority culture.

Implementation

To implement this policy the College identified five major areas of action. These are admissions policy, administrative structure, school liaison, course content and staffing policy. It is under these headings that I shall also make reference to the guiding assumptions for multicultural processes in teacher education and to the specific examples of good practice found within the institution which particularly relate to teacher training programmes.

Admissions policy

The College recognises that many students from minority groups may be prevented from participation in the mainstream success experience by the 'deselection' involved in the traditional streaming and examination processes. It is with this recognition that the College practises affirmative action policy for students from ethnic minority backgrounds. The provision of a variety of alternative programmes of study which lead to the secondary qualifications required for many educational and work careers may not have a specific multicultural label but are an essential feature of the strategy for serving the needs of a multiethnic population. These are particularly important for teacher training courses as they provide potential ethnic minority students with the qualifications to enter teacher training, and, for those in training, models of educational alternatives which they will need to become competent teachers. The stated objectives for the DipHE programme which leads onto the BEd (Honours) degree course include:[14]

> The College will pursue an affirmative policy towards students from ethnic minority backgrounds and endeavour to ensure a balanced and varied mix of students within permitted admissions procedures.

In designing a course which led to the award of a DipHE and also gave access to degree courses (BEd and BA) the College aimed to provide a unit based programme of study designed to develop a range of skills relevant to careers in education and administration within a course framework of issues of urban, industrial, multicultural society and with a progressive vocational focus. The four categories of students whose needs were borne in mind in the 1975 submission included:[15]

(a) those with a clear commitment to a course of higher education;
(b) those who have a firm commitment either to teaching or to a career in administration;

(c) those students, probably young, who want higher education but are uncertain of the mode and prefer to defer their choices;
(d) those students, probably mature, who seek an extension of their general education without a clearly defined career objective.

As a direct response to the patterns of choice revealed by students during 1975–80, a greater priority has now been given to students in the first two categories. The course aims have also been revised and reordered to reflect a more intensive focus on ethnic minority groups, gender, differentiation and social interaction. A requirement is now made that all students who lack formal qualifications shall be admitted to the course only after a successful interview and the submission of satisfactory written work completed in College as part of the admissions procedure. Successful completion of the Mature Students course of Bradford College is also a normal qualification for entry to the DipHE course.

The diagnostic and support programmes in Literacy and Numeracy as well as the structured 'Return to Learning' programme are designed to meet the identified needs of students entering the course.

Applicants who wish to proceed to the BEd degree but who lack O level maths and English (DES requirement for entry to Teacher Training programmes) are advised to acquire them before the end of the second year of the DipHE course.

Another significant change has been to remove the requirement that students wishing to select the major optional course unit in South Asian studies must demonstrate an oral fluency in one Asian language and an understanding of spoken Hindustani as a condition of entry to the entry to the option. This has enabled a large number of indigenous students to take up this option. However, students selecting this option are strongly recommended to take advantage of opportunities offered within the College to learn one Asian language. The introduction of Caribbean studies as an additional major option unit has served to strengthen the multicultural focus of the course. At the time of writing this very popular and efficiently-run major option had to be withdrawn temporarily.[16]

Administrative structure

The College had opened up its teacher education programme by placing it in the context of community education. This meant that interchange between staff engaged in teacher education and those in other community-related areas of work was inevitable. The staffing structure facilitated community experience for teacher educators and enabled those directly concerned with community provision to contribute to courses of teacher education. By rejecting the principle of exclusivity and by ensuring that no member of the academic staff would be totally committed to teacher education, the College had acted, however unwittingly, in the interest of its staff. When more teacher training institutions had to be closed because of further reduction in the teacher training numbers, the School of Community and Teaching Studies could not be identified exclusively as a teacher training institution any more than its staff could be as teacher trainers.

School liaison

To prepare students for schools 'as they really are' it was recognised that College staff should have a regular and systematic attachment to a school. The attachment was designed to foster the collaboration between teachers from the schools and tutors from the College and to help the tutor to become familiar with the specific implementation of theory into practice. In particular such attachments help establish the necessary practical arena for students to develop the skills and practices to achieve credibility in schools 'as they are' and develop an appropriate commitment to community education. It was hoped that through staff exchange school teachers can be involved in the design of teacher education courses or in staff development. Such an 'interchange' can strengthen real partnership between the schools and the College which is otherwise limited to a one way process of college using the schools as a teaching practice place.

In 'Teaching in Schools: The content of initial training' (1983), HMI have proposed that the teaching profession should be involved as a matter of course in the design and planning of all courses, in the selection of students, in the teaching and supervision of students and in the final assessment of who should or should not be given 'the licence to practice'.[17]

The paper also suggests for the staff involved in pedagogy on the training course that more of their time should be spent actually teaching in schools, perhaps exchanging with school teachers for part of each year; and perhaps an increase in the system of joint appointments, whereby individual teachers spend part of their time in training institutions, and part of their time in school.

Such good practice does exist in a limited way in Bradford. Currently four school teachers have been attached to the College for one term to work on a RE curriculum development project with a particular multi-faith focus.

The school experience aspect of teacher training as well as the actual teaching practice in schools provide another dimension for a collaborative partnership between the schools and the College. By using its inner city location, the College can ensure sufficient opportunities for students to demonstrate their growth in confidence, competence and potential as teachers in a multi-cultural context. Each teaching practice is normally undertaken in a different school. In addition to teaching practice blocks and associated preliminary visits, the students are required to work in schools in small groups for one day per week with teachers and College tutors. This school experience is seen as an interactive experience in four senses:[18]

- shared experience for both staff and students;
- a means of illustrating and translating into practice the general issues raised within the various core units;
- a focus for bringing together interrelated elements within the individual course units;
- a vehicle for the acquisition of and practice of teaching skills appropriate to teaching practices.

Each of the three school experience periods can be seen as a means of preparing students for each of the three teaching practices. The exercise also provides an additional base for work in College founded upon a recognition of the immediate and future needs of students. For students it is an opportunity to work as 'junior colleagues' with tutors and class teachers in an inner city multiracial school chosen as a model of good practice.

Such a partnership with schools and the greater use of school experience and teaching practice referred to 'as the central power house of the training course' has in fact been the main thrust of the College's BEd programme since 1980. It is hard to tell whether this thrust would continue in its present form in the new higher education programme currently under discussion.

Course content

The actual course content of the initial teacher training programme derives from the specific needs of the inner city multicultural, multiracial and multilingual schools. The courses are designed for those students who have a predisposition for working with people rather than those who seek a less functional approach to higher education. It is through this emphasis on the functional nature of knowledge and the permeation of multicultural focus that the College has taken cognizance of the educational challenge presented by the multicultural society in designing and implementing appropriate curriculum change. Considerable discussion had taken place to formulate specific multicultural guidelines[19] for the DipHE, and in order to assist their implementation, the following statement of intent had been agreed:[20]

> Bradford College's Dip.H.E. is committed to developing within its students an understanding of British society and the position of ethnic minorities therein. It is also committed to exploring in a scholarly and dispassionate way the many competing positions that are taken up in describing the nature of that society and the role of race and ethnicity in social relations as part of a balanced and coherent academic programme.

The professional preparation of teachers for work in urban multicultural schools also requires that the knowledge students acquire must be related to how communities are composed, and to how they relate to society at large, and to how contemporary schools and the present educational and social services respond to these communities. In relating these perceptions to practice, the aim is to provide a much more cyclical and interactive relationship between placements, school experience, formal lectures and workshops. The concept of workshops is used to describe both a teaching strategy and a place where students, tutors, visiting teachers and school children can work.

Consistent with the principle of 'permeation', the course content of all units is oriented much more positively towards multicultural education. The selection of materials for curriculum courses reveals a heavy emphasis on the mastery of teaching skills in English language and mathematics, while creative studies and environmental studies provide vehicles for learning about integrated approaches to the curriculum. BEd students are encouraged to build on the DipHE compulsory units of Human studies, Industrial society and Professional studies.

All the major optional courses in the DipHE also seek to complement this emphasis, but South Asian studies, Caribbean studies and Urban Geographical studies seek to increase the students' understanding of the multicultural society more specifically and progressively through the two years' study. Other minor options within the DipHE which examine particular multicultural issues include:

Christianity in a multiethnic context;
Islam, Hinduism and Sikhism in Britain;
Communities and Community Relations;
The Historical Background to Multicultural Britain (withdrawn in 1980);
Theories of Race and Racism (introduced in 1980).

With regard to the BEd, the two 'professional years' are an integral and cumulative part of a four-year programme in which the first two years have sensitised the students to the nature of the multicultural society within which the schools operate. During the BEd there is heavy emphasis on Teaching studies, Reading and Language development and Mathematics. In addition, the curriculum workshops are concerned with the development of the students' personal practical skills in connection with the various school experiences. The responsibility for establishing a multicultural inner city perspective on the curriculum, previously assumed by the electives and the curriculum workshops, has now been incorporated in the teaching studies. For their 'Individual Curriculum Study' students are encouraged to consider issues which are specifically multicultural so that a student can relate on an individual basis the previous and current academic experiences to an actual in-depth study of some aspect of the content or process of teaching and learning in a multicultural context. A similar opportunity is available in the fourth year where a student can, as part of the chosen elective, focus on a case study with specific emphasis on multicultural issues. The Language in Education elective offers opportunities for students to acquire specialist linguistic skills based upon current theory and research related to first-language acquisition and second-language learning.

For students concerned primarily with speakers of English as a second language and for those concerned with bilingual education there is a further opportunity to follow an intensive study of these areas. Community Education, on the other hand, is intended to broaden the students' understanding of the relationship between the educational process in school and in the wider community in order that community-based teaching may be more informed and realistic.

While certain aspects of course content are identified as having particular relevance for students intending to teach in multiracial schools, all course units throughout the four-year programme are required to indicate the ways in which they contribute to the implementation of agreed multicultural guidelines.

The context in which present teacher training programmes are operating results from a sensitive response to its own community and to the policies of the College. The changes made during the last five years are responses to the normal developments expected within an innovative course and are in line with requirements of its validating body, the Council for National Academic Awards. The CNAA working group on multicultural education outlined the needs of schools, pupils and society which teachers have to meet, and which institutions need to bear in mind in designing courses of teacher education. These included:[21]

(1) to be equipped to prepare all pupils for life in a multicultural society;
(2) to be able to teach in the 'multiethnic' classroom;
(3) to have an awareness of the issues of intercultural relations.

The major aim of the DipHE, BA and BEd programme at Bradford College and its related functional aims go a long way towards meeting these needs. This has been further substantiated by CNAA examiners' reports. The following are some examples:

> The College commitment to multiethnic/cultural studies and problems comes through clearly in much of the work seen and this is to be commended. (BEd Hons 1979–80);[22]
>
> This [synoptic paper] proved a challenging and rewarding form of examination and one with great potential in revealing the students' grasp of the issues raised by multiethnic, multicultural education. (BEd Hons 1978–79);[23]
>
> Much good work was seen. Students were committed to the profession and to the task of teaching children. There were excellent relationships with schools. Teachers and headteachers had been drawn into a close working relationship with the College and the students had benefited from this relationship.[24]

These comments also demonstrate that the professional skills required of a competent teacher are not in any way less developed by focusing on the preparation of teachers for a multicultural society. On the contrary, such teacher training courses equip teachers to be far more competent to teach in all schools thus making the 'professional skills' versus 'multicultural society' argument redundant. The headteachers in Bradford who initially had any reservations about appointing our teachers were very quickly convinced of the quality of their performance in the classroom.

Staffing policy

> The staff teaching B.Ed. courses are predominantly male, middle-aged or older, have no recent teaching experience, have been engaged on teacher training for over 10 years and have remained in the same institution for over 10 years. The overwhelming majority gained their teaching experience in secondary schools. Very few served in junior, infant or nursery schools and this typically only for a short time. Half the staff teaching on junior courses and two thirds of the staff teaching on infant courses have no experience of teaching these age ranges themselves.[25]

This was the conclusion of the research team engaged in a DES-funded study of the background and experiences of staff teaching BEd courses in seventeen institutions from the LEA, voluntary and university sectors.

While the general staffing situation in Bradford College was no different from the one described by the DES study, the principle of involving all teacher training staff on other courses within the School of Community and Teaching Studies and of attachment to schools meant that at least some of the staff concerned were able to renew their teaching experience in multiracial schools and to develop a sympathetic understanding and a broad perspective of the different cultures and races that now make up our society.

One of the more obvious manifestations of the principle of permeation is the participation of staff with ethnic minority backgrounds in planning and teaching on all the main courses of teacher education. The staffing policy of Bradford College did encourage such involvement and also attempted to recruit staff whose experience had been in multicultural education and of working with ethnic minority groups. This was intended to ensure that programmes of teacher education are community informed.

The placement of staff in schools and in the community and

their involvement in courses other than teacher education essentially provided a basis for staff development. However, further measures to continue such development to sensitise teacher trainers to the needs of student teachers and to engage them more productively in the partnership between school teachers, teacher educators and community educators.

The College programme for teacher education has achieved its coherence and credibility in so far as it proved consistent with its own academic policy which stresses multicultural education. The open-community-informed teacher education programme has proved to be capable of establishing in its students a sensitivity to the interaction between the local community and wider social groupings in a multicultural context. The ideology of multicultural education as practised by the teacher trainers is illustrative of a dynamic process which not only prepares teachers for schools as they are but also for bringing about the necessary changes in schools that are resistant to change. The schools which can combine good practice in the context of multicultural education with an interest in curriculum development and evaluation are the ones that can help students to gain the necessary knowledge to judge what values to hold, what methods to use and what criteria to develop to evaluate their effectiveness. No doubt they will also have to cope with the far from idealised conditions that characterise most urban multicultural schools. Such credibility is essential to ensure their own personal development as teachers and to expand their range of techniques and skills to meet the complex demands of teaching in a multicultural setting.

The present case study may give a dangerous appearance of coherence and integration to a set of activities that are frequently filled with conflicts and at times border on chaos. What the description does do is to identify the diverse elements that make up the multicultural *intent* of the College's teacher training. The difficulties in the process of implementation and management of more recent changes have to be acknowledged. However, external evaluators, including Her Majesty's Inspectorate, local headteachers' comments on students on teaching practice, and the employment record of these students within Bradford Local Education Authority support the College's belief that the contribution it is making is distinctive and that its students are approaching the multicultural schools with confidence and maturity.

The other danger, and a very real one for teacher training at Bradford College in particular, has been the effects of an endless series of mergers. The latest and the most recent one, i.e., the merger with Ilkley College, has highlighted one factor that must be accepted as an inherent feature of the multicultural stance taken by Bradford College, and that is CONFLICT. The forms of affirmative action around multicultural education inevitably confront accepted curriculum standards, practices and beliefs. Conflict of this kind can be anticipated and to some degree managed and sometimes reduced. The processes of management and resolution of such conflict are unfortunately not so explicitly identified at Bradford College at the best of times. Consequently the decision to form a separate School of Community and Teaching Studies with its identifiable teacher training staff and the process of designing a new teacher training programme has thrown into sharp focus the deeply ingrained residues of years of professional training and experience that are inconsistent with the forms of multicultural education.

As the merger has caused a complete reshuffle of staff in both the Bradford and the Ilkley campuses, both comfort and survival have pushed staff to return to secure positions within their particular disciplines. It has also resulted in a complete change of teacher training staff, thus making the original multibase teacher training team totally unviable. The interests and actions of these differing groups are not likely to move easily and neatly together without producing a range of tensions. Implied are a wide range of changes in course goals, methods and processes that staff in both campuses are used to. Individuals from Bradford who were involved in the validation of the teacher training package currently in operation and are members of the new course development group are no doubt making every effort to maintain the multicultural focus of these courses, whereas staff from Ilkley are engaged in maintaining a subject-oriented thrust characteristic of secondary teacher training. What is needed is a process which will provide leadership, support and a sense of protection for both staff and students. Without such processes, the consequence will be a drift of staff back to familiar ways and then movement away from effective multicultural programmes.[26]

It is hoped, though, that as long as an institutional structure has been created within which programmes can be adapted to the needs of an urban multiracial, multicultural and multilingual community and as long as the College acknowledges a responsibility for social action and a continuing need to provide teachers with a conceptual framework which enables them constantly to re-examine their own knowledge and skills, it will continue to progress along the lines it has taken over the last ten years or so.

This does not mean that there is no room for improvement. Far from it. The ways in which 'permeation' and preparation for 'schools as they are' operate may mean that many teacher education programmes will not appear to be multicultural in respect of either their content or their processes, but if they are available to students of ethnic minority backgrounds because they have privileged access to them, they become significant. The challenge to the College is to allow this access in ways that ensure recognition of ultimate qualifications at par with 'normal' qualifications and whereby the College can effectively reach out into the community groups whose educational needs are often unknown to educators. It will succeed in doing this only if its planning remains coherent. The Multicultural Education Unit was set up to assist such planning. Its objectives include the development of a comprehensive action policy throughout the College, the monitoring and teaching of courses, promotion of staff development and training to increase linguistic, cultural and racial awareness, formulation and implementation of research policy in multicultural education and promote greater participation of ethnic minority communities in the life of the College and its services.

As an integral part of the College structure this Unit is essentially seen as a servicing unit. As part of a School, it does provide a tidy management structure for the whole institution and thus a uniform line management system. It may make the co-ordination of all College-wide support services somewhat easier as well. But its policy development and monitoring role may appear less significant to outsiders, and its right to direct negotiation with outside agencies as well as with other section heads within the institution may remain at only a theoretical level.

But one cannot overlook the issues of differences in administrative and line staff concerns. Curiously enough, what was written about this institution in 1979 is even more true today.[27]

> It is one thing for the leadership to speak clearly on its desire to emphasise multicultural education, it is quite another thing for the line staff to implement such efforts.
>
> Unless administrators and line staff work closely together in setting goals and priorities, aspects of multicultural education, rather than penetrating to the central core of line work, merely become tacked onto the marginal and easily ignored periphery of work.

There is thus a strong case for developing an overall policy for teacher training colleges and for monitoring its implementation to ensure a comprehensive programme of multicultural education. What are likely to work are coherent approaches that span units and individuals, approaches which somehow integrate with each other. A comprehensive policy of staff support and staff development to prepare staff for their changing roles and continuation of local schools involvement is absolutely vital for multicultural programmes to be effective. Also important is the level of minority groups participation in the form of recruitment of staff and students, participation as consultants, advisers and as Governors to ensure involvement in crucial decision making processes.

While Bradford College has endeavoured to ensure that all its courses leading to qualified teacher status are permeated by the multicultural ethos and that such an ethos is reflected in the focus and make-up of staff, the opportunities to mix with a variety of students and the social and physical arrangements of the College, CNAA, the validating body of its teacher education courses, has not yet seen fit to declare their commitment to multicultural, albeit anti-racist, education. The CNAA working group on multicultural education did actually produce a statement[28] in October 1982, but its status is as yet unresolved. In fact there is no indication that a policy statement on these lines will be forthcoming.

Similarly the Polytechnics' Council for Education of Teachers (PCET), while declaring its commitment to education for a multicultural society seems to suggest: 'This may be achieved by the inclusion of specific course units or by a multicultural dimension being added to existing areas of study.'[29] This is indeed a very narrow interpretation of multicultural education and one that sees 'adding on' of cultural elements as the answer. This implies that multicultural education is relevant only for multiracial schools. Those colleges, polytechnics and universities who do identify their main concern as teacher education for a multicultural society have been restricted to a limited age-range and have therefore been unable to help shape the total programme of schooling for children from ethnic minority backgrounds. The present categories of subject specialisms and the tight limits on 'age-ranges' imposed by the DES restrict opportunities for developing an adequate response to the needs of ethnic minority groups through the teacher education system.

Radical reappraisal of the present provision of teacher training is a necessary step in an appropriate direction to raise the quality of the professional preparation of teachers and with it the quality of the education offered to children in our schools. At the same time a clear recognition by the DES of multicultural education as an essential element of such training and a greater degree of institutional flexibility in determining admissions and selections policy will go a long way towards achieving a working partnership between professionals in schools, in employing Authorities and in providing institutions.

Finally, qualifications and training alone do not make a good teacher. Successful experience of teaching in multicultural classrooms can provide the kinds of strength and insights which can equip all teachers to teach as competently in urban multiracial schools as it can in rural, suburban multicultural schools.

The 'deficiency model' emphasis on difficulties, differentiation and disadvantage, especially presented in a theoretical way and totally unrelated to the classroom, must be avoided at all costs. In the words of John Eggleston, 'Teachers need practical examples of successful multicultural teaching and not consciousness raising.' He goes on to say:[30]

> Some of the more enlightened teacher training institutions are now coming to see very clearly that it is only when teachers have had the opportunity to experience success with black children are they likely to be ready to respond fully to the aspects of their courses that are designed to remove such impediments to multicultural teaching as the use of racist books, the assumptions of racial inferiority and the deficiencies of cultural understanding.

Notes and references

1 'Academic Policy Statement: Underlying Principles', Bradford and Ilkley Community College, March 1983.
2 These figures are from City of Bradford Metropolitan Council Employee Headcount by Ethnic Origin, May 1983.
3 Raminder Singh, *The Sikh Community in Bradford*, Bradford College, 1978.
4 'Bradford's Black Population', Policy Unit, Bradford Metropolitan Council, (undated).
5 Ken Polk, 'Multicultural Education Programmes at Bradford College', IMTEC case study, 1979.
6 Bradford College before its merger with Ilkley College.
7 The programmes referred to will include the Post Graduate Certificate in Education. However, the 'policy for teacher education' does apply to all teacher training programmes within the institution.

8 Julian Dakin, 'A Survey of English Courses for Immigrant Teachers', CILT Reports and Papers 5, 1971.

9 University of Leeds, *Institute of Education Handbook* (1970–1), pp. 180–9.

10 Peter Chambers and Jacki Proctor, 'Initial Teacher Education in a Multicultural Community Setting: An institutional response' (paper prepared for 'Teacher Education in the 1980s and 1990s' conference), 1981.

11 F.M. Newman and D.W. Oliver (1967), 'A Proposal for Education in Community', in John Raynor and Jane Harden (eds)., *Readings in Urban Education*, vol. 2, Routledge & Kegan Paul, 1973.

12 Op. cit. (5).

13 Bradford College, 'A Policy for Teacher Education', Margaret McMillan School of Community and Teaching Studies, Bradford, 1980.

14 Bradford College application for re-approval of DipHE, BA (Hons), BEd (Hons) (Dec. 1980), vol. I (CNAA validation document), Bradford College, 1980.

15 Ibid.

16 This was due to the resignation of the Caribbean Studies tutor. The new appointment has now been made.

17 Pauline Perry, Chief HMI for Teacher Training, 'The Training of Primary Teachers: Current Teachers and Future Trends', *Primary Education Review* (The Training of Primary Teachers in the Balance), NUT, no. 16, spring 1983.

18 CNAA validation document, op. cit. 13, 14.

19 Ibid.

20 Ibid.

21 CNAA Committee for Education, 'Working Group on Multicultural Education', CNAA, 1982.

22 Comments of chief external examiner (CNAA) for BEd (Hons), 1979–80, in CNAA validation document, vol. II (op. cit., n. 14).

23 Comments of chief external examiner (CNAA) for BEd (Hons), 1978–9.

24 External examiner's report on the examination and on teaching practice for the degree of BEd, July 1981.

25 Pauline Perry, op. cit. (n. 17).

26 Ken Polk, op. cit. (n. 5).

27 Ibid.

28 Op. cit. (n. 21).

29 Statement of the Polytechnic Council for the Education of Teachers, 1983.

30 John Eggleston, 'Ethnic naivety', *The Times Educational Supplement*, 11 March 1983.

Chapter 14

In-service mis-education

Dave Dunn

The mere mention of in-service training is enough to raise a groan. The topic reeks with boredom. For many teachers it conjures up images of being told what to do by ageing lecturers remote from classroom realities. For administrators, too, this field is the poor relation in education. Incessant exhortations for more and better in-service work are all too often coupled with actual cuts and inadquate budgets. I shall not repeat these exhortations, except by quoting two national reports.

The first quotation comes from a study of eleven in-service courses which I and my colleague, Madhu Anjali Purewal, carried out between 1979 and 1981, and on which much of this chapter is based: 'Our investigations have left us in no doubt about the fragmentary and incomplete provision of in-service teacher education for a multicultural society. Indeed it appears non-existent in many areas and in none does it seem wholly adequate.[1]

The second observation was made by a parliamentary committee[2] not generally noted for intemperance:

> The issues involved have now been kicked around by interested parties for so many years that it is no longer acceptable to wait for the complex administrative structure of teacher training to come to terms in its own good time with the challenge presented by the multiracial classroom. It is against a background of justified weariness and impatience that we consider how teacher training must now tardily adapt to this challenge.

Interviews with teachers attending in-service courses emphasised the need, for the courses were in general very far from 'preaching to the converted'. Some participants made racist generalisations. Thus one secondary head of department castigated his West Indian pupils by saying, 'They've got no ambition – all they want to do is get down the Arndale Centre and get mugging.' Others exhibited considerable ignorance about their ethnic minority pupils, like an experienced inner-city first school teacher in Bradford who classified her pupils as 'Hindus' and 'Pakistanis – they're Muslims aren't they?' when she also had a number of Sikh children in her class.

Some teachers were unsympathetic to any changes for the benefit of their black pupils: 'I don't believe in bending over backwards to cater for foreigners.' Others were only a little less reluctant: 'Whatever my own feelings about it might be, I've got to face up' to the presence of 'immigrants' in her school. Participants' statements frequently revealed underlying assimilationist attitudes: 'I've got one little Indian boy in my class. He does the right thing, he fits in'; 'it's just trying to fit them in'; 'they have to adjust'.

By no means all teachers attending courses are racist, ignorant or assimilationist, but those who are not are frequently highly critical of their schools and colleagues. A teacher in a west London school reported the reluctance of her head to accept a Sikh boy as a prefect: 'He obviously thinks that if that boy stands up at prizegiving it presents a difficult atmosphere . . . and the image of the school is liked to be kept as a white school.' Where participants were happy with their own schools, they were often dissatisfied elsewhere:

> 'Something seems to happen when they get to the Juniors. What it is I don't know, but there's a very negative attitude – "They're thick, they don't understand, what can you do with them": that sort of thing. Nobody seems to be able to pinpoint what happens – an almost dramatic change.'

It should be the job of an in-service course to help such teachers to pinpoint what happens, but course providers in multicultural education[3] are faced with a number of severe difficulties in doing so. I have already alluded to one of these – the diversity of attitudes and knowledge among participants. An in-service course in, say, developments in primary mathematics can attract a relatively homogeneous group by comparison. But courses in multicultural education recruit teachers of a variety of subjects and age-groups. Some have little or no knowledge of relevant issues, but are concerned to enhance their mobility or career prospects. Some are educationally active in furthering what they deem to be the interests of their pupils or society at large, and seek practical or academic support for their initiatives. Others are attracted in the hope of solving specific 'problems' they feel they face in their classrooms.

In the face of this variety it will come as no surprise that there is much criticism of courses which do not meet individuals' expectations. Most frequently this arises from a perceived lack of relevance to the classroom: 'The whole course wasn't practical enough.' Sometimes this could be attributed to defects in organisation – 'Someone would suddenly think, "Oh dear, now we've got to relate this to the classroom and it would be about ten minutes to go" ' – but deficiencies in expertise were also noteworthy. These arose both from some organisers' lack of current experience in schools, and from a lack of knowledge and experience of the situations of ethnic minorities.

The more highly regarded courses are sensitive to the individual situations of participants, and provide individual 'research', experiential or innovatory activities which necessitate self-motivated learning and analysis. Their providers also possess or import as guest speakers people whose expertise is apparent to participants. Thus teachers were frequently notably appreciative of contributions by ethnic minority lecturers and participants who were perceived as offering insight, experiences and knowledge not available to many white speakers. However, as with any other type of course, efficient organisation and effective presentation can over-ride other considerations. Participants were particularly impressed by 'charismatic' speakers.

Teachers are also often critical of the coherence and progression offered by courses in multicultural education. Coherence is difficult when 'each week was a separate entity, different people talking about different things'; while progression was sought but not always achieved: 'The thing I was looking for was unification – getting it all together.' The difficulty for course providers in attaining these ends is severe and arises from the extent of the knowledge that could be offered to participants. The potential domain of courses in multicultural education (as understood in contemporary Britain) is so great that choices must be made to include or exclude certain topics. Such choices are, I believe, not always wisely made.

One possible way of summarising this domain is seen in Figure 14.1, which is an attempt to illustrate the inter-relationships between key concepts employed or employable in discussing the issues involved in multicultural education. Thus providers tend to select a social context (e.g. Britain, Birmingham or Bog Lane Comprehensive) and examine aspects of the inter-relationship

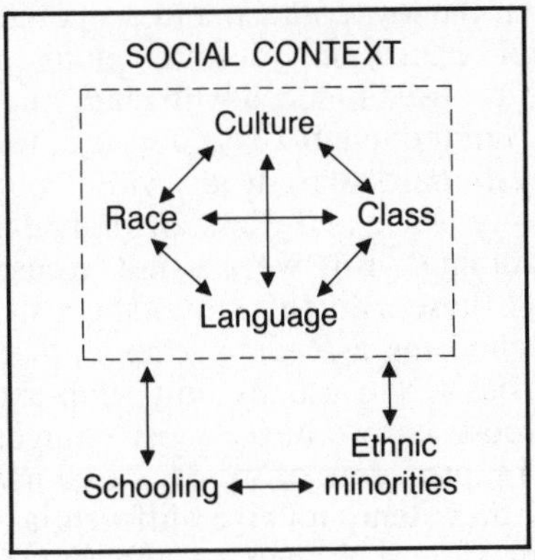

Figure 14.1

between the process of schooling and the situations of ethnic minority individuals or groups (such a selection can of course include aspects of education affecting white pupils' attitudes and knowledge relating to minorities, as 'minorities' exist only within the context of an associated 'majority').

Course providers then select for discussion issues associated with the concepts of race, class, culture and/or language, and their inter-relationship with the theory and practice of schooling and the position of minorities. The particular issues selected may then be considered within specified disciplinary perspectives – for example political, sociological or historical – or may be discussed as individual topics with evidence brought to bear from a variety of academic disciplines or from personal accounts. Longer courses leading to in-service diplomas or BEds are more likely to emphasise overtly a particular perspective and may even have units called 'Sociology' or 'Linguistics', but thematic topic-based approaches (e.g. 'Britain's Response to Minority Group Pupils') occur on both long and short courses.

My analysis at this point may seem to be needlessly complicated, but it has several purposes. The first is to emphasise that the theory of multicultural education includes not only most of what is conventionally understood to constitute the theory of education, but also necessitates an analysis of social context with reference to how British society was, is, and should be constituted in respect of inter-ethnic and inter-racial divisions and classifications. To simplify, and to beg all the vital questions, it is about good education in a good society.

My second purpose is to re-emphasise the problems of course

providers. Given the low political and economic priority accorded to multicultural education (despite pious utterances to the contrary), they are usually faced with clarifying a complex field in courses of very limited length. Teachers are, to some extent, used to thinking about particular dyads within our system of inter-relationships – say 'Race and Class' or 'Language and Culture' or 'Class and Schooling'. But we are not accustomed to thinking clearly about all these elements simultaneously. We do it only in action – when choosing a reading scheme, disciplining a child or devising a syllabus – and usually only semi-consciously.

My final purpose is to criticise most stringently the selections actually made by providers of in-service courses in multicultural education, for they tend to give differential treatment to the elements of our system. Language and culture are given much attention, if not always in an appropriate manner, but race and class make less frequent appearances and are all too often given minor roles.

By 'culture' I am referring to 'that complex whole which includes knowledge, belief, art, morals, law, custom, and any other capabilities or habits acquired by man as a member of society'.[4] This catch-all category does frequently serve to fulfil a demand from teachers wishing to learn about the sensibilities of their pupils. Virtually all courses treat cultural issues explicitly, dealing with phenomena such as religion, family life, dress, child-rearing practices and the arts. At best, such approaches can fruitfully enhance teachers' relationships with their pupils and parents, and provide helpful information for changing school organisation or curricula. At the worst they can lead merely to the creation of more sophisticated stereotypes and a pandering to what white teachers may see as exotic, where South Asian 'culture' is represented by 'sari soirées and curry evenings'[5] and the West Indies by the inevitable steel band.

A particular problem with the concept of culture is that cultures are too often seen as static and homogeneous. This difficulty arises with the recurrent 'torn between two cultures' model of minority youth in Britain. This model can occasionally be appropriate to illuminate the dilemmas of individuals, but in general it ignores social change, the multifaceted nature of inter-ethnic interaction, individual differences and sub-cultural variation. It can also serve to de-emphasise the commonalities of experience and aspiration between ethnic groups in a manner which obscures the processes of schooling which may affect all pupils whatever their ethnicity.

Language, or linguistic issues, is also given prominent attention by most in-service courses. Topics may include general linguistic principles, consideration of linguistic diversity and associated social phenomena, and issues relating to the teaching and learning of ESL and community languages. The last-mentioned is noteworthy, for there is probably no topic other than racism itself which can occasion such antagonistic and prejudiced reactions from participant teachers. Explosions of 'They're in England now, so they should speak English' are likely to occur before any detailed arguments have been considered – let alone the comparative behaviour of the English abroad.

Unlike culture and language, some courses give race no overt consideration, and others disguise the existence of racism by utilising mystificatory euphemisms such as 'Intercultural Relations'. In stressing the importance of the concept of race I am not referring to its use in biology, for there it has 'little value, no exactitude, and in itself explains nothing'.[6] I am referring to social aspects of racial classification and differentiation, which may vary widely between societies and have a potency which affects individuals or groups irrespective of their cultural or linguistic attributes.

Many studies have shown that racial prejudice is so prevalent in Britain that it must be considered in some sense to be a normal characteristic of white British people. One review[7] of this research estimates that 85 per cent of this population may undertake discrimination on racial grounds in certain circumstances. The saliency of race for discrimination in employment and housing is also well documented.[8] For example, in tests of applications for jobs it has been shown that Hungarians or Italians may suffer a certain amount of discrimination – but British people of West Indian or South Asian origin are affected much more extensively even when they have equivalent qualifications to the white applicants. It is race, not language or culture, which is the key element in inter-ethnic discrimination in Britain. Why then do many in-service courses underplay the role of racism, and some ignore it altogether?

The educational establishment has until recently been reluctant to acknowledge the prevalence of racism in Britain. The statement that 'racism, both intentional and unintentional, has a direct and important bearing on the performance of West Indian children in our schools'[9] was unusually direct for a semi-official source. The more customary quiescence means that some teachers come to in-service courses denying the very existence of discrimination: 'I assumed, well, it's qualifications and the competition you're facing.' Another reported that staffroom colleagues believed 'the only groups that were discriminated against were whites, and that the dice were far too loaded in favour of ethnic minorities.' Such nonsense is heard in many schools, and is at times given credence by the media and implicitly by certain actions of the law and state. Given this support, the historical preconditions for the existence of English racism and range of explanations for its perpetuation it comes as no surprise to find that many teachers are reluctant to acknowledge the importance of race.

They can be adept at ignoring racial conflict between their pupils, utilising a variety of devices to put the blame elsewhere. With the 'original sin' technique, racial name-calling can be safely ignored, as, 'They naturally tease each other about anything . . . children are cruel.' Conversely, some maintain their pupils' innocence: 'It's all love and peace . . . obviously my own opinions are coloured by the way I was brought up and I feel it's the same with the kiddies in the playground, both parties.'

Many teachers are reluctant to discuss anything to do with race in their classrooms. On one in-service course a group of infants teachers were shocked by another who had done so: 'You know she really had discussed colour of skin!' They were clearly amazed by her temerity: 'You've got to tread very carefully.' 'Are you in that case making people feel they are different?' Their views can be contrasted with the non-conformist teacher: 'I always talked about it because I discuss everything in the infant class, and when we're painting and colouring we want to look at the different colours of skin and hair . . . You can't ignore anything that's so obvious so it's better to talk about it.' As children are aware of race at pre-school ages,[10] she may well be right – might not a conscious or unconscious repression of the topic reinforce the idea that there is something 'not quite nice' about blackness, and assist in the creation of a taboo?

The reactions of certain teachers on in-service courses make it appear that 'taboo' is not too strong a word. I will let a primary deputy head express the anger that some participants feel when the taboo is lifted:

> 'I thought it was biased: anti-police, anti-establishment, anti-everything . . . it made me cross, that everything had a racialist bias, cartoons in the newspapers and adverts on the TV. I remember writing in my notes, "Aren't we allowed to laugh at ourselves?" '

This reaction can cause difficulties for providers, but is by no means universal. An infants teacher who criticised others as being 'aggressively political' or 'aggressively evangelistic' stated, 'I can't actually imagine why so many people got uptight about it.' Six months later, the deputy head had adjusted her ideas: 'I don't feel the back hair bristle quite so much now . . . Obviously I was going through life with blinkers on.' The explanation for her change in views may lie in the thoughts of another teacher on the same course:

> 'I was fully convinced when I started the course that I had absolutely no racial prejudice whatsoever, and bitterly resented the preaching and lecturing during the early part of it. Then I began to think, "Well, if I resent the preaching so much, what am I actually worried about, why can't I just sit back, let it wash over me?" Then I began to realise that possibly I had considerably more prejudice inbuilt into me than I had realised, otherwise I wouldn't be feeling so strongly. So that came as a shock . . . I had certain sorts of prickly feelings of resentment, particularly when people began to talk very seriously about changing . . . curriculum in school with a bias actually towards the immigrant population, and that's when I began to feel "Yes, I must be slightly more prejudiced than I'd actually thought", because I felt quite resistant to the idea although logically I could see the need.
>
> I began to feel terribly possessive, and think "Why should we change our system? . . . Why should we as a nation, as teachers, actually have to alter things we love dearly, believe in, our traditions, our heritage, our literature; in order to make way for something else?" . . . Looking very closely, it was prejudice, actually. It's fine as long as one is visiting all these lovely foreigners on their territory. It's not quite the same when these foreigners are coming here, and then one is very territorial about this. It was prejudice, definitely. I still feel ambivalent about it, but it does mean that if I'm in a situation where it actually matters, I should be able to view it openly and honestly without having to dig away and think, "Well, what are my feelings on this?" I've now at least worked them out as far as I need to at this point.'

The extent of the changes in this teacher's views will not be sufficient for many readers, but at least there was a change. On in-service courses which ignored racism, which did not discuss the facts of racial inequality in Britain or the mechanisms underpinning those facts, there were no such changes. Racial injustice disappeared in a tangential 'celebration of cultural diversity' or an 'exploration of the richness of our human heritage'.

However, our heritage is not confined to literature, the arts, religion and family life. It includes the persistence of gross inequalities of income, wealth, prestige and power; the socio-economic differentiations that I have encapsulated in the term 'class'. It is notable that even where in-service courses in multicultural education do consider racial inequalities, few go on to make the necessary links with class inequality in Britain – necessary as these inequalities are often maintained by the same processes which are given added piquancy by the operation of racism.

Migrants came to Britain to enter a society with established divisions between social groups, and their British children or grandchildren participate in a school system which had an established selective role from its inception. For schooling in Britain is intended to divide. The examinations we set and mark have as their actual or eventual purpose the segregation of people into those with opportunities open to them and those to whom many doors are closed. As teachers we are gatekeepers, and we open the gates only to pupils who conform to our requirements. Over the years inequality has been maintained by 'the weighting of the dice of social opportunity according to class, and "the game" is increasingly played through strategies of child rearing refereed by schools through their certifying arrangements.'[11]

We demand conformity not only to the open requirements of school rules and curricula, but to all sorts of expectations about what kind of behaviour, interactions and people are acceptable to us. In any staffroom we hear or participate in conversations about bad pupils, bad parents, bad families, bad language and bad behaviour. We reject whole groups of children as 'the dregs', 'scum' or 'no-hopers', and significantly we will also reject entire schools as 'sink' or 'slum' schools.

Our assessments of 'standards' in schools tend to conform with our social judgments about what output such a school should attain from its pupils: 'Given the social background of the kids, it achieves quite well. Every child in the school underachieves.' If we transfer to another school, we do not usually expect to transform it, and we may soon come to terms with what we find. A teacher promoted to a multiethnic primary school in Birmingham would not have been disturbed to find her new pupils with dramatically lower attainments:

> 'I was taking First Year when I left, and I expected it to be about the same, as I'm now taking Third Year, but it isn't. I think the maths isn't quite as good as I would have liked it to

be but I suppose it's better than it could have been. I think the English is a bit lower . . . I was expecting them two years behind and I should say possibly not a year.'

It should also be noted that this teacher, like most of us, talks of the children being 'behind', not the school or the teachers. On the whole, life as a teacher is too complex and demanding to encourage critical reflection on our own roles and the institutions we serve. Such reflection can be uncomfortable, for compulsory education in Britain was created to deal with[12]

> an urban problem, as constituted by the threat of anarchy incipient in an urban working class. Thus the teachers of the urban working class were clearly a crucial sector of the agents of control within nineteenth century capitalist society . . . The ideology of professionalism and respectability and the process of 'being cultured' served to distance teachers from their own sociocultural origins and from any dangerous association with the organised working class.

Today we fulfil much the same role, though this is not the place for an explanation of all the intricacies of the structural position of teachers. But there can be little doubt that schools have been successful in facilitating the considerable acceptance by the white working classes of their relative position in British society. Schools, by rejecting certain working-class characteristics as inferior, have facilitated this acceptance of inequality by encouraging a counter-rejection of the forms of knowledge, thought and action associated with the expectations of teachers and schools. A number of studies[13] have explored such resistance among children who form groups which actively oppose the ethos of their institutions. There is also a growing awareness of how this rejection is not pathological or ignorant:[14]

> The lads' culture, for instance, is involved in making its own realistic bets about its best chances in a class society and about how best to approach an improverished future in manual work whilst their advisors are tying themselves up in humanistic, developmental knots.

A sad complement to the logic of these pupils' rejection of schooling is that there is also a certain logic behind the rejection by many teachers of the potential of some of their working-class pupils. A stressed teacher cannot always be expected to persevere with pupils whom prior experience suggests will not succeed at schoolwork. Those who recognise the existence of the 'untapped pool of ability' among their working-class children may not have the energy to struggle against the wider social and educational forces which perpetuate inequality in schooling. For even the very texture of schooling is mediated through a class-biased means of communication:[15]

> To presume inferiority for a man's language through the official education system is to assert and celebrate the objective dominance of those social forces which have appropriated the 'standard language', the major symbol system of man's intellectual effort, and made it into a class dialect . . . This is the social and political meaning of the 'standards' that teachers have been appointed to maintain: it is a deliberately exclusive doctrine since its requirements are known to be unattainable by the mass of the working population.

This established treatment of white working-class pupils is a vital factor in the treatment of ethnic minority pupils. For their parents or grandparents generally came to Britain to replace the most depressed section of the white working class. They tended to fill the least skilled and lowest paid jobs, and found themselves forced into areas of the worst and cheapest housing in declining inner-city areas. Their children were generally allocated to schools with an established record of failing to achieve credentials for white pupils. And how did teachers respond to their new pupils? Given the preference for the racially inexplicit, the answer was (and often is still) 'We treat them all the same here.'

'Treating them all the same' can be criticised in many ways, but here I shall only explore its corollary: 'They're all working class, really.' For the objective indicators of class position have *social* meanings attached to them, as illustrated by a response to accusations of overcrowding among migrants: 'That there was excellent precedent for this in the dormitories of Eton and Harrow went unnoticed and unremarked.'[16] These social meanings are used by teachers to predict and explain the performance of pupils. Those who come from overcrowded homes, with parents in unskilled jobs, with large families, from divided households, on shiftwork (and not attending parents' evenings), or live in 'rough' areas are not expected to do well in school. Yet these expectations are largely derived from an appreciation of the class structure in white Britain, and cannot be applied directly to the children of enterprising groups of migrants.

Minorities arrived in Britain with their own appreciations of class divisions, but these did not correspond to those existing here. For example, in the Indian Punjab, 'class consciousness does not develop easily where the individual identifies with a household whose members' economic positions are so diverse (this is especially so in the middle ranges of the rural hierarchy). Caste is a more accessible focus . . .'[17] Furthermore, migrants coming from low-income groups did not have the same attitudes towards education or social mobility as low-income white groups within Britain, as with the great importance ascribed to formal education by rural Jamaicans.[18] But the higher educational and vocational aspirations of black pupils were and are frequently rejected by white teachers as 'unrealistic', in part because they did not coincide with the depressed aspirations of white schoolmates who appeared to come from a similar objective class position. This rejection ignores the continuing evidence of greater persistence by ethnic minority students in aspiring to educational goals, as exemplifiied by their high participation rates in school sixth forms[19] and further education.

Differences in the ambitions of ethnic minority pupils are further obscured for teachers by their frequent adoption of behaviour in school which is similar to their white working-class peers, one example being the use of regional and class-specific forms of spoken English. These behaviours may be especially important in the vital stages of initial schooling:[20]

> The only special disadvantage which speakers of low-status dialects suffer in learning to read is one imposed by teachers and schools. Rejection of their dialects and educators' confusion of linguistic difference with linguistic deficiency interferes with the natural process by which reading is acquired and undermines the linguistic self-confidence of divergent speakers. Simply speaking, the disadvantage of the divergent speaker, Black or White, comes from linguistic discrimination . . . Rejection, then, and not dialect differences is the problem educators must overcome.

I shall finish my discussion of class factors with reference to differential attainment of pupils from Asian and West Indian ethnic origins. As these groups face equivalent racism in the employment market, their relative successes in school are sometimes 'explained' by teachers with the same tired and discredited techniques of 'blaming the victim' that have obscured so many issues in education:

> 'I think West Indians do underachieve. I won't be polite and say it's because they are being badly taught. I don't think they are – they are taught the same way as the Asians. I think it is

actually a basic character difference. They just don't seem to have the application and motivation to work in many cases.'

From the many ways in which teachers can affect their pupils' application and motivation I shall select just two – their perceptions of language and social behaviour. It seems possible that for some teachers the existence of Asian community languages acts as an educationally acceptable 'excuse' for English language usages that might otherwise be classified as 'poor' because of their class basis. Both individually and institutionally, more (if insufficient) tolerance and attention is paid to linguistic development. But most West Indian pupils are not shown such consideration. Not only will many speak low-status class dialects, but some may choose to converse in Creole which many teachers regard as a sub-sub-standard form of English, sometimes categorising it with racist terminology such as 'mumbo-jumbo' or 'jungle-language'.

The child-rearing practices of some groups of south Asian origin induces an apparent conformity in the classroom behaviour of some pupils – whose social habits may be viewed by teachers as equivalent to one white middle-class model of the obedient, co-operative child. But some West Indian pupils do not exhibit such conformity:[21]

> In terms of classroom behaviour, the black girls gave all the appearances of being disaffected. Along with many pupils they viewed school as 'boring', 'trivial', 'childish'; their intolerance of the daily routine and their criticisms of much that went on inside the school were marked. They displayed a nicely judged insouciance for most aspects of the good pupil role . . . [but] the girls were strongly committed to education and some aspects of schooling.

In such situations teachers must abandon their established preconceptions about which children are capable and ambitious. They must ensure that pupils are given work that is sufficiently demanding to fulfil their aspirations, and not reject individuals as having 'behaviour difficulties' when these are solely a function of a teacher's misplaced view of what is appropriate. The frequent dismissal of black pupils as 'having a chip on their shoulder' or being 'anti-' is insensitive, ignorant and has racist consequences – for the children may well have a much more acute realisation of their position in the social structure than do their teachers.

I have now stated that in-service courses in multicultural education tend to overemphasise the importance of language or

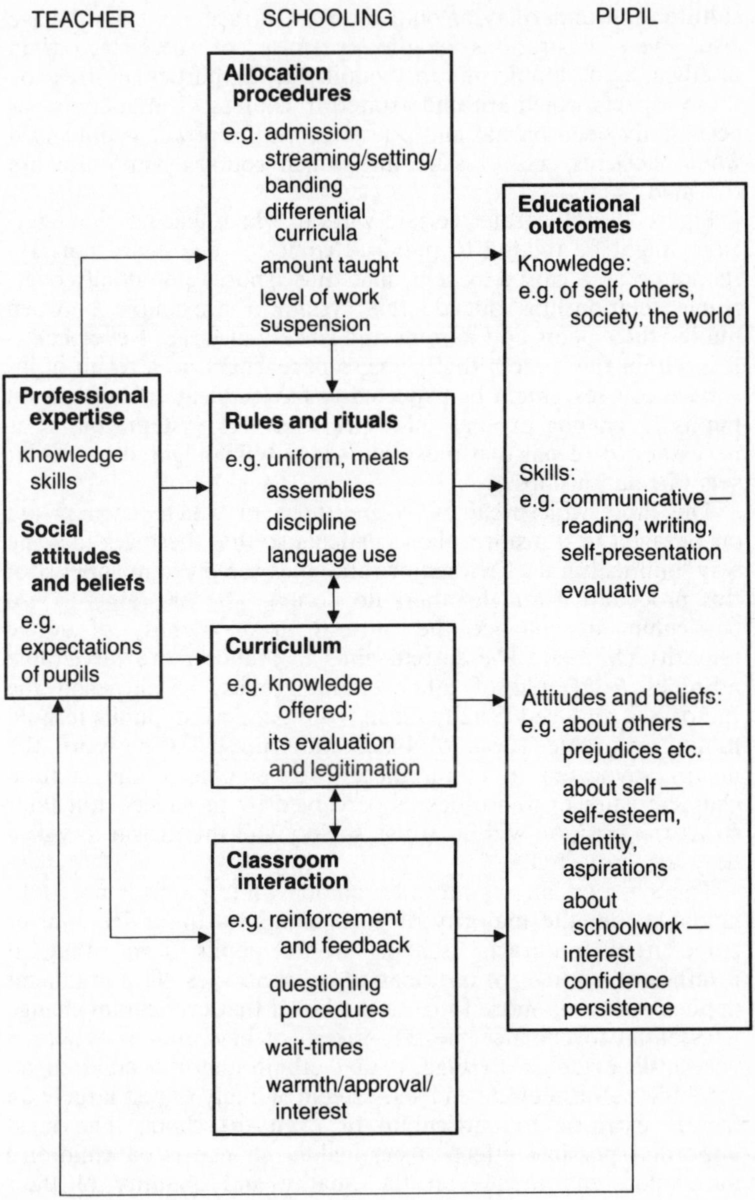
TEACHER
SCHOOLING
PUPIL
Allocation procedures
e.g. admission
streaming/setting/banding
differential curricula
amount taught
level of work
suspension
Professional expertise
knowledge
skills
Social attitudes and beliefs
e.g. expectations of pupils
Rules and rituals
e.g. uniform, meals
assemblies
discipline
language use
Curriculum
e.g. knowledge offered;
its evaluation and legitimation
Classroom interaction
e.g. reinforcement and feedback
questioning procedures
wait-times
warmth/approval/interest
Educational outcomes
Knowledge:
e.g. of self, others, society, the world
Skills:
e.g. communicative — reading, writing, self-presentation
evaluative
Attitudes and beliefs:
e.g. about others — prejudices etc.
about self — self-esteem, identity, aspirations
about schoolwork — interest
confidence
persistence

Figure 14.2

culture, and underplay or omit the role of race and class. I have also given illustrations of the operation of these factors in disadvantaging ethnic minority pupils, laying particular stress on those aspects which are understated in courses. The analysis has necessarily been partial and selective, but its power is enhanced when those aspects of schooling which courses emphasise are revealed.

Figure 14.2 illustrates certain ways in which teacher characteristics might be related to pupil outcomes.[22] The figure portrays schooling as a closed system, and thus ignores potentially overriding relationships outside this system, for example between pupils, their peers and parents and society at large. Nevertheless it is within this system that changes in teachers, as a result of in-service courses, might be expected to have educational effects on pupils. I cannot explore all aspects of this system, but it is necessary to reveal that most courses only highlighted particular sets of relationships.

The most widespread aims are those in which teachers are encouraged to transform their curricula so that these are in some way 'multicultural'. Two major rationales are given in support of this procedure (though others do occur). The first aims to use curriculum to enhance the self-esteem or identity of ethnic minority children. The second aims to induce more favourable attitudes to people of other ethnic groups, which when the rhetoric is removed usually means to induce white pupils to hold more favourable views of black minorities. Furthermore the means advocated to attain these ends emphasise the cultural characteristics of minorities as perceived by providers, not their structural position within British society and the racism to which they are subjected.

The aim of changing attitudes among white pupils is no doubt laudable, but the majority of participants on in-service courses come from multiracial schools where pupils have other, if insufficient, sources of information on minorities. This argument applies with even more force to the belief that curriculum change is essential to enhance the self-esteem of black pupils. There is very little evidence to suggest that ethnic minority children do have low self-esteem,[23] and self-esteem is likely to rest largely on factors extrinsic to curriculum or even to school. The most important possible effect of curriculum change is on children's motivation and thence on the quality and quantity of their schoolwork, but this is very rarely brought to the attention of course participants.

Overall, the emphasis on culture, curriculum and associated

attitudes exhibits a sadly deficient view of schooling: 'mopping-up operations against curricular relics of empire and nostalgic preservation of cultures that are fossilised and trivialised in the process.'[24] It is especially difficult to see a clear relationship between such changes and the enhanced acquisition of marketable skills and qualifications by older black pupils. For in the subject areas in which change is most simple it is not the content of an examination which matters to employers or admissions tutors but the mere fact of a pass at an appropriate grade. Curriculum change may be desirable for other reasons, but good grades are determined by the level and quantity of work performed in school. The level of pupils' work is largely determined by selective procedures within the process of schooling, not by the substance of individual curricula.

Allocative procedures are vital for ensuring that pupils are presented with the level of work appropriate to their aspirations, and that this work is then satisfactorily undertaken. Allocations to 'good' schools, or given suspensions and exclusions to any school at all, can operate unequally between racial groups. Within schools, assignment to different sets or bands can result in inexorable inequalities of opportunity: One Year Head told me: 'I have never known a child to be misplaced in the wrong band.' The criteria used in allocation may be covertly discriminatory, as when pre-existing results in a biased test or examination are used. Superficially objective criteria may be modified by social judgments about who is acceptable for a particular set; or assignment may openly be on social grounds, as in the allocation of West Indian pupils to ESN schools on account of their behaviour rather than their ability.[25]

Classroom interaction can have similar effects which result in inequitable education. A recent study notes that the primary-middle school boy of West Indian ethnic origin 'must, at times, wonder if there is anything more to classroom activity for him than criticism, questions and directives.'[26] Again, it is in the minutiae of interaction that teachers' assumptions about race and class might have their effect. For it is the nature of the classroom experience which will determine whether children's confidence and persistence will wax or wane.

Finally it must be stressed that in-service courses in multicultural education do have some valuable consequences, which have been reported elsewhere. They do contribute to the enlightenment of teachers in some respects. It is the possible effects on children which are much more tenuous. Until the relationship between course structures and the attainment of pupils is stressed more closely, this may continue to be the case. Let me leave the last word to a primary school teacher casting her verdict on one course:

> 'We haven't attacked any of the root causes of underachievement: the finance in schools, the areas the children are forced to live in, the staff they're taught by and the quality of staff – I've been in two secondary schools where there wasn't a single member of staff qualified to teach English, which wouldn't happen anywhere but the inner-ring . . . We spend a lot of time patting ourselves on the back for the tiny drops in the ocean that we've created, and we're doing very very little to alter the structure.'

Notes and references

1 J. Eggleston, D. Dunn and A. Purewal, *In-Service Teacher Education in a Multiracial Society*, Keele, 1980, p. 334. All subsequent unattributed quotations come from tape-recorded interviews conducted by the author, mainly in the course of research for this report.

2 House of Commons, *Fifth Report from the Home Affairs Committee*, Session 1980–81, *Racial Disadvantage*, vol. i, 1981, p. lix.

3 For this brief chapter I am not differentiating between multicultural, multiethnic, multiracial or anti-racist education for teachers.

4 E.B. Tyler, *Primitive Cultures*, 1871.

5 I owe this phrase to Madhu Anjali.

6 C. Bagley and G.K. Verma, *Racial Prejudice, the Individual and Society*, Saxon House, 1979.

7 G.A. Harrison, 'The race concept in human biology', *Journal of Biosocial Science*, supplement, no. 1, 1968.

8 e.g. D.J. Smith, *Racial Disadvantage in Britain*, Penguin, 1977.

9 A. Rampton (chairman), *West Indian Children in Our Schools*, Cmnd 8273, HMSO, 1981.

10 e.g. D. Milner, *Children and Race*, Penguin, 1975.

11 A.H. Halsey, 'Towards Meritocracy? The case of Britain', in J. Karabel and A.H. Halsey (eds), *Power and Ideology in Education*, Oxford University Press, 1977, p. 184.

12 G. Grace, *Teachers, Ideology and Control*, Routledge & Kegan Paul, 1978, p. 215.

13 e.g. D.H. Hargreaves, *Social Relations in a Secondary School*, Routledge & Kegan Paul, 1967.

14 P. Willis, 'Cultural Production and Theories of Reproduction', in L. Barton and S. Walker (eds), *Race, Class and Education*, Croom Helm, 1983, p. 110.

15 D. Holly, *Beyond Curriculum*, Hart-Davis, MacGibbon, 1973, p. 92.

16 A. Sivanandan, *Race, Class and the State*, Institute of Race Relations, 1976, p. 349.

17 U. Sharma, *Women, Work and Property in North-West India*, Tavistock, 1980, p. 81.
18 e.g. N. Foner, *Jamaica Farewell*, Routledge & Kegan Paul, 1979.
19 e.g. M. Craft, 'The Participation of Ethnic Minority Pupils in Further and Higher Education', *Educational Research*, vol. 25, 1, 1983.
20 K.S. Goodman and C. Buck, 'Dialect Barriers to Reading Comprehension Revisited', *The Reading Teacher*, October 1973.
21 M. Fuller, 'Young, Female and Black', in C. Cashmore and B. Troyna (eds), *Black Youth in Crisis*, Allen & Unwin, 1982, p. 91.
22 Stimulated by C.H. Persell, *Education and Inequality*, The Free Press, 1977, p. 133.
23 e.g. M. Stone, *The Education of the Black Child in Britain*, Fontana, 1981.
24 A. James, 'Why Language Matters', *Multiracial School*, vol. 5, no. 3, 1977.
25 S. Tomlinson, *Educational Subnormality: A study in decision-making*, Routledge & Kegan Paul, 1981.
26 P.A. Green, 'Male and Female Created He Them', *Multicultural Teaching*, vol. 2, no. 1, 1983, p. 5.

Chapter 15

The multicultural community and the school

Carlton Duncan

There is no universally accepted definition of community education, since it is one of these umbrella terms which conveniently means different things to different people. It has for example been considered synonymous with dual usage of school buildings for evening institutes, youth clubs and other recreational pastimes. Similarly it has been associated with play centres and information centres or all-embracing community colleges; while to others it has been seen as the organisation and process of learning through all the social and political relationships into which an individual enters at any point in his lifetime.

There is no logical reason why community education should not incorporate all the above ideas and more. For this chapter, however, emphasis will be laid on questions involving community participation, and control over educational resources; the community-based and/or -determined curriculum, with special reference to our multiracial, multicultural society and concomitant issues. These three issues and their multifarious implications will be considered.

Fundamental to the concept of any educational organisation should be the integration of that organisation and the community at large. The realisation of educational objectives will be a function of the extent of such integration.

If we eschew the philosophical controversies of what is right and what is wrong, it is not then difficult to postulate desirable aims and objectives of the educational institution. All that is required of the educationist in this task is a sufficiency or adequacy of past experience, an understanding of the present, plus a modicum of foresight. The difficulty is to translate 'ought' into 'is'. This is perhaps the major obstacle which tends towards the frustration of 'comprehensivisation' in some areas.

In contemplating the development of young minds, both personally and academically, the kind of arrogance – still typical of many of our educational establishments, which suggests that the school and its twelve or so subjects of the curriculum are all that are required to do the job – is the surest path to failure. Unless we view the job as one of shared responsibility among those who are interested in the individual's development, our hopes will remain hopes.

The education of the rising generation must realistically be the concern and responsibility of everyone within the community. Very little disagreement exists among educationists regarding what should be the aims and goals of educational institutions. Yet the same cannot be said of their methods; and the nature of such methodological conflicts reveals itself in the productive quality of such institutions . . . whatever measure is used.

It is a fair assumption that the economic and industrial survival of the individual, his social and moral skills, his sense of justice coupled with self-esteem, his sense of appreciation – aesthetically and otherwise – and a sense of enquiry and learning moved by a desire to contribute will be high on the list of priorities which a school would set as its developmental goals. But the theoretical situation is invariably easier than the practical. My contention is that without a realistic natural and free involvement of the rest of the community in the total life of the school it is difficult to see how the goals we set ourselves can be realised. It is impossible to set goals without an initial reference to society at large; it is even more difficult to achieve them without such reference.

We cannot isolate ourselves from what is real to the pupils we teach. Their present experience and understandings must be our starting-point. How else, then, can we expect pupils to understand and cope with the contradictions of their daily life? It makes nonsense to prepare young minds for industry, for further learning, for the business of citizenship without enlisting the aid of current soldiers from these fields.

For these reasons and others, the community school should be a laboratory of young people of compulsory school age; the parents of these young people; adults and young people over the school-leaving age; members of recognised and established groups; professional teachers; community workers; social workers; health visitors; politicians and other agents – all contributing in their own ways to the social, academic and other potential of the school; using as raw materials the community and its people, its culture, its successes and its failures to bring about change.

Our main task being to develop the individual in desirable ways, our curriculum structures, our pastoral structures and our social structures should be fully and realistically equipped for this task. If at any point of time we fail to see the relevance of our actions to the rest of what is existing around us, we are being artificial and perhaps too abstract.

What is less artificial, what is more natural than to establish and develop home–school links and gain parental understanding, co-operation and assistance in an environment which has the task of ensuring that every pupil is known and cared for as an individual? After all, parents have an interest in their offspring. They must be of valuable assistance in shaping programmes appropriate to the needs of the individual.

This kind of communal atmosphere, once established, sets the scene where everyone within it is undergoing simultaneous developments. Each person's development is affected by and influences that of the next. Everyone within the system must feel keen to achieve worthy personal standards. Personal examples on matters of taste, attitude to work, attitude to people and property become exemplary and are in fact copied.

There is then little or no place for a punitive system to extract what is deemed to be desirable from our fellow men. Naturally, there will be some need for constant vigilance – not in a policing sense – moved by a sense of genuine interest in the suitable development of all in all respects. Vigilance through dialogue, praise, examples and disapprobation of the anti-social. When all around us feel this sense of security, then we are achieving.

The pertinent issues of identifying developmental needs, resourcing such needs and measuring outcomes are not then left to artificial devices. The individual needs in terms of himself and the community are identified by those elements and members of the community with which and with whom he is most closely allied. He is provided for and assisted in the same light. We therefore assess the outcome in terms of what the individual got out of the system – the indicator being what he puts back into it.

In so far as we do not hope for absolutes or Utopia, we shall not then be surprised to find a percentage of individuals (not too large) who cannot function in the mass-model. They are not necessarily lost. It may be that our truants, aggressive types and 'anti-socialites' require a more individual menu – micro as opposed to macro treatment. On the other hand, we require the kind of flexibility to enable us to provide for the individual with special gifts. My argument is that it is the school whose point of reference is always the immediate community that will be most able in executing its responsibilities to these just as worthy individuals.

This is true, whatever the nature of the community with which partnership is sought. Admittedly, greater ingenuity is required of us, in the pursuit of our community educative philosophies, where that community is multicultural than where we have a monocultural situation. But there are at last two good reasons why we should not be deflected from our task: viz. difficulties are never a sufficient reason to abandon worthwhile tasks and multiculturalism is now a reality the world over.

I stated earlier that the realization of educational objectives will be a function of the extent of the integration of the school and the community at large.

Meaningful integration with the community, it is submitted, is impossible if the community is not viewed as equal partners in matters of school government to the extent of positive involvement in and commitment to the day-to-day issues in the school. One possible model was as practised at Sidney Stringer School and Community College,[1] where the author was Deputy Head and Director of Personal Development, 1976–82.

School and Community Association

Various groups of people could make up the life of the Community School, and they could be brought together in a School and Community Association (see Figure 15.1). Each person could join the School and Community Association by buying a leisure card, as though a member of a club.

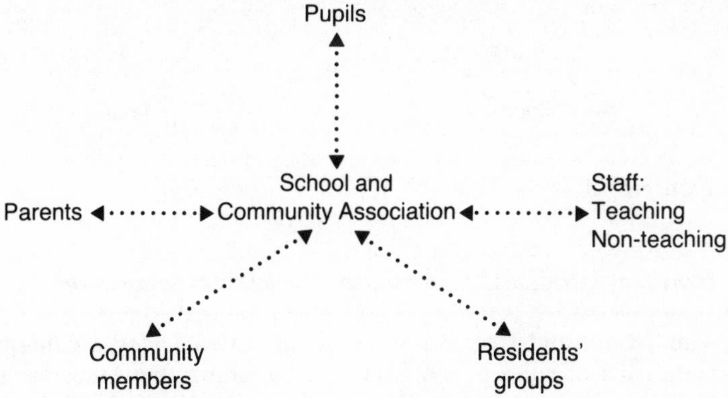

Figure 15.1

Tasks of the School Community Association

Examples of the kinds of decisions which the School and Community Association, and particularly the Council of Standing Committees, will have to make (Figure 15.2):

Rules for members and membership fees.
Who can be members.
How money is to be raised and spent by the Association.
How the building and facilities will be used, by whom, and at what cost, if any.
Opening times of the bar and prices of drink.
Decide on and set up new community projects, in association with the community staff.
Set up new activities for the Association.
Provide for various groups living in the area, for example pre-school children, old age pensioners, non-English-speaking Asians.

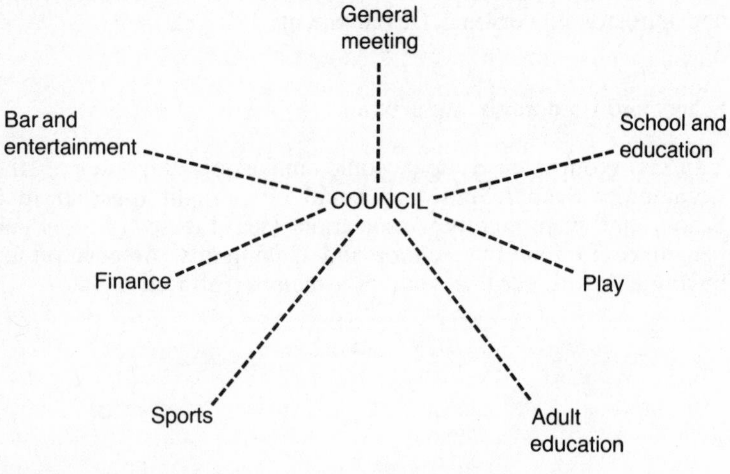

Figure 15.2

How the School and Community Association would work

The School and Community Association will need a constitution (i.e. a list of rules to say how and by whom the Association will be run). It is proposed that the main body of the School and Community Association will be the Council, consisting of about fifty representatives of the various groups. Since the Council will be so large and the work of the Association is so varied, it is suggested that most of the discussions take place in Standing Committees, covering various areas of the Association's work.

Decisions taken by the Standing Committees will have to be approved by the Council. A general meeting of all members will be able to over-rule or make decisions for the Council.

The School and Community Association and the Local Education Authority

In the last resort, the Local Education Authority is responsible for the school, both in law and since it provides most of the money to run it. In the Community School, however, the School and Community Association will be expected to raise some of the money necessary to finance activities, particularly community activities. The actual amount for this will be negotiated each year by the Board of Governors and the Local Education Authority. This means that the Board of Governors will be responsible for virtually all contact between the School and Community Association and the Local Education Authority. How the system will eventually work will be discovered only as it develops over a period of time and practice. For this reason, it is essential to establish a strong School and Community Association from the beginning, so that the powers offered by the Local Education Authority may be used to their full advantage.

The Board of Governors

By law, each school must have a Board of Governors (i.e. a body of people who instruct and advise the Headteacher on how the school will be run). Normally, people on the Board of Governors are well-known local people, who are nominated by the Education Committee of the Local Authority.

The Board of Governors will be like an Executive Committee for the School and Community Association, consisting mainly of elected representatives of the Council of the School and Community Association. In this way, it is hoped that the legal requirements will be fulfilled and the Community School will be run democratically by those who use it (Figure 15.4).

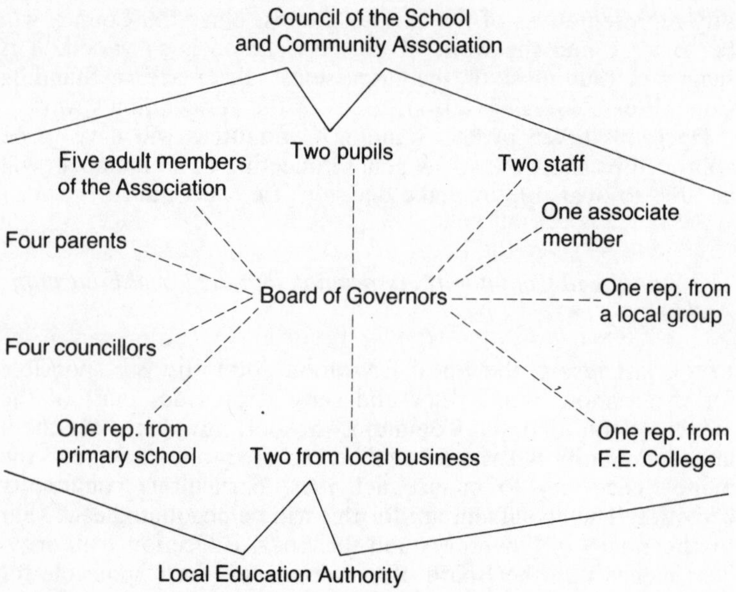

Figure 15.3 Arrangements for a possible Board of Governors

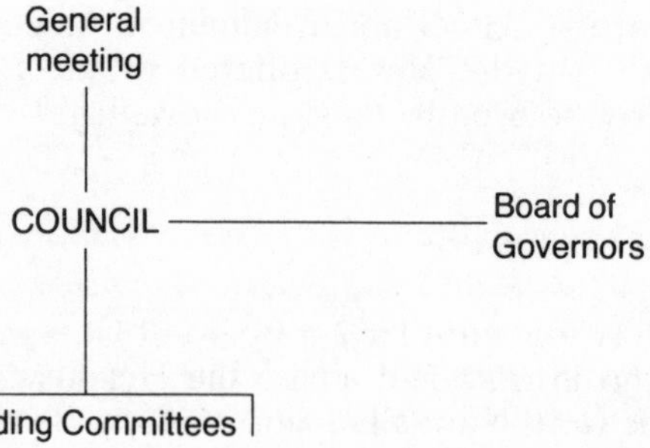

Figure 15.4

Tasks of the Board of Governors

The Board of Governors will have to:

Liaise with and prepare reports for the Local Education Authority for the efficient running of the school.

Prepare estimates for the financial needs of the School and Community Association.
Appoint the Headteacher, and if necessary dismiss him/her.
Determine what staff are needed, appoint them and grade staff, in consultation with the Headteacher.
Decide how the money available should be spent on the upkeep of the buildings and equipment.
Determine the overall policy framework of the Community School (although the Local Education Authority still has a lot of power).

As an Executive Committee, the Board of Governors will work with the School and Community Association, not make decisions for it.

The decision-making machinery clearly offers the opportunity for full participation of the community at large, but two problems are immediately obvious, given that the community is a truly multiracial, multicultural, multireligious and multilinguistic one. These are the problems of communication in order to encourage the necessary involvement and commitment, and the nature of democracy in relation to minority groups.

Unless steps are taken to ensure effective communication via the language media in which different people are most at ease, it would in reality tantamount to no more than lip-service; and the machinery as set up becomes a sham. Clearly the efforts, financial and other expenditure must be found if the system is to be truly effective, just and equitable.

Since democracy approximates to majority decisions, it will nearly always follow that minority groups will be at a disadvantage. If the community project is to avoid subscription to tokenism, it must ensure either that minorities are represented effectively in terms of voting powers – or that means exist to take positive notice of minority view-points. Positive discrimination must not be excluded where such actions would lead to the interest of all. It is only when initially all members of the community are truly convinced of the institution's seriousness of purpose in relation to their interest that they can be expected to develop and maintain the kind of commitment which is so vital to the self-perpetuation of the institution and its ideologies.

Another problem which must be given serious attention is the question of committee procedures. What measures can be taken to ensure that no section of the community is at a disadvantage? It will be recognised that those who are best at procedural activities are better able to make their viewpoints prevail.

Any system which goes so far towards ensuring equity and fairness in its operation could produce some interesting outcomes on matters such as the wearing of uniforms, corporal punishment, appointment, dismissal and promotion of staff – not to mention the curriculum.

With the foregoing considerations in mind, this model is in process of development at the author's own direction at Wyke Manor Upper School,[2] where he has been Headteacher since April 1982.

A community-based curriculum is one which is derived from market research among the community. Much could be gained from a Neighbourhood Group system, whereby the school's catchment area was widened and divided into several neighbourhoods. All members of the school's teaching and community staff could be attached to a neighbourhood. They could literally knock on the doors of all homes in their neighbourhoods, whether at weekends, evenings or other times. There would need to be a time-off-in-lieu (TOIL)-system to compensate.

The idea is to take the school's messages to the community and at the same time to discover what the community would wish the school to do for it. This method has been known to result in daytime adult classes in child care, young mothers' group, beginners, etc., English classes – mainly for Asian mothers – and crèche facilities. Similarly, many out-plant activities, for example, off-site youth work and living rooms (one-off) lessons in welfare rights thus results. In this way the traditional paternalistic and arrogant approach to educational provision is avoided with good effect.

But the community curriculum implies more than just market research. What is provided must do justice for all its consumers in the interest of creating a just society. It follows that the traditional Eurocentric approach to curricula provision must be abandoned for a multicultural approach. Many recent reports, including the Rampton Interim Report, *West Indian Children in Our Schools*, have identified the Eurocentric curriculum as a major cause of ethnic minority children's failures. A truly equitable community education project will avoid this at all cost. In the United Kingdom, progress in multicultural education has had many setbacks, for example:

> Subject to the provision of this section, the Secretary of State may pay to Local Authorities who, in his opinion, are required to make special provision in the exercise of any of their functions, in consequence of the presence within their areas of

> substantial numbers of immigrants from the Commonwealth, whose language or customs differ from those of the community, grants of such amounts as he may, with the consent of the Treasury, determine on account of expenditure of such descriptions (being expenditure in respect of the employment of staff) as he may so determine . . . (S.11 of the Local Government Act, 1966.)

S.11 has been variously misinterpreted and abused. But one particular misinterpretation still bedevils progress in comprehending the true nature of multicultural education. It is still a common experience to have cited the schools' or Local Authority's provision for the teaching of English as a second language to children, mainly of Asiatic origin, as evidence of informed commitment to the pursuit of multicultural education. As long as this view persists, little real progress can be expected in coming to terms with the important issues which will benefit all children – indigenous and ethnic minorities alike.

Similarly, the largely discredited idea that multicultural education was synonymous with 'Black Studies' or some curriculum module or unit which had to justify its worth in competition with the more established subjects for a slot on the timetable has greatly retarded the understanding of multicultural education. Evidence of this view is still prevalent right across this country: educationists are still at pains to stress either that they have a steel band, or they do Caribbean Studies, or that they need to do nothing special since they haven't got a 'problem' – because of the absence of ethnic minorities in their domain.

Here, both these approaches are disclaimed. They might be credited with a claim to being aspects of a greater whole, but no more.

The medium through which we shape young minds formally is the school's curriculum – planned or hidden. This is not to ignore the roles of other social institutions in terms of education. Their contributions are 'recognised' and are rated with no less importance than what happens in schools.

Haringey LEA advances the following definition of multicultural education (Rampton Report, p. 27):

> one which is appropriate to the education of ALL pupils, whatever their background, by reference to a diversity of cultures. The variety of social and cultural groups should be evident in the visual images, stores and information disseminated within the school. However, this selection should not be made in such a way as to reinforce stereotyping of life-styles,

occupations, status, human characteristics or one particular culture.

This is an excellent description of the vehicle that should carry the multicultural passenger, and one which finds full endorsement in the Rampton Interim Report.

Wrapped up in the above definition are ideas which will challenge almost every aspect of school organisation and practice – and even those of the wider society. If this definition of the multicultural curriculum is accepted, and I believe it should be, the following implications are clear:

(a) major reforms in the schools' planned and hidden curriculum are indicated:
(b) the attitudes and expectations prevalent amongst teachers, and which get inculcated into the young minds of the indigenous white peers of ethnic minorities, must be the subject of rapid change;
(c) decision-making in education, in schools and elsewhere must rid itself of its institutionalized racist complexion for a more equitable appearance, and –
(d) the positive effects of role-models upon motivation, image-building and consequential performance must be quickly recognized.

Going into practice is not really impossible, but it will require commitment, and the will to question deeply-held values and beliefs – whether they be one's own or those of others.

It is good practice for subject departments in school to hold their subject fields under constant review – hence, there is already an allowance, in terms of financial cost, time and direction for subject review. It is submitted that little or no new cost is necessitated in adopting the multicultural curriculum. What will be new is a shift in emphasis and approach.

We are sometimes told that our emphasis and approach are dictated by the constraints of examination syllabuses. Apart from the fact that it is we teachers who write examination syllabuses – be they modes I or III – one fails to see how children's examination chances in history could be jeopardised because they not only know of Wilberforce's and Lincoln's contribution to the emancipation of slavery, but are also able to measure their contribution alongside the contributions and human sacrifices of black politicians. Surely it cannot be examination suicide in geography to reflect Third World countries as major contributors to Western civilisation and not just as recipients of aid. And, really, if space allowed, each subject of the curriculum could be similarly shown to be Eurocentric and dangerously misleading to all our children in schools. The scope for multicultural education, via subject areas such as physical education, domestic science, religious education, mathematics, science, etc., is enormous.

To the negative images of ethnic minorities which are often reflected in textbooks and other teaching materials might be attributed many of modern-day educational and social problems. Peer grouping implies equality. Yet, this is hardly the case in some multiracial schools, where, largely because of stereotyping and negative images in relation to ethnic minorities, such children or people are perceived to be less than equals by their peers.

The mere fact that other people's languages, religions, festivals and values are not treated as worthy of equal rank with their European counterparts sends negative and silent messages to young minds. Yet, with commitment and organisation, full representation of all these areas might very well be reflected in all we do in schools and to the benefit of everyone.

The Taylor Report, and more recently legislation, have provided us with avenues through which to alter the structures of our Governing Bodies, thus ensuring equity in representation on decision-making bodies. What is in the interest of Man is what he takes interest in. Perhaps the time is well overdue when ethnic minorities should be defining their own problems and sorting them out themselves. Greater consultation and involvement at all levels of school organisation is called for with much rapidity.

Areas such as Coventry, Birmingham, Bristol, Ealing in London and Manchester in the north should long ago have shown their pupils – ethnic minorities and white indigenous ones alike – that members of ethnic minorities can be headteachers of major comprehensive schools. The informed and enlightened LEA that also possesses the necessary commitment to equity and fairness also has S.71 of the 1976 Race Relations Act on its side in bringing about a truly representative multiracial teaching force in terms of employment and promotion – all in the interest of the hidden curriculum for the benefit of all.

A major obstacle to practice relating to both the planned and the hidden multicultural curriculum must be expected in the areas of teacher attitude and expectations of ethnic minorities. We encounter this in the way children are classified and grouped; the kinds of stereotypes which are emphasised and indeed the way institutions are organised, and the way they work. There are, then, clear implications for both initial and in-service training – perhaps the areas of greatest financial cost in pursuit of this noble goal. But herein lies the test of true commitment and willingness of the powers in control.

Community education is about the sharing of information, effective communication, justice and equality.

Notes

1 Coventry Local Education Authority.
2 Bradford Local Education Authority.

Further reading

Comprehensive Education (Report of a DES conference, December 1977), HMSO, 1978.

A. Rampton (chairman), *West Indian Children in our Schools*, Cmnd 8273, HMSO, 1981.

Gerald Haigh (ed.), *On our Side*, Maurice Temple Smith, 1979.

Roy Evans and Mollie Lloyd (eds), *Early Child Development and Care*, vol. 10, no. 4, Gordon & Breach, 1983.

Compass (University of Warwick, Institute of Education), vol. 3, no. 1, autumn 1982.

Colin Fletcher and Neil Thompson, *Issues in Community Education*, Falmer Press, 1981.

Norman Garner, *Teaching in the Urban Community School*, Ward Lock, 1973.

John Sharp, *Open School*, Dent, 1973.

Pauline Jones, *Community Education in Practice: A review*, Social Evaluation Unit, Oxford, 1978.

Eric Midwinger, *Patterns of Community Education*, Ward Lock, 1973.

H. Morris, *The Village College*, Cambridge University Press, 1924.

'A Case Study in Management: Sidney Stringer School and Community College', The Open University E321, 'Management in Education', Unit 2, 1976.

Chapter 16

Pastoral care and guidance in the multicultural school

Carlton Duncan

It is not long ago that the major emphasis on pupil development was, to the practitioner, discipline and excellence in examination performance. Under the old tripartite system parents, teachers and indeed pupils were mainly preoccupied in the outcome of the now outmoded 11+ examination. Once this outcome was determined, the drive then was to do the best one could for youngsters in developing academically, especially in the grammar schools. In the secondary modern schools a parallel emphasis on the more technical skills was found. Admittedly the sizes of schools, as they then were, facilitated this limited view of pupil development. It was not easy to see the effects of such unimaginative approach to education, since the ease with which teachers often managed to know their pupils in many ways compensated for a wider definition of care and development.

Comprehensivisation must really be credited with the drift towards recognising pastoral care (though at first this was synonymous with discipline) as an essential part of any school. As schools became larger and teachers were denied smaller numbers with whom to work and the social context of the school became widened with varying degrees of problems, necessity became the mother of invention.

Illustrating the varied tasks which have become part of the teachers' duties, Eric Midwinter wrote:[1]

> Apart from the ordinary routines of any school, there are truants to be mopped up, injuries, sores and boils to be treated, adults to be advised on a range of topics from marital breakdown and housing to crime and punishment, emotional outbursts to be tended, family and other feuds to be quelled, and a host of other social disasters and miseries to be met. The

> E.P.A. teacher must be sleuth, nurse, solicitor, confidante, psychiatrist and pal all rolled into one society's representative on the other side of the tracks, along with a clergyman here and a social worker there.

Midwinter may have been describing the tasks of teachers who work in Educational Priority Areas, but it would be naïve to consider that comprehensives outside such areas are not captured in Midwinter's quotation.

The quotation aptly describes the nation's comprehensive schools today. Travels undertaken on behalf of the DES National Inquiry into the education of ethnic minorities[2] have given me many experiences of comprehensives right across the country – and such experiences have confirmed this general view of the demanding nature of the tasks of teachers in these large schools, admittedly more so in inner city schools.

It follows that pastoral care must now be seen in much wider terms than discipline and getting youngsters to concentrate on passing examinations. Indeed, even if passing examinations is our ultimate objective, it is realised that attention to other areas of our youngsters' development will enhance the opportunities for the kind of development which we seek. Pastoral care is thus defined as relating to the total development of the individual. In this way, we must become concerned with the numerous issues indicated in Midwinter's description of the EPA teacher's tasks. Care has to be comprehensive, since any area of development will necessarily affect development chances in other areas.

Experience has shown that if the teacher is to be effective in executing care in this comprehensive sense, he will need a certain minimum amount of information about the youngsters for whom he cares. He will need to know (a) how the child performs in a classroom situation, (b) how he performs independently, (c) how he performs under stress, and (d) what constitutes the child's background. Knowledge about classroom performance will be gained simply by following the timetabled activities provided by the school. The other pieces of information, however, will require greater and planned effort by the teacher. Knowledge about independent performances, for example, will call for observation of the child at play, in social circumstances and the like. The careful setting of tasks to be performed at home and so forth, and the monitoring or checking of these tasks, will similarly reveal a great deal about independent performances. Again examination or test arrangements will be instrumental in providing us with the kind of information we need to know about the child in stress situations. Of course, the same kind of information could be gained by using other measures. Most importantly, though, information about the child's background will require organised effort by the teacher. Of course much of this kind of information might come to us by chance or because it has been volunteered. But such information is incomplete, and incomplete information is as likely to hinder our operations as lack of information itself. The school should thus organise itself in order to go in search of the kind of information it considers vital in its system of care.

Only when we are armed with these minimum pieces of information about our youngsters can we be justly confident in the guidance we give them or what we write about them. But, above all, to motivate them it is important that we are able to start where they the pupils are. Surely, background information on our pupils must be the best indicator about where they are.

In schools where the need for a pastoral organisation is recognised, some arrangements – either horizontally, vertically or a combination of these – will have been instituted. Each system has its pros and cons, but the combined systems, while attempting the best of both worlds, also display the evils of both worlds, quite apart from being rather expensive to run. In the end, the important factor is recognising the need for and instituting a system for care.

Even in a monocultural situation, the task of caring for youngsters can be a very delicate matter for two very important reasons. First, of necessity we will be handling at times very sensitive materials which if not handled with utmost care could plunge all parties into rather embarrassing situations. Second, though the school is monocultural, society at large or the world at large is not. Part of caring for youngsters requires us to be as humanly accurate as we can in the kind of information and guidance we impart. Hence, even children in a mono-cultural school have to be prepared to take their places in a multicultural society.

Increasingly, however, schools in their compositions are reflecting the situation which is found in the wider society. There will be brown and black faces as well as white faces, and this normally means that different cultures, religions, values, languages, etc., are interplaying. Any system of care will have to take account of this fact if it is to be effective and just for all its pupils.

Many teachers when confronted with this reality, in my opinion, seek to take the easy or lazy way out of having to come to terms with the situation. They declare that it is not necessary to do anything special in such circumstances since all they need to do is to 'treat all pupils alike'. But this is a rather dangerous position to take, as is here illustrated. What does this statement amount to? Does it mean fostering our own values, religious ideas, linguistic tastes on those who do not share a common background with us in these areas? Or should we be seeking to motivate all youngsters by starting where they are? What more significant pointers are there to where a person is besides his linguistic, cultural and religious make-up – in short, the important elements of his value system?

Some illustrations of cultural conflicts at work will suffice to indicate the hidden dangers which are embedded in the equal treatment for all principle. Consider for example, my own experiences in two different situations soon after my arrival in this country from Jamaica. At a London polytechnic where I repeated my general education I had cause to borrow my neighbouring colleague's ruler to underline a piece of work. I had committed the most unforgivable sin in not asking his permission, and I was told off in no uncertain terms. I really could not understand what had provoked the onslaught. It was not until several weeks later that I started to appreciate the dynamics which were at work. I had recently come from an environment where nothing was wrong with using and replacing an object in the given circumstances, albeit without permission. My colleague was of an environment which valued permission before use. The seeds of cultural conflict were thus placed in a fertile medium. Only a full appreciation of the values involved would have enabled my colleague and I to make the adjustments which were called for in the circumstances.

Another illustration will help. As a boy in Jamaica, it was inculcated into me that I should always address my elders as 'Sir' and 'Ma'am'. How was I to know that this would not be generally true in England? At first it was difficult to understand the looks of incomprehension on the faces of older English men whom I had addressed as 'Sir' either in conversation or at introduction. I later realised that many wondered whether I was making fun of them or was I just plain stupid?

At a school in Birmingham, the case of the West Indian girl who enthusiastically flicks her fingers at the teacher to indicate that she knows the answer to the question provides us with yet another interesting illustration of cultural conflicts. The teacher felt that the girl's conduct was rude. The girl thought it was a way of expressing keenness and enthusiasm.

The teacher or police officer who might have occasion to admonish a West Indian youth may well deduce insolence on the part of the youth who persists in not looking his accuser in the face. But while this might be *prima facie* insolence in relation to British culture or value system, it is regarded elsewhere as a mark of respect and remorse to hang one's head in shame when confronted with your wrongful deed. It is not necessary for me to indicate here the difficulties which could arise from these illustrative situations. What, however, must be indicated is the error involved in treating all children alike in spite of the good intentions of fairness.

From the very early days both at Aylestone School[3] in London and Sidney Stringer School and Community College[4] in Coventry I was involved in exploring ways and ideas to avoid the difficulties which are likely to follow upon inadequate care of the pupils in our charge. It became obvious that the teachers' first job was to ascertain their own ignorance and devise a strategy for enlightenment. Accordingly, a number of measures indicated themselves. Living in the relevant communities can help, especially if this is done as a participant – visiting mosques or temples. In-service courses, well selected, and holidays designed for learning are also measures that will contribute to the vital initial process of finding out. No one measure will suffice; it is the cumulative effect of all useful measures that will eventually have the desirable impact.

As the Deputy Head and Director of Personal Development at Sidney Stringer School and Community College, it fell to me to ensure that pastoral care had the wide comprehensive meaning that it should have. Little emphasis was placed on discipline, though of course it was an integral part of the means of ultimately ensuring that pupils advanced academically. Pastoral care, therefore, had to be seen equally in relation to the kind of curriculum diets our young people received, with where they are placed, whether CSE, GCE or remedial streams, and so forth. I was concerned too with all the issues that would inform my judgment in identifying and servicing the needs of my pupils whether in relation to their placement, their academic achievement or their social development. It follows that in a school of mixed culture, religion, values, language and race my job was not going to be easy. But one thing which was also certain is that it was going to be a most interesting worth-while and challenging experience.

At the time, Sidney Stringer was composed of some 54% Asian (mainly Sikh background), 38% indigenous whites, 6% West

Indians, plus another 2% Chinese and others among its pupil population. There was an internal structure in which to operate, but in 1976 when I joined the school this structure or organisation took no account pastorally of the fact that needs might be different.

Similarly, external provisions by the Authority were there in the usual forms, that is: Social Service, the Educational Psychologist and her team, the Careers Service, and even links with the police were clearly established. The main drawback, however, was that, as with the school organisation, everything was geared to one cultural point of view. Yet this need never have been the case.

Within the school historical accidents had caused up to eleven Asian members of staff to be present (though even this in itself was inadequate, for they were all men in a mixed school of 1,200+ pupils, aged 11 to 19+ in some cases); one member of the staff was Chinese in background, though he resented this definitive reference. At first I was the only West Indian on the staff. There was, however, a female West Indian secretary who was later succeeded by an Asian secretary. Both were called upon from time to time to lend their particular skills and expertise.

Immediate action was to redistribute staff and responsibilities to ensure that the values and input in policy-making would draw substantially and appropriately upon all the different cultures represented in the school. Simultaneously, representations were made to the Authority to the effect that the external supporting statutory services needed to reflect the communities and the society which they served. No immediate responses were made, but well organised and constant pressures meant that the changes, at least in some quarters, came later. But while we at Stringer awaited the change, compensatory measures had to be adopted.

An obligation[5] has been placed on us to start the day with an act of corporate worship. There was no place on the premises where the whole school could come together, but we were able to meet in different house groups. This gave us the much used opportunity to draw upon the expertise of different members of staff, senior pupils, their parents and indeed members of the community through voluntary organisations in arranging our assemblies throughout the school. The view was taken that the Education Act did not specify a particular religion, and so, as long as what we did was kept fair and balanced with no deliberate omissions or neglect, we were discharging our obligation.

The same principle, of varied involvement of staff and relying upon voluntary expertise where they were available, applied in connection with diciplinary matters. This means that the school at any one time had to incorporate a variety of disciplinary philosophies to ensure social order. Corporal punishment was frowned upon by the headmaster, and therefore little used. But it would be grossly inaccurate to suggest that it was never used. Clearly, what was necessary to reflect a just society was not consistency in terms of the type of measure used to establish social order. In our school community it was necessary to adopt a variety of measures born out of discussion, with a wide body of interested parties. What was important was the consistency showed in rejecting anti-social or non-productive behaviour – whatever the measure used to reflect this disapprobation.

It became part – the most important part – of the school's pastoral policy that every pupil's home should be visited (except in the very rare case where a parent would prefer this not to happen) at least once each year, whether for negative or positive recognition. In reality this happened much more frequently for a variety of reasons. For example, in many cases it became common for teachers simply to call into homes for a cup of tea and a chat, and the reverse situation also developed; again many pupils had to be visited several times, though admittedly for negative purposes. In addition, the policy of the school was for parents just to drop in when they felt like it. No appointments system was established, since it was felt that the need to do that was itself a barrier which must be avoided. In any case, the argument in favour of appointments is that teachers would be disturbed in a free system, but our philosophy was that the best place for a parent to see a teacher was on the job – in the classroom. The job of home visiting was that of the House Head, but he or she was encouraged to delegate appropriately and where necessary in order to cash in on the varied talent which we had on the staff. It is little wonder that the discipline at the school and parental involvement in school activities were of such a high standard.

It helped enormously, too, that the school was a community school. Parents and other members of the adult community were at liberty to join all the ordinary classes held at the school for the pupils, in addition to those specifically laid on for them as determined by them. This meant that there was a constant flow of adults, staff and others betwen 8.30 am and 10.30 pm for five days a week, and all day on Saturdays and Sundays. Few signs of graffiti and vandalism were evident. In this conjunction of staff, pupils, their parents and other adults, a great deal of in-service training was happening. The school adopted a policy that everyone had something to offer, and created the atmosphere in which things could happen.

It was important to us that no child was misplaced. Since our multicultural composition ensured that no test could ever guarantee us the kind of assessment which would avoid misplacement, the school adapted a mixed ability structure from age 11 to 19+. At the mock examination, however, we were forced to decide which public examination pupils would take. But even here double entries were often used to guard against possible injustice in some cases.

Finally, it fell to me as an individual to keep meaningful and indicative statistics along ethnic lines – if for no other purpose, they were clear indicators of how the different groups in the school were performing. I am happy to report that of the forty or so whom we managed to send to university, polytechnic or teacher training each year, the different groups reflected their proportionate representation within the school. Perhaps there is something, after all, in this multicultural approach to pastoral care?

Our own internal assessment relied on tests and examinations, but it soon became clear that, if for no other reason, equity demanded the most accurate and carefully planned profile of each of our pupils. Above all, each profile had to be authorised and authenticated by each pupil's home and community before it left the school.

It was vital, too, that in giving careers advice, teachers' preconceptions did not always prevail, and therefore much use was made of specialist advice drawn from our various communities in giving guidance to all our young people. Justice, equity and successful endeavours prevailed in these circumstances.

Notes and References

1 Eric Midwinter, 'Children from another World', in Bruce Kimble (ed.), *Fit to Teach*, Hutchinson Educational, 1971, pp. 148–9.
2 A. Rampton (chairman), *West Indian Children in our Schools*, Cmnd 8273, HMSO, June 1981; and the Swann Inquiry, published March 1985.
3 Brent LEA, 1971–6.
4 Coventry LEA, 1976–82.
5 Education Act, 1944, S.25 (1).

Further reading

Carlton Duncan, 'Discipline and the Multi-cultural School', ch. 5 in Gerald Haigh (ed.), *On our Side*, Maurice Temple Smith, 1979.

Invited paper by C.G. Duncan in *Comprehensive Education* (Report of a DES conference, December 1977), HMSO, 1978, pp. 31–3.

Carlton Duncan, 'The Multi-racial Aspects of Community Education', in Roy Evans and Mollie Lloyd (eds), *Early Child Development and Care*, Gordon & Breach, 1983, pp. 311–25.

Pauline Jones, *Community Education in Practice: A review*, Social Evaluation Unit, Oxford, 1978.

'A Case Study in Management: Sidney Stringer School and Community College', The Open University E321, 'Management in Education', Unit 2, 1976.